Juliette Drouet
to Victor Hugo

Juliette Drouet and Louis Guimbaud

Alpha Editions

This edition published in 2022

ISBN: 9789356577565

Design and Setting By

Alpha Editions

www.alphaedis.com

Email - info@alphaedis.com

Contents

FOREWORD

A POET, a great poet, loves a princess of the theatre. He is jealous. He forces her to abandon the stage and the green-room, to relinquish the hollow flattery of society and the town; he cloisters her with one servant, two or three of his portraits, and as many books, in an apartment a few yards square. When she complains of having nothing to do but wait for him, he replies: "Write to me. Write me everything that comes into your head, everything that causes your heart to beat."

Such is the origin of the letters of Juliette Drouet to Victor Hugo. They are not ordinary missives confided to the post and intended to assure a lover of the tender feelings of his mistress: they are notes, mere "scribbles," as Juliette herself calls them, thrown upon paper hour by hour, cast into a corner without being read over, and secured by the lover at each of his visits, as so many trophies of passion.

When Juliette Drouet's executor, M. Louis Kock, died in Paris on May 26th, 1912, he had in his possession about twenty thousand. He had added to them the letters of James Pradier to our heroine, those of Juliette to her daughter, Claire Pradier, and the answers of Claire Pradier to her mother.

This collection of documents passed into the hands of a Parisian publisher, Monsieur A. Blaizot, who has been so good as to allow us to examine them and compile from them a volume concerning Victor Hugo and his friend.

At first sight the task presented grave difficulties—nay, it seemed almost impossible of execution. To begin with, it would have been futile to think of publishing the whole of the twenty thousand letters; in the second place, it might appear a work of supererogation to reconstruct from them in detail the story of a *liaison* well known to have been uneventful, almost monotonous, and more suggestive of a litany or the beads of a rosary than of tragedy or a novel.

We have attempted to surmount these objections in the following manner:

In the first portion we present the biography of Juliette Drouet in the form of a series of synthetic tableaux, each tableau summarising several lustres of her life. We thus avoid the long-drawn-out narrative, year by year, of an existence devoid of incident or adventure.

In the second, we publish those letters which strike us as peculiarly eloquent, witty, or lyrical. In the light shed upon them by the preliminary biography, they form, as one might say, its justification and natural sequel.

At the outset of her *liaison* with the poet Juliette does not date her "scribbles"; she merely notes the time of day and the day of the week, until about 1840; we have therefore been obliged to content ourselves with the classification effected by her in the collection of her manuscripts, and preserved by her executor.

From 1840 she dated every sheet. Consequently our work simultaneously achieves more precision and certainty.

When its difficulties have seemed insuperable, we have derived valuable encouragement from the sympathy of the literary students and friends who had urged us to undertake it, or were assisting us in its execution. We have pleasure in recording our thanks to the following: MM. Louis Barthou, Beuve, A. Blaizot, François Camailhac, Eugène Planès, Escolier, etc. b We have often wondered what the charming woman whose ideals, tastes, and habits have, by degrees, become almost as familiar to us as her handwriting, would have thought of our efforts. As far as she herself is concerned there can be but little doubt. She would have made fun of the undertaking. By dint of moving in the society of men of high literary attainments she had acquired a very modest estimate of her own wit and talent. In 1877, when the architect Roblin one day discovered her sorting out her "scribbles," he thought she was attempting to write a book and gravely asked her "when it was to be published." "What an idea!" she cried, and burst out laughing.

Such was not the opinion of Victor Hugo, however. That perfect artist attached the utmost importance to the writings of his friend. Each time she wished to destroy them he commanded her to preserve them. Whenever she proposed to bring them to a close, he insisted upon her continuing. We possess an unpublished letter from the poet in which he exclaims:

"Your letters, my Juliette, constitute my treasure, my casket of jewels, my riches! In them our joint lives are recorded day by day, thought by thought. All that you dreamed lies there, all that you suffered. They are charming mirrors, each one of which reflects a fresh aspect of your lovely soul."

Surely such a phrase conveys approbation and sanction sufficient for both Juliette Drouet and her humble biographer.

THE CHÂTEAU OF FOUGÈRES IN 1836.
Unpublished drawing by Victor Hugo.

PART I
BIOGRAPHICAL

CHAPTER I

JULIENNE GAUVAIN

AN irregular outline, sombre colouring, a tangle of towers, steeples, high gables and ramparts, steep passages built in the form of steps: such was the town of Fougères at the beginning of the nineteenth century. The principal features of its surroundings were a turbulent river waging unceasing conflict with numerous mills, uncultivated wastes, more footpaths than lanes, and more lanes than high-roads.

This former hot-bed of *chouans* was an appropriate birthplace for a heroine of romance—and there, on April 10th, 1806, was born Julienne Joséphine Gauvain, subsequently known as Mademoiselle Juliette, and later still, as Madame Drouet.[1]

Her father was a humble tailor living in a suburb of the town, on the road between Fougères and Autrain; her mother kept the little home. Madame Drouet was somewhat proud of her humble origin; she wrote: "I am of the people," as others might boast "I am well born"; she wished thereby to explain and excuse her taste for independence, her fiery temper, and her impulsive nature. She might equally have attributed these to the neglect she suffered in early infancy.

For she had no parents to guard or train her. Her mother died on December 15th, 1806, before the infant could lisp her first words. On September 12th in the following year the father dragged himself to the public infirmary at Fougères, and there breathed his last. The infirmary took over the charge of the orphan, and was about to place her with the foundlings—indeed, the necessary formalities had already been complied with—when a protector suddenly came forward, a certain worthy uncle.

His name was René Henri Drouet. He was thirty-two years old, a sub-lieutenant of artillery, had seen active service in eight campaigns under Napoleon, and been wounded in the foot by the blow of an axe. The wound was such that some very quiet employment had to be provided for him. The ex-artilleryman was turned into a coast-guard, and dawdled out a bored existence in the little Breton port where fate confined him henceforth. He claimed Julienne, and she was handed over to his care.

It would be foolish to pretend that this retired warrior was a suitable person to undertake the training of a little girl. He understood only how to spoil and caress her. Never did child enjoy a wilder, more vagabond childhood. Julienne never got to the village school, because on the way thither glimmered a large pond bordered by clumps of bushes. Among the latter she would conceal her shoes and stockings, and, wading into the water, blue as the skies above, gather starry water-lilies. When she came out, more often than not she failed to find the hiding-place, and ran home bare-footed, with hair floating in the wind and a frock torn to ribbons. But she only laughed, and was forgiven because she made such a winsome picture in her tatters and her wreath of flowers. Those were halcyon days—days filled with innocent joys and elemental sorrows: a fruit-tree robbed of its burden under the indulgent eye of the old coastguard in his green uniform, the death of a tame linnet. All her life Julienne's memory would dwell pleasurably on those early delights. Nothing could curb her natural wildness, not even the gate of a cloister or the rule of St. Benedict.

Among René Henri Drouet's female relations he counted a sister and a cousin, nuns in a great Parisian convent, the Bernardines-Bénédictines of Perpetual Adoration. Their house was situated in the Rue du Petit-Picpus. When Julienne was ten years old he easily managed to have her admitted to the school attached to the convent, and thenceforth the orphan's path in life seemed settled: she should first become a distinguished pupil, then a pious novice, and lastly a holy nun. But, as events turned out, Julienne was only to carry out the first part of the programme.

From the description left us by Madame Drouet and transcribed in full by, Victor Hugo in *Les Misérables*, the house in the Petit-Picpus was none too cheerful; its first welcome to the child was more sombre than any drama she was to figure in, later, as an actress. Padlocked gates, dark corridors, bare rooms, a chapel where the priest himself was concealed behind a veil—such was the scene; black phantoms with shrouded features played the parts; the action was composed of interminable prayers and stringent mortifications. The Bernardines-Bénédictines slept on straw and wore hair shirts, which produced chronic irritation and jerky spasms; they knew not the taste of meat or the warmth of a fire; they took turns in making reparation, and no excuse for shirking was permitted. Reparation consisted in prayers for all the sins and faults of omission and commission, all the crimes of the world. For twelve consecutive hours the petitioner had to kneel upon the stone steps in front of the Blessed Sacrament, with clasped hands and a rope round her neck; when the fatigue became unbearable, she prostrated herself on her face, with her arms outstretched in the form of a cross, and prayed more ardently than before for the sinners of the universe. Victor Hugo, who gathered these details from the lips of Madame Drouet, declared them sublime, while she who had personally witnessed their painful passion, retained a profound impression for life, coupled with a strong sense of Catholicism, and the gift of prayer.

Outside of these austerities the pupils of the school conformed to nearly all the practices of the convent. Like the nuns, they only saw their parents in the parlour, and were not allowed to embrace them. In the refectory they ate in silence under the eye of the nun on duty, who from time to time, if so much as a fly flew without permission, would snap a wooden book noisily. This sound, and the reading of the *Lives of the Saints*, were the sole seasoning of the meal. If a rebellious pupil dared to dislike the food and leave it on her plate, she was condemned to kneel and make the sign of the cross on the stone floor with her tongue.

Neither the licked cross nor the meagre fare ever succeeded in damping Julienne's spirits. She preserved the beautiful spontaneity and love of fun of her early years. She was the spoilt child of the convent where her aunts, Mother des Anges and Mother Ste Mechtilde, appear to have wielded a kindly authority. She soon became its *enfant terrible*. Once, when she was about twelve years old, she threw herself into the arms of a nun and cried, devouring the outer walls with her eyes: "Mother, mother, one of the big girls has just told me I have only got nine years and ten months more to stay here: what luck!" And another time she dropped on the pavement of the cloister a confession written on a sheet of paper so that she might not forget its items: "Father, I accuse myself of being an adulteress. Father, I accuse myself of having stared at gentlemen."

One might well ask who were the gentlemen concerned, for in the convent of Petit-Picpus there were no male professors; only the most distinguished among the nuns assumed the duty of instructing the young boarders. Judging from the eloquence which will be found later in Madame Drouet's letters, the Bernardines-Bénédictines must have accomplished their task with great thoroughness. Julienne learned from them, if not orthography and cultivated style, at least sincerity, and the point that, before attempting to write, one should have something to say. She also studied accomplishments. Mother Ste Mechtilde possessed a beautiful voice. She was consequently appointed mistress of ceremonies and of the choir, and used to train her niece and other pupils. Her habit was to take seven children and make them sing standing in a row according to their ages, so that they looked like a set of girlish organ-pipes. History does not relate whether Julienne sang better than the others, but a little later she began to nurse in secret the idea of utilising her gifts as a virtuoso. At Petit-Picpus she also learned to sketch and paint in water-colours. She owed this instruction to the favour of the pious nuns, who, as a special breach of their rule, authorised her to take lessons from a young master, Redouté.

It may not be too bold to declare that Julienne imbibed at the convent those qualities of tact and restraint, and that air of distinction she exhibited later in the drawing-rooms of Victor Hugo. To the Convent of the

Bernardines was attached a sort of house of retreat where aged ladies of rank could end their days, as also nuns of the various orders whose cloisters had been destroyed during the Revolution. Some of these preserved within their hearts a generous instinct of maternity, which Julienne easily managed to waken. She fell into the habit of running across to break the rule of everlasting silence in that fairly cheerful environment, and, in defiance of the prohibition against intimacy, she turned the old ladies into personal friends. She listened attentively, and remembered much, and forty years later she could describe correctly the names, appearance, and habits of that picturesque group, somewhat archaic, but invariably courteous and witty.

Perhaps because of this slight lifting of the veil, Julienne began already, at the age of sixteen, to fix her eager gaze beyond the cloister and the gate. Perhaps also some instinct of dignity and self-respect urged her to learn something of the world before entering the novitiate to pronounce her vows. However this may be, it seems certain that, on the solemn occasion of her presentation to the Archbishop of Paris, Monsignor Quelen, as a postulant, she managed to convey that her vocation was of the frailest, and her desire for the world, deeply rooted. The prelate understood, and signified to the nuns that this particular lamb desired to wander. That very evening Julienne left the convent.

Here follows a somewhat obscure interlude in the girl's life. We meet her next among the pupils of the sculptor Pradier, in 1825.

James Pradier: to those of our generation this name recalls merely a number of groups and statues: statues more graceful than chaste, groups more elegant than virile; the work of a master who aimed at rivalling Praxiteles, but only succeeded in treading in the footsteps of Clodion.

Pradier, however, only needs a careful biographer to acquire another kind of celebrity: that of an artist, *grand viveur*, magnificent and vain, careless and weak, born too late to lead without scandal the frivolous life he loved, too early to acquire by industry the fortune needed for the indulgence of his tastes.

Twice a week his studio was transformed into a drawing-room, and his receptions were attended by a most varied company: painters and poets, models, actresses, dames of high degree, politicians and men of the sword—all society, in short, liked to be seen in the Rue de l'Abbaye.

Clad in high boots, cut low in front, in violet velvet trousers and a coat of the same material decorated with Polish brandebergs, flanked by a Scotch greyhound almost as big as himself, the master of the house received his visitors, listened to them, talked with them, without interrupting his work; he created fresh marvels with the chisel while the conversation flowed unrestrained, and thus his labours became simultaneously a gossip and a spectacle.

In the novel excitement of surroundings so brilliant, so varied, and of morals so easy, Julienne committed the imprudence which was to settle the fate of her whole life. Thanks to her independent spirit, and still more to her beauty, she very soon established her position in Pradier's house. She came there often, remained long, and consented to pose for him.[2]

And when, one day, the sculptor desired for himself this flower, so superior in delicacy and aroma to those usually found in the studios, he had but to bend down and pluck it.

CLAIRE PRADIER AS A CHILD.
From an unpublished drawing by Pradier.

He made Julienne his mistress in 1825. In 1826 she gave him a little daughter whom we shall meet again later. But now arose difficulties of a practical nature. James Pradier, ex-Prix de Rome, Chevalier de la Légion d'Honneur, Membre de l'Institut, Professeur de l'École des Beaux-Arts, could not with propriety, according to his ideas, marry a model. He does not dream of it for an instant, but, as he wishes to do the girl some kindness, however unsuitable, he manages to insinuate her into the theatrical world, and to put her on the boards. Having friends in Brussels, he decrees that she shall go thither to study and make her first appearance; and, as she needs guidance, advice, and protection, he writes her almost every day long letters, in which platitudes alternate with vulgarity. The correspondence continues, wordy and trivial, interminable and foolish, a repulsive mixture of boasting and preaching. Does Julienne show distaste for vaudeville, Pradier proclaims that form of acting to be the most charming in the world, and places it far above tragedy, which he pronounces tiresome and chilling. If Julienne complains that she has but one dress, Pradier tells her that only the leading lights of the stage possess more. If she ventures a timid request for money, he answers that he has none himself, and offers her a book of fairy-tales illustrated under his supervision.

She had to keep herself alive somehow, and when the poor thing had pledged everything she possessed at the pawnbroker's, she wrote plaintively: "This is the only money my talents have earned for me so far." She might perhaps have been reduced to some desperate measure, had not chance placed her in the path of Félix Harel.

Although an incorrigible Bonapartist, and consequently a conspirator by trade, Harel seems to have been above all a man of the theatre: in the midst of his political preoccupations, one can always discern his predilection for things pertaining to the stage. He also had a very definite conviction that politics and the drama, statesmen and ballet-dancers, have always been closely linked together. So, whether he was for the moment pamphleteer, financier, or prefect, whether he was holding an appointment, or in full flight, he always had a finger in some theatrical pie, either as a director, a manager, or a private adviser. At the time he first met Julienne, he was filling the latter capacity at the Théâtre Royal, in Brussels. He presented the young woman. Without further training than that which Pradier had directed from afar, we know that she made her first appearance in Brussels, at the beginning of the year 1829—to be exact, on February 17th.

On that day she informs Pradier that her début has been successful, and that the Brussels press is favourable. He at once thanks Providence and decides that she can henceforth support herself by her talent. He writes: "Is not this a great pleasure to you? Does it not lift a weight from your heart, you who have such a noble soul? How sweet is the bread one has earned so honourably! For my part, I feel that all your faults are condoned by the trouble you are taking. Your perseverance will be rewarded, never doubt it.

Go on working! Time can never hang heavy when one is labouring honestly; study carries more flowers than thorns."

Having spoken thus, the artist returned to his business and his pleasures, not without having exhorted Julienne to remain in Brussels as long as possible. He was not ignorant of the passionate desire of the young woman to see her babe once more, but he feared that, if she should not find an engagement in Paris like the one she enjoyed in Brussels, she would again be, morally at least, on his hands. Therefore, redoubling his cautious advice and his counsels of prudence, he implored her not to relinquish a certainty for an uncertainty.

However, nothing deterred her. Julienne, as she used to say afterwards, would rather have trudged the distance that separated her from her child, on foot, than waited any longer. The events of 1829 spared her the trouble. Owing to certain evidences of internal discontent, the government of Charles X was developing liberal proclivities. Among other political exiles, it allowed Félix Harel to return, and with him his illustrious mistress, Mlle. Georges. Julienne shared their lot. She accompanied them, not only to Paris, but to the Theatre of the Porte St. Martin, which, under Harel's influence, rapidly became the stronghold of romanticism, and on February 27th, 1830, she made her début on its boards in the part of Emma, in *L'Homme du Monde*, by Ancelot and Saintine. Then she migrated almost at once to the Odéon, of which Harel had just undertaken the management, without, however, resigning that of the Porte St. Martin. She played various parts there throughout the year 1831.

We shall hear later on that she was beautiful, but for the present we must confine ourselves to the question of her talent and dramatic qualities. It has been hinted that she owed her success solely to her lovely face and graceful figure, and that she was one of those ephemeral favourites who reap popular applause in return for the exhibition of their charms. The truth seems to be that "la belle Juliette," as she was already called, gave proofs of distinguished powers, although one is fain to admit that, at this distance of time, it is not easy to define her capacity with any exactitude. For one thing, it was never Juliette's good fortune to play an important part which has since become a classic, and by which her true qualities could be gauged: in Harel's troupe the first-class parts were already justly monopolised by Mlle. Georges and Madame Dorval. Also, nearly all the plays in which Juliette appeared are nowadays looked upon as antiquated and sometimes even absurd. In fact, it is difficult to conceive how they ever could have been given. It will be wiser, therefore, to rely mainly on Pradier's letters to discover what were the natural gifts which could have inspired that artist to make of his mistress an actress, and even a tragedian.

Pradier, then, considered Juliette well equipped by nature in respect of sentiment, intelligence, and voice production; but he criticised in her a certain timidity and lack of assurance, sufficient to mar her entrances and cover her exits with ridicule. He also thought fit to observe to her that, once she was on the scene, and had overcome her initial fright, she overacted her parts, and was not sufficiently natural; she forgot to address herself to the audience, and would speak into the wings, and neglect to vary her gestures, intonations, and pauses.

To sum up, fire, intelligence, and an adequate vocal organ, but shyness, awkwardness, monotonous delivery, and hesitation in gesture and gait: such seem to have been the dramatic qualities and shortcomings of "la belle Juliette." The testimony of Pradier has been confirmed by that of *L'Artiste.* If there is any need to say more, we can judge by an analysis of her engagements with Harel.

On February 7th, 1832, Harel signs a contract with her for thirteen months, to begin from the March 1st following. He brings her back from the Odéon to the Porte St. Martin, and promises her the modest salary of four thousand francs per annum, payable monthly. But he does not treat her as a "general utility" actress—on the contrary, he insists that she keep principally to the part of *jeune première* in comedy, tragedy, and drama; that she learn daily at least forty lines or verses of the parts which shall be allotted to her; that she furnish at her own expense all the dresses necessary for her parts; that she be present at all rehearsals called by the administration of the theatre. On January 13th, 1833, the two agree that the engagement shall be prolonged on the same conditions until April 1st, 1834. Between whiles, Juliette continued to create parts.

It must be confessed that she led the customary life of a theatrical star. From the Boulevard St. Denis, where she lived, to the Boulevard du Temple, which was then the hub of the social world and the centre of amusement, the distance was negligible. She was therefore present at every scene of this ceaseless round of entertainment. Her wardrobe enjoyed a certain renown. Her journeys, one of which was to Italy towards the end of 1832, helped to keep her before the public. Beautiful as a goddess, merrier than ever, her bearing unconcerned, her arm lightly placed within that of the chance companion of the moment, her eyes flashing fire, though her heart might be full to bursting, she sailed towards Cytheræa without apparent regret, without thought of return. It was at this moment that Victor Hugo succeeded in bringing her back into port, and keeping her there for ever, the slave of one master, the woman of one love.

CHAPTER II

PRINCESSE NÉGRONI

TWO portraits of Victor Hugo are extant: one by Devéria executed in 1829, the other by Léon Noël in 1832.[3] What a change is visible in the short space of three years! The "monumental" brow which reminded Théophile Gautier of the "fronton de temple Grec" is the same; but, whereas in 1829 it was instinct with lofty thought and pleasant fancies, in 1832 worry and suspicion have already scored it deeply with lines of care. In 1829 Devéria recognised and rendered the characteristic expression of the poet: that bright, upward glance which ten years before had caused the author of the *Odes* to be compared to a stained-glass archangel. In 1832 Léon Noël saw a fixed, overshadowed gaze, whose severity is further accentuated by knitted brows. In 1829 fleshy, sinuous lips always half ready for a smile or a kiss, indicate both sensuality and humour. In 1832 they are tightly compressed, their outline exaggeratedly firm; they give the impression of having forgotten joy and learnt to express only will. Even in the quality of the flesh-tints the artists disagree. According to Devéria the pallor natural to the poet bears the impress of health and placidity, whereas Léon Noël's rendering reveals sickliness and a sense of doom.

What, then, had happened between the dates of the two portraits? Had the whole character of the poet changed? Had he lost some precious article of faith or conviction, or was it that the mainspring of his enthusiasm had failed him? Nay—his soul still cherished the same treasures of idealism. The former penitent of the Abbé Lammenais still preserved at thirty his ardent, perhaps even narrow Catholicism, his cult of purity, his contempt for physical indulgence, his delight in the joys and duties of family life. Eager for self-sacrifice, rich in the hopes and illusions he confided to his few intimate friends, he dreamed of sharing everything with the people, towards whom the trend of events inclined him to turn; just as he had once written *Les Lettres à la fiancée* for a single reader, so he had now published for the crowd *Les Feuilles d'Automne*, the curious preface to that collection, and in the collection itself the sublime *Prière pour tous*. His was a soul profoundly religious, and a lofty mind which aspired to raise itself ever higher.

But he did not live by thought alone. Many of those who watched him working without intermission, with a method and a will that defied human weakness, who saw how numerous were his lectures, how varied his researches, and who witnessed the incessant travail of his imagination, thought that the author of *Hernani* and *Dona Sol* must be lacking in human sensibility. He protests against this. In a letter to Sainte-Beuve he says: "I live only by my emotions; to love, or to crave for love and friendship, is the fundamental aim—happy or unhappy, public or private—of my life."[4] He might equally have added: "That is why for the last two years my brow is no longer placid, why my eyes seek the ground, why my lips are so bitterly compressed."

The secret of the change in Victor Hugo's physiognomy lies in the treachery of his wife and his best friend. Love and friendship failed him together. His moral distress was immense, his pain unfathomable. They inspired him with plaints so touching that, after hearing them, one asks oneself whether it can ever be possible for him to forget or recover. One despairs of the healing of the man who writes: "I have acquired the conviction that it is possible for the one who possesses all my love to cease to care for me. I am no longer happy."[5]

Calmness did return to him, however. It was thus: For the last ten years, that is, practically ever since her marriage, Madame Victor Hugo had behaved in such a manner that when the day of the betrayal, in which she was the accomplice of his friend, dawned, the poet was able to consider her with contempt. Although fairly gifted in appearance, she possessed neither taste nor cleverness in the matter of dress; she had always shown herself to him in careless attire and unfashionable gowns. Absent-minded and limited in intelligence, she remained uncultured and oblivious of the genius of her husband, and of achievements of which she appreciated only the financial value. In addition, she had declined to share the noble ideal originally proposed to her by her twenty-year-old bridegroom: love considered as "the ardent and pure union of two souls, a union begun on earth to end not even in heaven."[6] The poet was thus authorised, and even forced, to seek happiness in the arms of some other woman. If Victor Hugo had wished to avoid that "other woman " he would have had to remain for ever concealed in his tower of ivory—which certainly did not happen.

VICTOR HUGO AS A YOUNG MAN.
In the possession of M. le D. F. Jousseaume.

He emerged from it in the spring of 1832, on May 26th, and appeared at an artists' ball. There he saw Juliette for the first time; but she was so beautiful and so captivating that he was afraid of her, and dared not address her. Five years later he recorded this impression of admiring timidity in the book in which they had agreed to celebrate all their anniversaries, namely the *Voix Intérieures*.[7]

For more than six months the poet lacked the courage to seek his vision again, but in the early days of 1833 he found Juliette among the actresses Harel suggested to him at the Porte St. Martin for his play, *Lucrèce Borgia*. He accepted her at once and gave her a small part, that of Princesse Négroni. Then the rehearsals began. Juliette admits in one of her letters that she showed herself very coquettish and mischievous.

According to her, the poet made up his mind the first day and the first hour. But matters did not really proceed so easily. Victor Hugo, who, as stated above, cherished the highest and purest moral ideal, must have carried his principles with him into the wings and on the stage. He was not partial to actresses; he was suspicious of them, and made no secret of the feeling. One must picture him rather as on the defensive than bold and adventurous.

His attire and appearance were not calculated to ensure his social success. We hear from Juliette herself that he wore his hair *en broussaille*, and that his smile revealed "crocodile's teeth." Allowing himself to be dressed by his tailor in the fashions of four or five years earlier, his trousers were firmly braced above the waist, tightly drawn over his boots, and fastened under the instep by a steel chain. To sum up, as a dandy who writes these details concludes, he was a worthy citizen desirous of being in the fashion, but unable to compass it.

Fortunately the said citizen could speak, and his words of gold were sufficient to gloss over any personal disadvantages. To men he discoursed of his hopes and plans, and even his forecasts for the future; to women of their beauty and the supremacy of such a gift. Men found his arrogance intolerable, and complained that they must always either listen, or talk to him of himself. But women liked him for abasing his pride before them; they appreciated his good manners, his urbanity, and the incomparable art with which he cast his laurels at their feet. The god took on humanity for them; they were careful to pose as goddesses before him. Juliette possessed everything needful to accomplish this end.

She was about to enter her twenty-sixth year; very shortly afterwards, Théophile Gautier wrote this fulsome description of her, to please the master:

"Mademoiselle Juliette's countenance is of a regular and delicate beauty; the nose chiselled and of handsome outline, the eyes limpid and diamond-bright, the mouth moistly crimson, and tiny even in her gayest fits of laughter. These features, charming in themselves, are set in an oval of the suavest and most harmonious form. A clear, serene forehead like the marble of a Greek temple crowns this delicious face; abundant black hair, with wonderful reflections in it, brings out the diaphanous and lustrous purity of her complexion. Her neck, shoulders, and arms, are of classic perfection; she would be a worthy inspiration to sculptors, and is well equipped to enter into competition with those beautiful young Athenians who lowered their veils before the gaze of Praxiteles conceiving his Venus.[8]

These elegant phrases probably represent very imperfectly the impression produced by Juliette. We have had the privilege of perusing some of the proposals addressed to her, and we have read the cruel novel Alphonse Karr prided himself on having written about her.[9] Everything conspires to show that she shone and dazzled especially by her all-conquering air of youth and ingenuousness. When she passed, spring was over. Her age, condition, manner of life, had made of her a woman, while her smile and movements kept her still a girl. Her gait was, in fact, so fairy-like that her admirers all make use, certainly without collusion, of the adjective, "aérien." Her face presented a perfect image of calmness and purity. Did she raise her eyes, a soft, velvety, sometimes mournful gaze was revealed—did she lower them, it was still the dawn, but a dawn concealing itself behind a veil.

All beautiful countenances have a soul; upon Juliette's could be read less contentment than unsatisfied ardour, more melancholy than serenity. Neither luxury, nor pleasure, nor flattery, was able to satisfy the dearest desire of her heart from the age of sixteen, which was, to become the passionate companion of an honest man. She lent herself to her lovers, but her eyes made it plain that she still sought the perfect one to whom she would some day capitulate. According to herself—and we have no reason to doubt her—she selected Victor Hugo as soon as she made his acquaintance. She expended herself in advances and coquetries, and infused into the study and expression of her small part all the art of which she was capable. In the third act of the play, when Maffio said to her: "*L'amitié ne remplit pas tout le cœur*," she had to query: "*Mon Dieu, qu'est-ce qui remplit tout le cœur?*" It seems that at rehearsals she did not wait for Maffio's answer, but turned subtly towards the poet and sought him with her eyes. He, however, still hung back; a tradition attributed to Frédérick Lemaître, which we have carefully verified,[10] informs us that he surprised even the actors of the Porte St. Martin by the respectful tone he maintained towards his beautiful interpreter. Far from addressing her in the familiar manner customary in theatrical circles, he called her Mademoiselle Juliette, kissed her hand, and bowed low before her. Frédérick could not believe his eyes.

At last the evening of the first performance arrived; the success of the piece was immediate. Juliette had her share of it. She was so beautiful as the poisoner that, as Théophile Gautier says, the public forgot to pity her unhappy guests and thought them fortunate to die after kissing her hand.[11] After the third act she received congratulations even from Mademoiselle Georges, who folded her in her arms and covered her with kisses. As for the author, we do not know what he did in the first blush, but the next morning he wrote thus:

"In *Lucrèce Borgia*, certain personages of secondary importance are represented at the Porte St. Martin by actors of the first order, who perform with grace, loyalty, and perfect taste, in the semi-obscurity of their parts. The author here thanks them. Among these, the public particularly distinguished Mademoiselle Juliette. It can hardly be said that Princesse Négroni is a part: it is in some sense an apparition; a figure, beautiful, young, fatal, which floats by, raising one corner of the sombre veil that covers Italy at the commencement of the sixteenth century. Mademoiselle Juliette threw into this figure an extraordinary virility. She had few words to say, but she filled them with meaning. This actress only requires opportunity, to reveal forcibly to the public a talent full of soulfulness, passion, and truth."[12]

Nothing could be better said or more openly declared, and the interpreter of the part was thus informed of the intentions of the author. He adopts her, makes her his own, is ready to share his own glory with the youthful renown of Négroni. For her he will conceive marvellous parts; she will create them.

Juliette understood him perfectly. With the ardour of a twenty-five-year-old imagination excited by love, she began to dream of her poet, of their two lives henceforward united in a common success. While Victor still wavered, still hesitated whether to seek this actress of whom thousands of alarming anecdotes were current, she made foolish projects, settled trivial details, savoured one by one those joys of the dawn of love which so many women prefer to the delights of possession.

He came at last on February 27th, Shrove Sunday, towards the end of the afternoon. The weather had been beautiful, one of those soft spring days that enhance the beauty of Parisian women and make the men pensive. The streets were littered with booths, noisy with fireworks, discordant with raucous voices. The Boulevard du Temple exploited a fair where, on that particular day, masks and songs added variety and movement.

Victor Hugo, who lived in the Place Royale and never drove in a cab, had to cross this scene on foot. His thoughts were still confused; he, who was ordinarily so determined in his plans, still debated whether he should mount the actress's stairs. After all, this child seemed fond of him—but whom was she not fond of? Who was there that did not figure on the list of her lovers? Yesterday, Alphonse Karr, loutish, a babbler, a writer of romances, fairly honest, but so ponderous in his pretentious and everlasting coat of black velvet! To-day a Russian Prince who was said to have offered Juliette a marvellous trousseau, copied from the wedding outfit of Madame la Duchesse d'Orléans. He was also credited with the intention of installing her in a sumptuous apartment in the Rue de l'Échiquier.... What should a poet, a great poet conscious of his mission, want with such a girl?

Then a voice sang in the memory of Victor Hugo, a voice almost supernatural, like those with which he used to endow the good fairies in the days when he covered the margins of his lesson-books with fancies. *"Mon Dieu,"* it wailed, *"qu'est-ce qui remplit tout le cœur?"* And at last the poet walked up to place the answer at the feet of his new friend.

Like all great hearts, Victor and Juliette fell head over ears in love, and thought of nothing else. The poet was no longer to be found in the Place Royale, or, if he was, he remained abstracted, a stranger at his own hearth. He, usually so precise, so punctual and methodical, now neglects his guests and is late for meals. When evening comes and his drawing-room is filled with voices, song, and discussion, and with women who smile upon him and men who render him homage, he forgets everything, even to be polite. His eye is on the clock, he longs for the blessed hour of the *rendezvous* at 9, Rue St. Denis. Sometimes he snatches up a stray sheet of paper and scribbles feverishly. Verse or prose? More often it is verse, for it will be offered to Juliette, and nothing flatters her so much as these poetical surprises created in the midst of the din and diversions of a social circle.

Neither did she give herself in niggardly fashion. From the very beginning she said to him: "I am good for nothing but to love you!" She threw herself thoroughly, magnificently, into the part.

Thus quoth she—and wrote likewise, for she, also, wrote from everywhere: from her room, from a friend's house, from her box at the theatre, from a chance café. For her tender "scribbles," as she calls them, any scrap of paper will serve, even an envelope or the margin of a newspaper; and for instrument a pencil, a blackened pin, even a steel pen, that novel invention of which every one is talking, but which she hardly knows how to use.

Of the form of her letters she takes little heed. No lexicon is needed to say that one loves. A woman in the throes of passion does not worry about grammar. Juliette is of that opinion, and that is why her early letters are so full of charm. They exhale the perfume of love, and also its timidity.

Her letters were not merely a means of giving vent to her feelings: they seemed to her the only occupation fit for a sweetheart worthy of the name, when the lover is absent or delayed. On February 18th, 1833, Victor Hugo had left her early in the morning. She had rushed to the window to follow him with her eyes as long as he was in sight. At the corner of the Rue St. Denis, as he was about to turn into the Rue St. Martin, he looked back; they exchanged a volley of kisses. Then she found herself lonely indeed, oblivious of her surroundings, like a somnambulist who walks and speaks and acts in a dream. Around her was an immense void, in her heart one sole desire: to see the poet again, and never to part from him. It was to fill that void and beguile that desire that she took up the habit of writing to him.

JULIETTE DROUET IN THE RÔLE OF LA PRINCESSE NÉGRONI.

He, on his part, repaid letters and messages as much as possible with his own presence. Any time he could snatch from his children and work and visits to publishers or theatre-managers, he gave to Juliette. As *Lucrèce Borgia* continued to reap a signal success—the greatest, from the financial point of view, that the Porte St. Martin had ever experienced—Harel asked the author for a new play. Victor Hugo wrote *Marie Tudor* in very few days, and the principal parts had just been allotted: to Mademoiselle Georges the Queen, to Juliette, Jane. Under pretext of rehearsing, we find our lovers lunching together almost every day. If there was really a rehearsal, they met again afterwards on the stage, and tasted the rare pleasure of sharing their work, as they shared their pleasure. When they did not rehearse, they hurried out of town. Furtively yet boldly, timidly but merrily, they started on one of those strolls, partly Parisian, and partly suburban, which, according to Juliette, were the chief enchantment of their *liaison*.

Paris was not then the dusty conglomeration of eight-story-high houses it now is. Instead of spreading over the surrounding country, it allowed the country to encroach upon itself. At the foot of Montmartre (which Juliette always calls a *mountain*), real windmills waved their long arms; along the Butte aux Cailles a genuine brook purled among the lilacs and syringa; on the summit of Montparnasse, when there was dancing, artists and poets, dandies and grisettes, trod actual grass, to the sound of fiddles! Juliette had always in her a strain of bohemianism. We may therefore picture her in short, striped, pleated skirt, tight at the waist but flowing out wide at the bottom over white stockings, a little silken cape covering her queenly young bosom, without concealing its fine lines, her head surmounted by a rose-trimmed bonnet with black ribbons, clasping the arm of her "friend" with sparkling eyes and cheeks as rosy as her headdress. Happiness, as she used to say in after-days, is so light to carry, that her feet hardly touched the ground. Her pride in her companion was such that her glance defied Heaven. "When I hold your arm," she wrote to him, "I am as proud as if I had made you myself."

She did *re*make him, to a certain extent, for it was she who insisted upon his becoming younger and smarter in appearance. He now trained his chestnut locks over his Olympian brow, in careful but unromantic fashion; his black eyes, with their blue depths, resumed their upward glance, when they were not plunged in those of his mistress; his complexion, which had been so pale, now gained colour, and soon, when Auguste de Châtillon paints the poet's miniature for Juliette's pleasure, he will be able to endow him with lips less eloquent than caressing, without straying from the truth. "The dear little fashionable," as his companion called him, compressed his sturdy figure into a really handsome blue coat opening over a shot waistcoat. His immaculate linen, and the scarlet ribbon of the order Charles X had bestowed upon him in his youth, stood out in pleasant contrast to the sombre hue of his coat. His tiny feet, and hands as delicate as Juliette's own, completed this somewhat incongruous exterior.

And the two made expeditions together, wherever they knew of, or hoped to find, moss and trees, and an attractive shelter. They went to Montmartre and Montrouge, to Maison Blanche and St. James, to Bicêtre and Meudon, Fontainebleau, Gisors, St. Germain-en-Laye, and Versailles. Sometimes the poet pondered his work as he walked. Silence was then the order of the day; so Juliette was silent. But more often they talked, made plans for the future, babbled merry nonsense, and exchanged kisses. Or else they discussed their past: Victor told of his studious childhood spent poring over books, of his early works, laborious and chaste. Juliette recalled her bare-footed school-girl pranks. Both gloried in the radiant memories of their youth.

But in the midst of those halcyon days of simple pleasures, Fate began to show herself unkind. First came the failure of *Marie Tudor*, then Juliette's disappointment at the Comédie Française, and, in addition, the persecution of her creditors and the consequent quarrels with Victor Hugo, with their subsequent scenes of tender reconciliation.

The poor girl was, in fact, overwhelmed with debt. When Victor Hugo, desirous of setting her free for ever, asked her to draw up a detailed statement of her affairs, she nearly broke down under the task, for there were not only ordinary bills, such as 12,000 fr. to Janisset the jeweller, 1,000 fr. to Poivin the glove-maker, 600 fr. to the laundress, 260 fr. to Georges the hair-dresser, 400 fr. to Villain the purveyor of rouge, 620 fr. to Madame Ladon, dressmaker, 2,500 fr. to Mesdames Lebreton and Gérard for dress materials, 1,700 fr. to Jourdain the upholsterer—but also fictitious and usurious debts intended to disguise money loans, and all the more numerous because they were for the most part invented under the direction of an attorney who answered to the name of Manière. She took good care not to reveal to Victor Hugo, whose own burdens, and practical, economical mind, she was well acquainted with, the amount of her expenditure and the magnitude of her liabilities. The moment came, however, when the creditors realised that they had to deal with a pretty woman inefficiently vouched for by a poet. They lost patience and threatened her, and it was then that Juliette had recourse to money-lenders. The remedy was worse than the evil. Stamped paper soon flooded her rooms. Her furniture was seized, and also her salaries from the Théâtre Français and the Porte St. Martin. She tried to save a few clothes, and was had up for illegally making away with the creditors' property. Her landlord threatened her with expulsion; she imagined herself homeless, and lost her head.

Instead of confiding in Victor Hugo, her natural protector, she had recourse to former friends. There were many such, from Pradier, the sculptor, to Séchan, the scene-painter of the Opera and other theatres. Pradier replied with advice; he was not without just pretext for refusal, for, since her intrigue with Victor Hugo, Juliette no longer wrote to the father of her child except *"par accident et monosyllabes"* or else in a school-girl's handwriting, calculated to cover the pages in very few words. Séchan and a few others were less stingy; they sent small but quite insufficient contributions. She was therefore forced to take the big step of revealing the whole truth to the beloved.

The scene was stormy, although Victor Hugo did not hesitate for a moment before complying with an obligation that was also a satisfaction, since it secured his possession of Juliette. Fussy and meticulous though he was in the small circumstances of life, he knew how to be generous and even lavish in the great—but Juliette's petty deceptions had infused doubts in his mind; moreover, he was in love and therefore jealous. Towards the end of 1833 and in the early part of 1834, suspicion, anger, unjust recriminations and noisy quarrels became almost daily affairs. As invariably happens in these cases, friends, male and female, interfered. Juliette was slandered by Mademoiselle Ida Ferrier, her understudy in the rôle of Jane at the Porte St. Martin—who would, if rumour may be trusted, have gladly understudied her also in the heart of Victor Hugo—also by Mademoiselle Georges, who was getting on in years[13] and could not forgive the lovers for not acknowledging her sovereignty in the green-room and drawing-room as they admitted it upon the stage. To aspersions and reproaches Juliette opposed, not only indignation, but angry words, violent retorts, and sometimes even insulting epithets; or else she protested in innumerable letters and notes, rendered eloquent by their sincerity. She complained that she was "attacked without the means of defence, soiled without opportunity of cleansing herself, wounded without chance of healing"; she affirmed her intention of putting an end to the situation by suicide or final rupture. Generally Victor Hugo arrived in time to calm her frenzy with a caress or a soothing word, and then Juliette would try to resign herself and let hope spring uppermost once more. But Victor Hugo, under the influence of some new tittle-tattle, resumed his grand-inquisitorial manner, and the tone, words, reproaches and even threats appertaining to the part. The creditors continued to harry her without intermission; so in the end the couple passed from words to actions.

As we have stated above, Juliette's furniture had been seized, and she was about to be turned out of her apartment in the Rue de l'Échiquier. She had endeavoured vainly to interest her friends, past and present, in her difficulties. Even Victor Hugo, disheartened probably by the difficulties of the task, had returned a refusal. The lovers therefore exchanged farewells which they thought final, and on August 3rd Juliette started for St. Renan, near Brest, where her sister, Madame Kock, was living. Happily she travelled by the Rennes diligence, and there were many halts on the way. From the very first of these she sent an adoring letter to the poet. She wrote again from Rennes, from Brest once more, and lastly from St. Renan. Victor Hugo responded with expressions of poignant regret and remorse, according to those who have read them. He promised to do his very best to find the few necessary banknotes to satisfy the biggest creditors. In the end, he set out for Rennes himself, and rejoined his friend. The lovers returned to Paris on August 10th.

Now commences the most singular period of the life of Juliette, one which has been aptly entitled an "amorous redemption after the romantic manner."[14] For nearly two years Victor Hugo, taking his mistress as the subject of his experiment, put into practice the theories, in part religious, and in part philosophical, which he professed concerning courtesans, namely: the expiation of faults by faithful, passionate, disinterested love; love itself being considered as a species of *sesame*, capable of opening wide the doors of science, and throwing light upon all hidden things.

The first condition of redemption was poverty, voluntarily, almost joyously, accepted. The furniture of the Rue de l'Échiquier must be sold and the beautiful rooms given up. A tiny apartment consisting of two rooms and a kitchen was taken for Juliette at No. 4, Rue du Paradis au Marais, at a yearly rental of 400 fr. There she shivered through the winter, and spent part of her days in bed to economise her fuel; but at least she proved that she loved truly and was deserving of love.

No more dresses or jewels ... every evening Victor Hugo repeated to his mistress that dress adds nothing to the charms of a lovely woman, that it is waste of time to try to add to nature where nature herself is beautiful; and proudly, as if indeed she were clothed in the hair-shirt of her former mistresses at the convent, Juliette wrote: "My poverty, my clumsy shoes, my faded curtains, my metal spoons, the absence of all ornament and pleasure apart from our love, testify at every hour and every minute, that I love you with all my heart."

But there can be no true reformation or conversion without work. So Juliette must work; she must study her parts, make her clothes and even some of Victor Hugo's, patch others, keep her little house in order, and spend what leisure she can snatch, in copying the works of the master, cutting out extracts from the newspapers, classifying and collecting his manuscripts and proofs.

When he had completed this splendid programme, of which almost every part, as we shall presently see, was carried out to the letter, the poet experienced an overpowering need to find himself alone somewhere with the woman he had finally subjugated. His mind was still quite Virgilian. He had not yet arrived at confusing duty with politics and happiness with popularity. His greatest enjoyment, next to love, was in rural pursuits, and for the indulgence of these he flattered himself he had discovered in Juliette a companion worthy of himself. The lovers had barely settled in the Rue du Paradis au Marais before they went off to the valley of Bièvres. Half mystics, half pagans, worshipping equally at the shrines of the forest divinities and those of the village churches, they entered upon the consummation of what they themselves called their "marriage of escaped birds."

JULIETTE DROUET IN THE RÔLE DE LA PRINCESSE NÉGRONI.

HOUSE IN THE VILLAGE OF LES METZ, IN THE PARISH OF JOUY-EN-JOSAS, SEINE-ET-OISE,
In which Juliette Drouet lived while Victor Hugo was staying at Les Roches. This is the house referred to in La Tristesse d'Olympio.

CHAPTER III

"LA TRISTESSE D'OLYMPIO"

IN the neighbourhood of Paris, about four miles from Versailles, nestles a valley which the modern devotees of romance should deem worthy of a visit. Not because it boasts of any special features, such as mighty torrents thundering from giddy heights into abysmal precipices below—on the contrary, its character is harmonious and serene, more like a French park decked with flowers by nature, and watered by chance—but because in these classic surroundings, about the year 1830, circumstances led the great men of the new school to seek temporary repose for their fretted souls. To us, these peaceful meadows, flanked by pensive willows weeping on the borders of the silent Bièvres, must evermore be peopled by those troubled shades: by Lammenais, the priestly keeper of consciences, Montalembert, the angelic doctor, Sainte-Beuve, the purveyor of ideas, Berlioz, the musician, and, lastly, by the poet, Victor Hugo, who followed meekly in the rear, while awaiting the glory of conducting the procession.

They used to arrive in the summer, some for a couple of days, others for weeks together, to stay with Monsieur Bertin, editor of the *Journal des Débâts* and owner of Les Roches,[15] a property situated midway between the villages of Bièvres and Jouy-en-Josas. Genial and lively, as Ingres represents him in his celebrated portrait, Monsieur Bertin loved to divine, promote, and, where needful, encourage their vocations and plans. His housekeeping was on a modest scale, but his hospitality delightful—a mixture of go-as-you-please and kindly despotism; perfect freedom outwardly, but, in reality, careful ministrations skilfully disguised. Louise Bertin, the eldest daughter of the old man, and one of the muses of the period, willingly divided her time between the kitchen and the drawing-room, cookery-books and poems. As an ardent musician, tolerably familiar with the best literature, her mind was full of quaintness, while her heart was instinct with kindliness. When, perchance, she had surfeited her guests with sonatas and song, she would be seized with fear lest she should be interfering with their habits or inclinations, and would hastily substitute anarchy, by commanding each one to choose his own occupation, and pursue his meditation, walk, or game unhindered.

Of them all, Victor Hugo seems to have been the girl's favourite, and the one who made the largest use of this generous welcome and charming liberty. As soon as the periwinkles blossomed, he settled his wife and children at Les Roches, while he himself came and went between Paris and Bièvres. Gradually he grew to associate the valley with his joys and sorrows; it became one of those familiar haunts to which one instinctively turns, with the comforting assurance of finding there the outward conditions suitable to one's moods. As a young father, he made it the fitting frame for family joys; when his love was flung back in his face and his friendship betrayed, he returned to seek, if not consolation, at least faith and hope for the future. A year later, again under the shelter of Les Roches, he thought he had found solace. The valley meant something more than an invitation to dawdle: it filled him with sensuous suggestion; he longed to place his ideal of an unquenchable love at the feet of a woman, and to pronounce the word "Forever."

With the connivance of Madame Victor Hugo, who shut her eyes, and that of Mademoiselle Louise Bertin, who smiled her toleration,[16] this happiness came to him at length; not indeed in the first year of his passion for Juliette, but in the early part of the second. He brought his mistress to Bièvres and to Jouy on July 4th, 1834, a little before the tragic crisis that so nearly separated the lovers, as we have related in the foregoing chapter.

Juliette immediately fell in love with the scenes the poet had so often and so eloquently described to her. Of their joint visit to the Écu de France, the little inn at Jouy-en-Josas,[17] she drew up, in fun, one of those mock official reports in which she excelled. They decided to return and lunch, no matter where, or how, provided it was neither too near nor too far from Les Roches. Then they set out in quest of rooms, which they eventually found in the hamlet of Metz, on the summit of the hill above Jouy on the northern side. They returned to Paris after paying over to the proprietor, Sieur Labussière, the sum of 92 frs. for a year's rent. Thither they came in September for a sojourn of six weeks, after the troubled interval described above.

The little house does not seem to have been altered at all.[18] It was originally built for the game-keeper of the neighbouring château, which belonged to Cambacérès. It still spreads its white frontage, pierced with green-shuttered windows, against the background of woods. It consists only of a ground-floor and an attic; a rambling vine covers its walls; around it are scattered a barn, some outhouses, and an orchard, whose steep sides slope downwards to a gate opening on to the Jouy road.

With the assistance of the landlady, Mère Labussière, as she calls her, Juliette undertook to perform the lighter tasks of housekeeping in the mornings, and it was understood that Victor Hugo should visit her every afternoon unless some grave impediment prevented him.

But the walk from Les Roches to Les Metz was long: not much under two miles, by rough roads. The lovers agreed therefore to meet half-way, by a path settled beforehand, and to abandon the Labussière roof-tree for some leafy bower. Thus began, as Juliette writes, their "bird-life in the woods."

Victor Hugo had a choice of three ways when he went to meet his lady. One led across the valley of Bièvres; another, along the pavement,[19] as the high road from Bièvres to Versailles was called; and lastly there was the woodland path, which they both preferred. Victor Hugo started by the Vauboyau road, plunged into the woods skirting the boundary of the Château of Les Roches, then, turning to the left, walked straight on as far as the four cross-roads at l'Homme Mort, and bore to the right towards the Cour Roland. There, in the hollow of a hundred-year-old chestnut-tree, all bent and twisted, his lady-love would be awaiting him.

Clad in a dress of white jaconet striped with pink, such as she usually affected, her head covered with an Italian straw hat, left over from the days of her former affluence, with swelling bosom, rosy cheeks, and smiling mouth, she resembled a flower springing from the rude calyx formed by the aged tree. A wide-awake flower, indeed, for, from the first sign of the approach of Victor Hugo, she would fly to him, and afford him one more opportunity of admiring the far-famed aerial gait, that fairy footstep, so light that it had been compared to the sound of a lyre.

Then followed kisses, caresses, a flood of soft words, more kisses, and a rapid rush into the cool green depths whither the twitter of birds invited them. When they issued forth again, silent now, Juliette walked first, making it a point of honour to push aside the branches and thorns before her poet; and he was content, gazing upon the tiny traces left upon the moss or sand by the feet that looked almost absurd by reason of their minuteness.

At the far end of a clearing a fountain burbled. Juliette made a hollow of her little hands and collected a delicious draught for their burning lips. Drops dribbled from between her fingers, and, seeing them, her lover knew that here was a fairy able to "transmute water into diamonds."[20]

We must not imagine, however, that the treasure of their love expended itself entirely in this sportive fashion. If it be true that passion is the stronger for an admixture of intellect, it follows that only persons of distinguished parts are capable of extracting the full measure of delight from sentimental intercourse. Victor Hugo was far too wise to neglect the training of the sensibilities of his young mistress. Like some block of rare marble, she submitted herself to this able sculptor in the charming simplicity of a nature somewhat uncultivated and rugged, as she herself owns, and he perceived in the formless material the growing suggestion of the finished statue he was soon to evolve. The forest was the studio whither he came every afternoon to cultivate, through novel sensations and delights, his own poetry and eloquence. The forest gave him colour for colour, music for music....

At other times Victor Hugo encouraged in Juliette an inclination for prayer and tearful repentance. He retained, and she had always possessed, strong Catholic sensibilities. The mere satisfaction of sensuality without the hallowing influence of absorbing love spelt defilement, from their point of view. Hence followed painful remorse for a past which the lover liked to hear his mistress bewail, and which she despaired of ever redeeming. Her *rôle* was the abasement of Magdalen; his, the somewhat strained attitude of an apostle or saviour.

Nothing could be more peaceful or uneventful than Juliette's evenings. She devoured with the appetite of an ogress the frugal supper put before her by Madame Labussière, repaired the damage done to her clothes by the afternoon's ramble, or studied some of the parts in which she hoped to appear sooner or later at the Théâtre Français. At ten o'clock she went to bed. This was the much-prized moment of her solitude, when she retired, as she says, into the happy background of her heart to rehearse in spirit the simple events and delights of the day, to recall the face of her lover, see him, speak to him, and hang upon his answers; then, as drowsiness gradually gained the upper hand and clouds dimmed the dear outline, to surrender to slumber. It was at Les Metz that she coined the happy phrase: "I fall asleep in the thought of you." Sometimes the wind moaning in the heights awoke her, and she resumed her sweet musing. The poet was in the habit of working at night; she would picture him in his room at Les Roches, bending over his writing-table. Then she "blessed the gale that made her the companion of the dear little workman's vigil across the intervening space."

As soon as dawn broke she was up again. She jumped out of bed, ran to the window, opened the shutters, and interrogated the heavens—not that she feared rain, any more than she minded "blisters on her feet or scratches on her hands"—but she had only two dresses, a woollen and a linen, and the condition of the weather controlled her choice of the two. Her toilet was rapid, her breakfast simple. She spent the remaining time copying the manuscripts confided to her by Victor Hugo. Then, lightly running, as she says, like a hare across the plain, she started for the rendezvous. As becomes a loving woman, she was always first at the trysting-tree. She scrutinised the intertwined initials she herself had carved upon its bark, or conned again from memory the verses she had found the day before in its hollow trunk. She "sings them in her heart," presses them to her bosom, and kisses the letters she has brought in answer.

CHURCH OF BIÈVRES, SEINE-ET-OISE.

For the chestnut-tree served them as a letter-box as well as a shelter. According to an arrangement between them, the first thing they did on arrival was to deposit within its friendly shade everything they had written in the course of the preceding day for, or about, one another. On Juliette's part, especially, the letters became more and more numerous: two, four, sometimes six per day. She no longer wrote, as at first, to expatiate upon her passion or assure the poet that she loved him with real love, or to relieve boredom and make the hours of her solitude pass more quickly. She wrote because Victor Hugo, who had formerly been indifferent to her "scribbles," now exacted them as a daily tribute, and reproached her if they were too brief or not numerous enough. This jealous lover had discovered the advantages of a pretty woman's mania for writing. When thus occupied, he reflected, she is contented. He also found that her letters were full of enthusiasm, humour, feeling, fun, and poetry, and he therefore desired that they should be preserved; one day, when Juliette had thrown a packet of them into the fire in a fit of temper, he made her write them all over again. Juliette might protest prettily, entrench herself behind her ignorance, and allege her want of intelligence; but the more she pleaded that she knew not how to write, the more her lover insisted upon her doing so. No one has ever carried to greater lengths that form of affectation which consists in vilifying oneself in order to gain praise. Having thus placed herself, as far as her style is concerned, in the kneeling position she prefers, Juliette remains there. It is at Les Metz that her letters commenced to be a hymn of praise in honour of her divinity. Adoration and excessive adulation are their basis; for form and imagery, Juliette does not hesitate to borrow from the sacred writings she had studied at the Convent of Petit-Picpus. Sooth to say, this mixture of religiosity and passion presents an aspect both disproportionate and pathetic. When love raises itself—or degrades itself—to this almost mystical adoration, one cannot be surprised if it ends by believing in its own virtue. Having adopted the forms of religion, it insensibly acquires its importance and dignity; it ennobles itself.

We do not possess Victor Hugo's answers, but partly from the note-books in which his lady-love punctiliously copied and dated the poems addressed to her, and partly from the dates inscribed at the bottom of each page in the collected works of the poet, we know which of his verses were composed during his sojourn at Les Metz. It is not too much to say that the author of *Feuilles d'Automne* was never more happily inspired. Nowhere did he more closely approach the classical model he had chosen at that time, the gentle Virgil.

The lovers returned to Les Metz twice: once in October 1837 for a few days, and again, for a day, on September 26th, 1845. In 1837 it was Victor Hugo who directed the expedition and took the lead. He sought one by one the traces of their *amours*; his eccentric genius admired nature's grand indifference, which had failed to preserve them intact for his honour and pleasure, and, deploring this ingratitude concerning outward things, he composed that masterpiece, *La Tristesse d'Olympio*. He laid it at the feet of Juliette, who accepted it, read and reread it, and learnt it by heart, without criticising it.

In 1845, the pilgrimage was hers; she planned it and begged for it, writing on August 19th: "I have an inexpressible longing to see Les Metz again. We absolutely must go there."[21]

They did. Early in the month of September Juliette arranged the little journey. Which dress should she wear? The striped organdy one, or the blue tarlatan shot with white, she had worn a few months previously, at the reception of St. Marc Girardin at the Académie Française? She chose the former because her lover preferred it; the same reason determined her to wear a straw hat "trimmed with geraniums above and below the brim." Thus decked, with cheeks rosier than usual, and eyes glowing, Juliette climbed with her poet into the omnibus from Paris to Sceaux.

Victor Hugo disliked omnibuses, and especially that one. He remembered his many drives in it with his friend Sainte-Beuve, at the time the latter was most assiduous in his visits to Les Roches, and in spite of himself he seemed to see the ghost of Joseph Delorme in the back seat, with his ecclesiastical appearance, and his mania for nestling cosily between two fat people. Silently the poet dwelt upon these memories, while Juliette volubly recalled others. She wondered whether they would find the beggar at the foot of the Bièvres hill, into whose hands she had often emptied her purse, in order that alms should bring them luck, and whether the baker in the Square still made those little tarts her lover used to be so fond of. At last the omnibus deposited them at Bièvres in front of the Chariot d'Or. The striped organdy dress created a great sensation among the village children. Juliette rushed off to the little church; nothing was changed—the same simplicity, the same silence, the same brooding peace as in the old days. The young woman fell on her knees, then, together, the lovers returned to the Chariot d'Or, breakfasted, and started to walk to Les Roches. There again, in Juliette's opinion, everything was unchanged. To the left, behind tall grasses, the river flowed unseen and unheard. In deference to the needs of man and those of the valley, its course had been diverted, and it now spread itself through meadows and orchards. Its presence could be divined from the abundance of flowers and reeds born of its moisture. When they reached Les Roches, Juliette insisted upon abandoning the valley for the forest. They ascended through Vauboyau to the wood of l'Homme Mort. She walked straight to a chestnut-tree which she said she recognised; then she found a mountain-ash upon whose bark she had once carved their interlaced initials; after that the spring, and the paths. She wished to revisit what she called "the chapels of their love," to pay at each one a tribute of devotion.[22]

At length they reached Les Metz and the house of the Labussière. Delirious enchantment! Everything was just as she remembered it: the gate, the bell, the kitchen-garden, the mile-stone upon which she used to sit to watch for her lover when the *rendezvous* was at the cottage; the bed, with its curtains of printed cotton, the rustic wardrobe, the oak table.... "Heaven," she cried, "has put a seal upon all the treasures of love we buried here! It has preserved them for us," and she longed to take possession of them all and carry them away with her.[23]

How charming Juliette is at this moment, and how superior to *Olympio*! How preferable is her enthusiasm, with its power of bringing back to life the dead past, to the melancholy which disparages and kills! One sole interest animates her. Her instinct is creative, for where the poet sees death she perceives life. The roses he thought faded and scattered, she admires in full bloom; she can still breathe their perfume. From the dust and ashes he has tasted and bewailed, she draws the savour of honey. In this instance, surely, her love does not merely aspire to sit on the heights with the poet's genius, as she claimed—it soars far beyond it.

CHAPTER IV

THE SHACKLES OF LOVE

VICTOR HUGO never succeeded in making Juliette adopt his conception of love. He craved something calm, placid, regular as a time-table in its manifestations; but she was wont to object: "Such a love would soon cease to exist. A fire that no longer blazes is quickly smothered in ashes. Only a love that scorches and dazzles is worthy of the name. Mine is like that."

And indeed it would not be easy to name an object that this woman did not cast into the crucible of her passion between the years 1834 and 1851. Everything was sacrificed—comfort, vanity, renown, talent, liberty. Then she turned to her poet. She adopted his tastes, his ambitions, his dreams for the future; she shared his joys and sorrows; she exaggerated his qualities, and sometimes even his faults. She lived only in him and for him.

We are about to witness a completeness of self-abnegation that raises Juliette Drouet almost to the level of the mystics of old; afterwards we shall scrutinise one by one the details of the cult she rendered to Victor Hugo.

I

After selling the bulk of her furniture and quitting the luxurious apartment she occupied at 35, Rue de l'Échiquier, Juliette, it will be remembered, had settled down in a tiny lodging costing 400 frs. a year, at 4, Rue de Paradis au Marais. She and Victor Hugo determined to live there together, poor in purse, but rich in love and poetry.[24] The said love and poetry must indeed have filled their horizon, for they have left no account whatsoever of that first nesting-place.

On March 8th, 1836, Juliette removed again to a somewhat more commodious apartment: 14, Rue St. Anastase, at 800 frs. a year. It comprised a drawing-room, dining-room, one bedroom, a kitchen, and an attic in which her servant slept. This district has fallen into decay, and is now dull and dreary. In those days it was chiefly occupied by the convent of the Hospitaliers St. Anastase, whence the street took its name, and a few houses more or less enclosed by gardens. The convent and gardens endowed it with a provincial tranquillity and an impenetrable silence which occasionally weighed upon Juliette's spirits.

Her mode of life was not calculated to enliven her. A degree of poverty bordering on squalor simplified its details. Little or no fire: Juliette sometimes even lacks the logs she is by way of providing for herself. Then she spends the morning in bed, reading, planning, day-dreaming. She keeps careful accounts of her receipts and expenditure—accounts which Victor Hugo afterwards audits most minutely. When she rises, the cold does not prevent her from writing cheerfully, "If you seek warmth in this room you will have to seek it at the bottom of my heart."

All luxuries in the way of food were reserved, as in duty bound, for the suppers the master honoured with his presence after the theatre. The rest of the time Juliette ate frugally, breakfasting on eggs and milk, dining on bread and cheese and an apple. When her daughter visited her she treated her to an orange cut into slices and sprinkled with a pennyworth of sugar and a pennyworth of brandy. The same simplicity reigned on high-days and holidays.

Juliette also denied herself useless fripperies and reduced to the strictest limits the expenses of her wardrobe. Everything she was able to make or mend, she made and mended, and it gratified her to compute the money she saved thus in dressmakers. The rest she bought very cheaply or did without. In the month of August 1838, when she was about to start on a journey with Victor Hugo, she found herself in need of shoes, a dress, and a country hat. She bought the shoes, manufactured the dress, and had intended to borrow the hat from Madame Kraft; but this lady, who held some minor post at the Comédie Française, only wore feathered hats, so Juliette curses the extravagance that places her in an awkward predicament. A little later, on May 7th, 1839, she wanted to furbish up her mantle with ribbon velvet at 5d. a yard; but she found that she could not do with less than eight yards and a half. She bemoans her extravagance, saying, "Why, oh, why have I let myself in for this!"

In studying Juliette's financial position one wonders that so much privation should be necessary, for, from the very beginning, Victor Hugo allowed her 600 or 700 frs. a month. He afterwards increased this sum to 800, and finally to 1,000 frs. in 1838, when he began to get better terms from publishers and theatre-managers. Surely such a sum should provide ordinary comforts—there should be no suggestion of squalid poverty?

The fact is that, in 1834, Victor Hugo had only paid off the most pressing of Juliette's debts; but the result of his doing so was to rouse the energies of the rest of the creditors, and Juliette was overwhelmed by them. Sometimes she managed to pacify them by quaint expedients. For instance, to Zoé, her former maid, she offered, in place of wages, a box for *Angélo*; to Monsieur Manière, her legal adviser, she promised that, if he would extend her credit, "Monsieur Victor Hugo should read with interest" a certain plan of political organisation of which the said Manière was the author, but which alas, does not yet figure in the archives of the French constitution! But more often she was forced to pay, and she had to save off food or dress. Then it was that money was skimped from the butcher and grocer to satisfy the former milliner or livery-stable keeper. In the month of May 1835, out of 700 frs. received, the creditors obtained 316; in June they got another 347; in July 278. Another cause for pecuniary embarrassment was the irregularity of Pradier's contribution to the maintenance of his and Juliette's child. Very often, but for Victor Hugo's assistance, this item would have been added to the sum-total of her debts. But Juliette bore everything with the blitheness of a bird. She, who had hated accounts and arithmetic, now devoted her attention to them every day, sometimes more than once a day; she, who loathed poverty, encountered the most sordid privations with a smile; she, who once throve upon debts and promises to pay, now exclaimed: "I would do anything rather than fall into debt. How hideous and degrading such a thing is, and how splendid and noble of you, my adored one, to love me in spite of my past!"[25]

VICTOR HUGO ABOUT 1836.
From a picture by Louis Boulanger (Victor Hugo Museum).

In these circumstances, it is not surprising that she began to seek in work, especially theatrical work, an addition to her private resources. She took her career as an artist very seriously, and it was a great disappointment to her that her lover failed to desire her as an interpreter of his parts. He certainly did not. He allowed his jealousy full play, and wished to keep Juliette for himself alone. His tactics seem to have been to dangle promises ever before her, but to give her nothing; to procure dramatic engagements for her, and prevent her from fulfilling them.

In February 1834 he introduced Juliette to the Comédie Française, but a year later he declined to give her the smallest part in *Angélo*, which was produced there. In the course of 1836, 1837, 1838, he allowed Marie Dorval to monopolise all the important *rôles* in his former plays, and never once attempted to put Juliette's name at the head, or even in the middle, of the bill. Yet he gave her fine promises in plenty, encouraged her to learn long passages from *Marion* and *Dona Sol*, and vowed he would some day write a play for her alone.

Thus kept in the background, Juliette passed through exhausting alternations of despair and confidence, gratitude and jealousy. For, as may easily be imagined, she was terribly jealous, and her suspicious mind exercised itself chiefly concerning actresses, whose lively manners and easy morals she knew, by professional experience. There was Mlle. Georges, already growing stout, no doubt, but ever ready to raise her banner and exercise her accustomed sovereignty. There was Mlle. Mars, who, though her looks were a thing of the past, still endeavoured to attract attention. Above all, there was Marie Dorval.

Ah, how Juliette envied Dorval! How she studied her in order to arm herself against her fancied rivalry! How often she took her moral measure! She knew that she was of the people, that she tingled with vitality from head to foot, that, though her primary impulses were virtuous, nature was yet strong within her.... She was well acquainted with "the voice that quivered with tears and made its insinuating appeal to the heart."[26]

Could Juliette fail to dread such a woman, one so versed by the practice of her profession in the wiles that attract men? Could she refrain from warning her lover against her, day after day, like one draws attention to a danger, a scourge, or a tempest? Far from it—she threatened to return to the theatre, to act in her lover's plays, to be present at every rehearsal, to vie with her rival in beauty and talent and ardour. She learnt parts, and whole scenes, and filled her solitude with the pleasing phantoms her lover had once created, and that she dreamed of restoring to life on the stage.

Months passed; delicate circumstances obliged her to relinquish her plan of appearing at the Théâtre Français.[27] She was on the verge of despair when, one evening in the spring of 1838, her lover brought her a new play he wished to read to her, according to his invariable custom. It was *Ruy Blas*. She at once claimed the part of Marie de Neubourg, and fell in love with the melancholy little queen who was hampered and hemmed in by the trammels of étiquette, as she herself was imprisoned within the limits of her icy apartment in the Rue St. Anastase. Victor Hugo asked for nothing better. He intended *Ruy Blas* for the Théâtre de la Renaissance, which was under the management of his friend, Anténor Joly. He requested the worthy fellow to engage Juliette, and the agreement was signed early in May.

We can picture the delight with which Juliette set about copying the play; nevertheless, she was assailed by melancholy fears: "I shall never play the queen," she wrote; "I am too unlucky. The thing I desire most on earth is not destined to be realised." And it is a fact that the part was taken from her almost as soon as it was given.

After 1839 her longing to go back to the stage calmed down gradually. At the end of that year it had completely faded. Her love's tranquillity was greatly increased thereby, while she was driven to immerse herself still more completely in her amorous solitude and the disadvantages pertaining thereto.

For, in the same degree that he deprecated her being seen on the stage, Victor Hugo detested the thought of her going out alone, and he had managed to extract a promise from her that she would never make one step outside the house without him. She was, therefore, practically as much a prisoner as any châtelaine of the Middle Ages, or heroine of some of the sombre dramas she had formerly played. She had not even permission to go and see her daughter at school at St. Mandé, and, rather than trust her by herself, the poet would escort her to the dressmaker and milliner, or on her visits to the uncle whose name she bore, and who lay dying at the Invalides, to the money-lender's, and curiosity-shop, and even the ironmonger's!

When Victor Hugo thus lent himself to her needs, all went well, and Juliette, proud and happy, arm in arm with her "dear little man," chattered away blithely. But a time came when the lover, monopolised by other cares, perhaps by other intrigues, was no longer so assiduous. Then the mistress protested and rebelled, with the fierce rage of a prisoned beast of the forest, bruising itself against the bars of its cage, in its agony for freedom.

Victor Hugo met her remonstrances with gentle reasoning and persuasive exhortations. However far Juliette went in her transports of anger, he was always able to pacify her. On September 27th, 1836, at the end of a long period during which the poet had not been able to give his friend even what she called the "joies du préau"—that is to say, a walk round the Boulevards—Juliette threatens to break out. For several weeks she has been attributing the sickness and headaches she constantly suffers from, to her sedentary life. Losing all patience, she addresses an ultimatum to him, proposing an assignation in a cab on the Boulevard du Temple. He does not appear. For three hours she waits inside the vehicle, then, in the certainty that he has failed her, she writes a letter in pencil, dated from the cab, No. 556, stating her intention to fetch her daughter and go off somewhere, anywhere, alone with her. "Thus," she writes, "I shall free myself for ever from a slavery which satisfies neither my heart nor my mind, and does not secure the repose of either of us."

However, the next day she did not start. She did not go out at all. She had resumed her chains and her prison garb. Her anger always evaporated thus, and turned to melancholy and resigned gentleness. In the end she came to feel that nothing existed for her, save a lover who sometimes came and sometimes stayed away. If he was present, she was alive; if absent, her mainspring was broken.

But Victor Hugo continued to lead an ordinary life, while his mistress spent her days in the confinement of a cloister. It was probably about this time that Juliette resolved to set up in that cloister an altar for the cult of her lover. Finding herself impotent to attract and keep him by the sole charm of passion, she endeavoured to win him over by devotion, minute attentions, tender interest in everything he undertook, and by unbridled adoration of his person and work.

II

According to Juliette, who secured several stolen meetings in the poet's own house,[28] Victor Hugo suffered from a complete absence of the most ordinary comfort at home. His lamps smoked, as did his chimney on the rare occasions when a fire was lighted; he worked in a "horrible little ice-house," with insufficient light and a half-empty inkstand; his bed was wretched, the mattress stuffed with what he termed nail-heads; when he dressed he found his shirts button-less and his coats unbrushed—as for his shoes, Juliette was ashamed of their condition. We learn from Théophile Gautier that the author of *Hernani* was a hearty eater, but that his meals were served up in confusion: cutlets with beans in oil, beef and tomato sauce with an omelette, ham with coffee, vinegar, mustard, and a piece of cheese. He made short work of this extraordinary mixture, and no doubt was often reminded of a line his mistress had once written to him on the subject: "When I think of what you are and what you do, and of the discomfort in which you live, I am filled with admiring pity."

With the instinct of a loving woman and the resource of a clever one, Juliette was quick to take advantage of the human side of her god, and to supply him with the personal care he needed. She trained herself to be a *cordon bleu* and a sick nurse, a tailor and a cobbler. If Victor Hugo went to the theatre he found on his return to the Rue St. Anastase, a dainty repast of chicken, salad, and the milky puddings he liked, and all the year round a dessert of grapes, a fruit he had always been fond of. Juliette served him "kneeling"—so at least she affirms. She took umbrage if he did not allow her to select for him the biggest asparagus and the thickest cream. He was happy, so was she. If he had an attack of that "cursed internal inflammation which sometimes affected his head and sometimes his eyes," his mistress would prepare liniments, tisanes, herb soups, which the romanticist meekly swallowed. She assumed a maternal manner, kissed him, coaxed him with soft words, tried to feed him with her own hands, and regretted that she could not give him her own health and take his indisposition upon herself. If he complained of the paucity and untidiness of his wardrobe, Juliette mended his socks and linen, ironed his white waistcoats, removed grease-stains from his coat, made him a smoking-jacket out of an old theatre-cloak, and manufactured "a capital greatcoat lined with velvet, with collar and cuffs of the best silk velvet, out of another." Thus she managed by degrees to collect nearly all the poet's clothes in her own room; his ordinary suits, as well as those he wore on great occasions, such as a reception at the Académie, or a sitting of the House. On one occasion she writes, in gentle self-mockery: "I was sorry, after you went, that I had not made you put on your cashmere waistcoat to-night; it was mended and quite ready for you. This morning I have been tidying all your things. Your coat occupies the place of honour in my wardrobe; your waistcoat and tie hang above my mantle, your little shoes and silk socks below. In default of yourself I cling to your duds, look after them, and clean them with delight."

But Juliette's great achievement, her triumph, was to create in her tiny apartment the right atmosphere for her poet to work in. His custom was to collect his thoughts during the day, and work them out at night. Juliette made him a cosy corner in her bedroom, close to her bed. She fitted it up with a table, an arm-chair, a lamp, and an ink-pot. Above the chair she hung portraits of his children, to make him feel at home. On the table, sheets of paper and freshly cut pens attested the presence and care of a devotee of genius. Whenever he came in the evening the poet settled down in what he himself called his work-room. His methodical habits and strong will enabled him to abstract himself from his environment and devote himself strictly to his labours as an author. Besides, he was under the impression that Juliette was fast asleep; but in that he did her less than justice. Sleep while he worked! Juliette could never have brought herself to do so. She watched him, and admired him. Sometimes she seized a pencil to scribble on any scrap of paper the expression of her veneration, and when the poet had finished he would find little notes such as the following: "I love to watch even your shadow on the page while you write."[29]

That a poet should allow his person to be thus worshipped is nothing new; that he should desire to be admired in his works is still more natural. Juliette guessed this, and acquired the habit of applauding the slightest achievement of the master with loving enthusiasm. Part of the day she spent in copying his manuscripts, classifying them, making them as like as possible to printers' proofs; and it may easily be imagined that she occupied much time reading them over and over again. Everything he wrote was equally sublime in her eyes. If she permitted herself to show preference for this or that work, it was only on condition that she should not be supposed to be depreciating some other. In 1846, Victor Hugo having arranged to make a speech in the House on the "consolidation and defence of the frontier," Juliette read it no less than three times: once in *La Presse*, again in *Le Messager*, and a third time in *La Presse* again. She made extracts from it and put it away among his archives; she then wrote gravely to the author, that he had never been more pathetic or more eloquent. In the same manner she hoarded all his most trivial sketches and poorest caricatures, and pasted them into albums which she carefully hid. She was envious of Léopoldine, the poet's daughter, who was doing the same thing, and naturally had more opportunities than herself of adding to the collection.

She was more greedy still of his theatrical output, for there her jealousy came into play. It is safe to affirm that for more than fifteen years, namely from 1834 to 1851, she interested herself in every single representation of the dramas of Victor Hugo. She was present at the Théâtre Français on the first night of *Angélo* on April 28th, 1835, and wished to go again on all the following nights, in spite of the bitter disappointment the play had caused her, through the frustration of her ambition to take part in it. She was there on February 20th, 1838, for the revival of *Hernani*; and on March 8th following, it was she who applauded Marie Dorval loudest, at the revival of *Marion Delorme*. While *Les Burgraves* was being written she demanded to know all about it from its earliest conception, and achieved her wish. When Victor Hugo read the play to her, she was very much moved and said: "I hardly know how to descend to earth again from the sublime altitude of your conception." She took part in the distribution of the *rôles*, and intrigued against Mlle. Maxime and Madame FitzJames, whom she did not want for Guanhumara.[30] She championed Madame Melingue, who, in consequence, obtained the part. At last the first night arrived. There was a cabal, a violent, aggressive cabal, a sign of the reaction of the new practical school against the romantic school. Who sat in a prominent box and opposed the firmest front to the hissing crowd? Juliette! Who ventured to accuse Beauvallet of murdering the part of the Duke Job? Juliette again! "To applaud thus your beautiful verses," she wrote on March 13th, "and hurl myself into the fray in their defence is only another way of making love. Ah, I wish I could be a man on the nights the play is given![31] I promise you the subscribers of the *Nationale* and the *Constitutionel* would see strange things!"

The afternoons hung heavy in the lonely apartment of the Rue St. Anastase. Sometimes the poet looked in for a moment to bathe his eyes, or claim some other domestic attention; but, as a rule, his visits were made in the evening, after the parties and the theatre. His mistress, therefore, begged, and obtained, permission to receive a few of her friends. They were insignificant, but warm-hearted folk: Madame Lanvin, the wife of one of Pradier's employés, who acted as intermediary, partly honorary and partly paid, between the sculptor and the mother of Claire Pradier; Madame Kraft, an employée of the Comédie Française who affected literary culture; Madame Pierceau, a worthy matron, and, lastly, Madame Bezancenot, a tried ally.

As a rule, Victor Hugo tolerated the presence of this little company; but, democratic though he might be in principle, it palled upon him before long, and he made some remonstrance. Then Juliette revealed to him that her need to talk about him had driven her to institute a regular course of "Hugolatry" among the good ladies. They made a practice of reading his poems, declaiming his plays, and showering praise on the independence of his character and the dignity of his life. In the face of such delicate proofs of the affection she bore him, it is not surprising that the poet should have entrusted to Juliette his most sacred hopes and ambitions. She was one of those in whom a lover may always confide, in the certainty of being ever sustained, encouraged, and approved. Thus it came about that she was cognisant of every effort Victor Hugo made, every step he took, and even of the intrigues by which he climbed gradually to the Académie Française, then to the Tuileries and the little court of Neuilly, and finally to the Chambre des Pairs.

III

Not that Juliette herself ever cherished special veneration for kings, princes, peers, or Academicians. Democratic and republican by the accident of birth, as she herself wrote, she likewise detested, on principle, everything that seemed likely to attract or keep Victor Hugo away from the Rue St. Anastase. Her first inclination, therefore, was to criticise with acerbity Academies, drawing-rooms, politics, and Courts; but the poet's determination was not of the quality that is easily weakened by remonstrances. Juliette knew this. As soon as she realised that the *habit vert* was really the object of her idol's desire, and that he had set his whole heart upon obtaining it, she abandoned her opposition and only indulged in gentle mockery calculated to cover the retreat of the unsuccessful candidate, and deprive it as much as possible of bitterness.

For Victor Hugo was, above all, an unfortunate candidate, at any rate of the Académie. In February 1836 he was refused Lainé's *fauteuil*, and it was given to a vaudevilliste of the period, called Dupaty. At the end of November of the same year, Mignet was preferred before him, for Raynouard's vacancy. In December 1839, rather than select Hugo, nobody was appointed in the place of Michaud. In February 1840, precedence over him was given to the permanent secretary of the Académie des Sciences, Monsieur Flourens. It was not until January 7th, 1841, that he was elected to Lemercier's *fauteuil* by seventeen votes, against fifteen given to a dramatist called Ancelot, whose name an ungrateful posterity no longer remembers.

In all the peregrinations required by these five successive candidatures, Victor Hugo was invariably accompanied by Juliette. On December 24th, 1835, she writes to him: "One point on which I will tolerate no nonsense, is your visits. I insist upon accompanying you, so that I may know how much time you spend with the wives and daughters of the Academicians. I shall, by the same means, be able to gather up a few crumbs of your society for myself, which is no small consideration."

The visits were begun between Christmas and the New Year, in cold, dry, sunny weather. Clad in black according to prescribed custom, Victor Hugo fetched his friend every day from the Rue St. Anastase, got into a cab with her, and showed her the plan for the afternoon: at such and such a time they must lay siege to Monsieur de Lacretelle; after that, to Monsieur Royer-Collard; then to Monsieur Campenon. Monsieur de Lacretelle was too diplomatic not to give plenty of promises and assurances; Monsieur Royer-Collard too good a Jansenist to fail in a blunt refusal to the author of *Hernani*. As for Monsieur Campenon, he had the reputation of being an honest man and an excellent amateur gardener. His conversation bristled with graftings and buddings. How should he humour him about his favourite pursuit, Victor Hugo asked his friend. Should he select roses or pears, myrtle or cypress? As the good creature was getting on in years, and counted more summers than literary successes, Victor Hugo unkindly inclined towards the last.

Juliette laughed merrily, and the poet would climb up numerous stairs, and return with a stock of entertaining anecdotes, which filled the cab with fun and colour and life. Then followed calculations of his chances; if they seemed promising, Juliette congratulated her "immortal," as she called him in anticipation; if not, she made fun of the Académie once more.

At the end of the year the whole performance began over again. As in 1835, Juliette pretended not to attach much importance to the election of her lover, but this did not prevent her from hotly abusing the Académie when, a month later, the society again closed its portals to the leader of the romantic school.

It is the privilege of the Académie Française to be most courted by those who have oftenest sneered at it. No institution has ever been the cause of so much recantation. Juliette herself was to eat her words. On Thursday, January 7th, 1841, when Victor Hugo had at last triumphed over his brother candidate, it was no longer a mistress who wrote to him, but a general addressing a panegyric of victory to a hero: "With your seventeen friendly votes, and in spite of the fifteen groans of your adversaries, you are an Academician! What happiness! You ought to bring your beautiful face to me to be kissed."

Victor Hugo yielded to her gallant desire, as may be imagined, and forthwith began to prepare for his reception. The poet aimed at a magniloquent and comprehensive speech which should embrace all the great names and ideas of the past, present, and future; something as vast as the empire of Charlemagne, and as noble as the genius of Napoleon. Juliette, on her side, dreamed of a dress of white tarlatan mounted in broad pleats and decorated with a rose-coloured scarf, like the one she had once admired on the shoulders of Madame Volnys, a hated rival at the Comédie Française.

Although the speech was only to be delivered in June, Victor Hugo had it ready by April 10th; he read it to his admiring friend the same night. The white tarlatan dress, alas, was longer on the way. Several reasons conspired against its completion. First of all, Juliette declared that she would concede to nobody the honour of presenting the new member with his lace ruffles: this involved an expenditure of about 23 frs., a heavy toll on the exchequer of the lovers. Secondly, Victor Hugo's reception was to fall upon nearly the same date as the first communion of Juliette's daughter, Claire Pradier, which was yet another cause of expense. The young woman bravely sacrificed her frock, and, having consoled herself by making a fair copy of the master's splendid speech, she awaited the great day. But at the very moment she hoped to see it dawn without further disappointment, malicious fate brought her, and consequently Victor Hugo and the Académie, face to face with a fresh dilemma of the gravest importance, namely, the question of the pulpit for the momentous occasion.

The time-honoured affair was a wooden erection of mean appearance, stained to represent mahogany. On ordinary days it was contemned and relegated to the lumber-room of the Bibliothèque de l'Institut; but, on the occasion of the reception of a new member, custom prescribed that it should be placed under the cupola, in front of the agitated neophyte. Étiquette demanded that the latter should place upon it his gloves and the notes of his address; but the rickety thing had already borne so much eloquence in the past, that it tottered under the weight of its responsibilities. It stood weakly upon a crooked pedestal, in imminent danger of subsidence. Instead of being a haughty pulpit, equal to any occasion, it seemed to offer humble apology for its absurd existence.

Such was the farcical object Victor Hugo had to interpose between himself and Juliette, on the day of the great ceremonial. She lost her sleep over it; for a time, even the lace ruffles, and the speech, and the white tarlatan dress and rose-coloured scarf, retired into the background: "I am in a state of inexpressible agitation and worry over this wretched pulpit," she wrote. "I shall be just at the back of it. I am in perfect despair! Truly, since this apprehension has taken possession of me, I have become the most wretched of women. I think if I cannot see your handsome, radiant face that day, nothing will keep me from bursting into sobs of rage and misery. The very thought fills my eyes with tears."[32]

In spite of himself, Victor Hugo shared one characteristic with Jean Racine: he could not bear to see a pretty woman cry. He therefore took decisive measures, and managed to assuage his friend's grief. Juliette was assured that, whatever happened, she should contemplate her "dear little orator" at her ease—that is to say, from head to foot. Unfortunately, it was ordained that calmness should not inhabit this passionate soul for long together. The night preceding the reception, Juliette felt frightfully nervous, and, while Victor Hugo sat up correcting the proofs of his discourse at the Imprimerie Royale, she retired, saying irritably: "I am like the savages who take to their beds when their wives give birth to children." At 4.30 a.m. she was already up, wrote several letters to her lover, dressed, and hurried to the Palais Nazarin, where she took up a position in the front row, before even the platoon of infantry detailed for guard had arrived.

According to the testimony of Victor Hugo's enemies as well as of his friends, the reception surpassed in dignity and brilliancy anything the cupola had previously witnessed. The Court was represented by the Duc and Duchesse d'Orléans, the Duchesse de Nemours, and the Princesse Clémentine, in a tribune. Fashionable society and the world of letters jostled each other on the benches. There were women everywhere, even beside the most ancient and prim of Academicians. Old Monsieur Jay was partially concealed under billows of laces, gauzes, silks, and satins, worn by his neighbours, Madame Louise Colet and Mlle. Doze. Monsieur Étienne waggled his head between two monstrous hats so beflowered that, with one movement, he disturbed the *fleurs du Pérou* of Madame Thiers, and with the next, he ruffled the bunches of roses on Madame Anais Segalas' head.

"LE CITOYEN VICTOR HUGO JOUANT AU CONGRÈS DE LA PAIX."
Political caricature, 1849.

Juliette saw nothing of all this; neither did she heed the irrelevant babble of her neighbour on the right, Monsieur Desmousseaux of the Comédie Française, or of her guest on the left, Madame Pierceau. She was in a state of painful, yet delicious turmoil, and when Victor Hugo made his entry, she nearly fainted. Fortunately, the poet gave her a smiling look before beginning his speech, which restored her to life; and she settled down to listen to his eloquent words, as if she had not already written them out until she knew them by heart. To-day they seemed invested with fresh beauties, and she gave herself up to the enjoyment of the moment. The magnificent imagery which decked Victor Hugo's first address at the Académie, concealed calculation of the most worldly wise description. Victor Hugo aspired to the Chambre des Pairs as a stepping-stone to a power which would assist him to develop the moral and social mission he deemed to be the true function of a poet. To achieve this aim it was necessary that he should first belong to one of the societies from among which alone the King could legally select the members of that Assembly. The Académie was one of these, hence the successive candidatures of the poet, and the special tone of his discourse, in which all the political parties were blandished and caressed alike; hence, finally, the visits to Court, which increased in frequency after 1841.

Just as Juliette had practically burned in effigy almost all the Academicians of her time before she had the opportunity of becoming acquainted with them and finding them charming, so she began by criticising and censuring Louis Philippe and his children with the greatest severity. Were not these people going to wrest her poet from her? And for what? For the sake of empty honours and useless occupations! Therefore we find Juliette preaching to her lover the contempt of earthly greatness. She was fiercely jealous of the citizen-king.

In order to calm her apprehensions, Victor Hugo had only to reveal to her his secret plans; from the first moment that he mentioned the Pairie to her, she became complacent and Orléaniste. Whether the poet went to harangue the widow of the soldier-prince in the name of the Académie, after the accident of 1842, or whether he paid her a private visit, Juliette always insisted upon accompanying him to Neuilly, and there she would wait, sitting in a cab outside, whilst her lover coined honeyed phrases inside the palace.

The Duchesse was German, simple, a good mother, and deeply religious. Of Victor Hugo's works, the only one she was familiar with was No. XXXIII. of the *Chants du Crépuscule, Dans L'Église de....*

"C'était une humble église au cintre surbaissé,
L'église où nous entrâmes,
Où depuis trois cents ans avaient déjà passé,
Et pleuré des âmes."

The good lady probably thought these verses had been composed in a moment of deep fervour, in honour of a respected spouse. She congratulated the poet, quoted some of the lines to him, questioned him minutely about his children—and, while he enlarged on these domestic topics, the real heroine of the beautiful poetry so dear to the Duchesse, sat waiting below in the cab ... dreaming of the future peer of France; she already saw him in imagination descending the great staircase of the Luxembourg, with a demeanour full of dignity. For her part, she was more than ever content to remain at the foot of the steps, in a posture of humility, among the crowd of watchers.... When the poet issued at last from the ducal apartments, she would tell him her dream, and he would complacently acquiesce.

The appointment of Victor Hugo to the Pairie appeared in the *Moniteur* of April 15th, 1845. It must be left to politicians to determine in what degree the presence of "Olympio" could profit the councils of the nation; but to Juliette's biographer the entry of her lover into the Luxembourg seems a felicitous event. From that moment, in fact, the young woman ceased to be cloistered. Busier than ever, and perhaps less jealous, the poet permitted his mistress to accompany him to the Luxembourg and to return alone to the Marais. At first Juliette hardly knew how to take this unfamiliar freedom. With her lover absent, she had grown accustomed to semi-obscurity. The blatant sunshine seemed to mock her loneliness. She writes: "Nobody can feel sadder than I do, when I trudge through the streets alone. I have not done such a thing for twelve years, and I ask myself what it may portend. Is it a mark of your confidence or of your indifference? Perhaps both. In any case, I am far from content."

Gradually, however, she fell into the new ways. She used to walk back from the Luxembourg by way of the Pont-Neuf and the Quais. She amused herself by trying to trace the footsteps of Victor Hugo and fit her own little shoes into them. When she reached home, she immersed herself deeper than ever in the preoccupations of her lover.

Occasionally, fortunately, she had a reaction. She read little: the letters of Madame de Sévigné, perhaps, or those of Mlle. de Lespinasse. She tended her flowers; for Victor Hugo had made her remove from No. 14 to No. 12 Rue St. Anastase, where her ground-floor rooms opened on to a garden.[33] There, in a space of sixty square feet, she had four bushes of crimson roses, and a few dozen prolific strawberry-plants, destined to furnish the poet's favourite dessert, throughout the summer. She attended to all the most trivial details in person, making them all subservient to her love.

In this wise—with the exception of a few bouts of jealousy of which we shall have occasion to speak later, Juliette's days flowed almost happily. She no longer brooded over her past; redemption through love seemed to her an accomplished fact. When she turned to the future, it was with ideas borrowed from Victor Hugo certainly, but none the less consoling, since they authorised her to hope for the eternal reunion of souls beyond the confines of this earth. On December 31st, 1842, the poet had dedicated some delicate verses to her, which she learned by heart. They were part of a creed by which Juliette hoped to fortify her soul against the arrows of fortune—hopes fallacious in the event. First death, then treachery, were about to rend her faithful heart as a child's toy is smashed.

CHAPTER V

CLAIRE PRADIER

ABOUT the year 1844, when Victor Hugo visited his friend on Sundays and holidays, he used to find seated at his private table, in accordance with his own permission, a tall girl of eighteen, very fair, very pale, with very black eyes—two prunes, as he said, dropped in a saucer of milk. Often she did not hear him enter. Bending her willowy neck and undeveloped bust over her books, she was immersed in study, perhaps also in rêverie. Sometimes he kissed her affectionately, at other times bowed formally. The lowly assistant-mistress of a suburban school, marvelling at the great man's condescension, would rise blushing, and submit her pale brow to his lips. She would then ask permission to return to her task: the examinations were near at hand, and, as she was going in for a diploma, she must work.

Sometimes Victor Hugo smilingly took up the books scattered on the table, weighed the value of each with a glance, then, pushing them all aside with the back of his hand, sat down, saying: "Now then, Claire, I will be your tutor to-day," and the lesson began, vivid, enthusiastic, brilliant as a poem.

The reader would be justly disappointed if we failed to relate the story of the girl to whom this "magician of words" thus unveiled the beauties of the French language. Besides, a deeper acquaintance with the daughter may lead to a better understanding of the mother; therefore, we append a short sketch of Claire Pradier.

I

She was born in Paris in 1826. Her father, the sculptor, undertook the care of her early childhood, while her mother, as we have learnt, was in Germany and Belgium. He put her out to nurse at Vert, near Mantes, with a married couple named Dupuis, and sometimes combined a visit to her with a little sport, in the shooting season.

He brought her back to Paris on October 15th, 1828. From letters of his which have been preserved, we are justified in believing that he derived some satisfaction from his educational rôle. His pen is prolific in praise of the child with "the locks of pale gold," "the roguish brown eyes," "the apple-red cheeks," whose "nose ends in a pretty tilt" which reminds him agreeably of Juliette's.

He discovers in his daughter a fine nature, plenty of intelligence, and so much feeling, that he hesitates for a time whether he shall apply his efforts to checking its development, or to cultivating it—in the first case, he would turn Claire into a semi-idiot in order not to let her passions become too strong for her happiness, and in the second, he might make of her an artist capable of the most splendid impulses and the noblest fulfilment.

If Pradier is to be believed, the child herself decided in favour of the latter. At the age of three, guided by paternal suggestion in the studio of the Rue de l'Abbaye, she chose for her favourite plaything a stuffed swan. From her games with this handsomely fashioned bird she imbibed a taste for pure lines and fine pose. She also listened to music given at Pradier's house by sculptors and painters who aped the art of Ingres. She derived so much delight from it that she could never afterwards meet any of these self-engrossed performers without begging for a kiss. Finally, by his studies of dress, his clever manipulation of draperies, which he always preferred to the higher parts of his profession, Pradier taught her to appreciate light and colour. She had a vivid appreciation of the latter, and, during her short life, a mere trifle such as the blue of the sky, or the tint of a rose, gave her the most exquisite pleasure.

Having thus cultivated the sensibilities of the flower committed to his charge, Pradier was rewarded by the prestige attached to his rôle of master and guide; the father reaped in tenderness what the artist had expended in intelligence and effort. From her earliest infancy Claire showed a marked preference for this man, so ardent, so gay, who taught her to breathe and live among works of art; all her life she felt for him an affection that neither his mistakes nor his carelessness, or even his injustice, could damp. Meanwhile, ever prolific in good intentions, always ready with vows and promises, the artist was forming high hopes and ambitions for his daughter.

"We must hope," he wrote to Juliette on that October 15th, 1828, when he took the child away from her nurse, "that she will live to grow up, and that we shall make a distinguished personage of her." A little later, on September 28th, 1829, he writes: "Dear friend, you are fortunate in the possession of a Claire who will be a great solace to you in your old age." Again, on July 4th, 1832: "Who can love her better than I do, especially now that I see her rare intelligence developing so satisfactorily and encouragingly for our designs?"

He planned for his little daughter the most singular and unexpected gifts: once it was to be the proceeds of his bust of Chancellor Pasquier, a commission he owed to Juliette and her friendship with the subject; another time it was the price of a house he possessed at Ville d'Avray and wished to sell; again, he designed to settle upon Claire the sum of 2,000 frs. he had lent to a cousin—fine words, as empty as the hollow mouldings that decorated the studio of the man. The cousin never returned the loan, the house at Ville d'Avray was sold, by order of the court, at a moment when the mortgage upon it far surpassed its value, and the bust of Chancellor Pasquier, though ordered, was never even rough-cast by Pradier.

Juliette had determined to live with Victor Hugo in the conditions of poverty indicated in a former chapter. Her natural delicacy prompted her to make the future of her child secure, and at the same time to release the poet from all anxiety on that score. In the latter part of the year 1833, therefore, she wrote to Pradier asking him to acknowledge Claire. The answer of the sculptor was as follows:

"DEAR FRIEND,

"Your letter did not displease me at all, as you seem to have feared that it would. Its motive was too praiseworthy to cause me any sentiment contrary to your own. The only thing that vexes me is that I should be unable to do at once what you desire, and what I fully intend to do eventually, though in a manner carefully calculated not to interfere with the future or tranquillity of any other person. It grieves me that you do not realise what I feel towards you and Claire! I believed that all your hopes were centred in me! I am so crushed with debt that I cannot think of executing my intentions at present. Good-bye, get well and hope only in me. You have not lost me, either of you—far from it! Good-bye, your very devoted friend, and much more,

"J. PRADIER."[34]

CLAIRE PRADIER AT FIFTEEN.
From an unpublished drawing by Pradier.

It is easy to guess how annoyed Juliette was at the receipt of such a letter. She expressed her disgust to Victor Hugo in various notes in which she abuses her former lover: "Wretched driveller, stupid scoundrel, the vilest and most idiotic of men, a coward without faith"—such are the principal epithets she applies to him.

It has been said that the author of *Lucrèce Borgia* interfered and obtained from Pradier the acknowledgment of Claire.[35] This is absolutely incorrect. It is probable indeed that the poet made the attempt; it seems certain that with the assistance of Manière, the attorney, he extracted from the sculptor the promise of an allowance; but there was no official recognition, and soon we shall find the father of Claire more disposed to repudiate her than to allow her the protection of his name.

For the moment he merely agreed that Juliette should put the child to school at Saumur with a Madame Watteville, whose Paris representative was a certain Monsieur de Barthès. He would have liked Victor Hugo and his friend to undertake the sole responsibility of the arrangements, but they prudently declined to do so, though they lavished kindness, caressing letters, advice, and treats, upon the little exile.

On May 28th, 1835, Claire, having suffered some childish ailment, received from her mother a doll and the following letter:

"Good morning, my dear little Claire. I hope you will be quite well again by the time you read this letter. Now that you are convalescent I can discuss serious matters with you. This is what I wish to say: Foreseeing that you may be in need of recreation, I send you from Paris a charming little companion who is most amiably disposed to amuse you. But, as it would not be fair that the expenses of her maintenance should devolve upon you during the time of her stay with you, I also send you a big purse of money for her upkeep. Spend it wisely, in accordance with your needs.

"Monsieur Toto is no less anxious about her, than devoted to you. He therefore adds an enormous basket of provisions. I hope the little girl will not have eaten them all up on the way, and that there will still be something left for you.

"This is not all. I have also been thinking of your clothes, dear little one, and I send you a shawl for your walks, a white frock with drawers to match, a figured foulard frock, a striped frock without drawers, and a sleeved pinafore.

"Good-bye, dear good child. You must tell me if my selection is to your taste. Love me and enjoy yourself, so that I may find you tall and plump and pretty, when I come to see you again.

"J. DROUET."

At other times, Victor Hugo himself wrote affectionately to his friend's child. It is necessary to read these letters, so full of thoughtful tenderness, to gain a better knowledge of the warmth of the poet's heart. Much should be forgiven him in consideration of it.

"We love you very much," he wrote to Claire on May 23rd, 1833, "and you have a sweet mother who, though absent, thinks a great deal about you. You must get well quickly, and thank the good God in your prayers every night for giving you such a good little mother, as she on her part thanks Him for her charming little daughter."[36]

And a few days after, in a postscript to a letter to Juliette: "Monsieur Toto sends love and kisses to his little friend, and wishes he could still have her to travel everywhere with him. But, above all, he would like to caress her and look after her as his own child."[37]

As his own child—those words were indeed characteristic of Victor Hugo's feeling concerning the little girl thus thrown across his path by chance, and unhesitatingly adopted by him. At first, Claire either did not realise, or was unwilling to return, his affection. She was jealous of the big gentleman who stole some of her mother's attention from her. She was reserved and disagreeable. Juliette was indignant, but the poet did not relax his efforts to win her. With the authority of Pradier, who was only too pleased to delegate it to him,[38] he placed Claire, on April 15th, 1836, in a school at St. Mandé, 35, Avenue du Bel-Air, kept by a Madame Marre. From that moment, whether he paid her a surprise visit in the parlour on Thursday afternoons, with a Juliette beaming from the enjoyment of the trip, or whether she spent Sundays with her mother, Claire Pradier insensibly grew to connect Victor Hugo with Juliette in her affections, to give to them both equal respect, and to link them together in her prayers. Exceedingly sensitive by nature, more eager for love than for learning, she fell into habits of day-dreaming in school, or out in the meadows, and only seemed to recover the brightness of cheeks and eyes when the lovers fetched her, and toasted her little cold, contracted fingers in their warm ones. Then the apartment in the Rue St. Anastase resounded with her merry chatter, and she joined eagerly in the rites of which Victor Hugo was the god and Juliette the priestess.

In 1840, when she had attained her fifteenth year, Claire's mother thought it right to confide to her the secret of her irregular birth. She told her also of Pradier's neglect, and Victor Hugo's goodness. She exhorted her to be simple in her ideas, and not to set her ambitions too high. Claire manifested much chagrin and vexation at first, but presently her natural piety awoke and Juliette was able to write: "Claire is for ever in church." Victor Hugo took upon himself to open the girl's eyes to the practical side of life, and to point out to her the necessity of preparing for a profession as early as possible.[39] In response to these appeals to her reason, Claire soon accepted her lot with a brave heart. It was settled that at the age of eighteen, that is to say in 1844, she should be engaged as an assistant mistress in Madame Marre's school, in exchange for board and lodging, but without salary. She agreed also to study for a diploma, and she hoped, when once she had gained it, to find some honourable and paid employment, by Victor Hugo's help.

Claire fell to work with an ardour, a good-humour, and an intelligence, that drew from Juliette the warmest commendation for her daughter and gratitude for Victor Hugo.

II

One cannot but wonder whether Claire Pradier was really happy at heart, or whether that eighteen-year-old brow, pure and fair as Juliette's own, perchance concealed a spirit weighed down by melancholy. She was good-looking certainly, and knew it. In her chestnut locks, her eyes, whose hue wavered between soft black and the blue of ocean, her rounded cheeks, often hectic with fever, the distinction of a tall figure and stately walk, she united—

"À la madonne auguste d'Italie
La flamande qui rit à travers les houblons."[40]

But beauty is no consolation to one who feels herself already touched by the icy finger of death, and who has, besides, no incentive to prolong the struggle for life. Claire felt thus.

Already, in earliest childhood, she had shown a delicate temperament, uncertain health, more nerves than muscle, more sensitiveness than vitality. During the whole of 1837, her cough never left her. In the years that followed, her figure scarcely showed any of the curves of youth. When her looks were praised, she smiled faintly, and her voice, which was lovely and caressing enough to recall to Victor Hugo the softest cadences of *Les Feuillantines*, scarce dared pronounce the word "to-morrow." Hence proceeded low spirits, which she was never able to shake off, though she usually managed to conceal them from her mother. Presentiments also beset her. "I often dream of those I love," she wrote to her mother, "and when I wake up, I long to sleep on for ever."

Mobile as the chisel he manipulated so skilfully, volatile as the dust of the plaster which powdered him, Pradier gave Claire neither regular assistance nor moral support. He had married, and was the father of several legitimate children. Unfortunate as was the celebrity of his wife and far-reaching the scandals provoked by her, he yet desired to preserve before his natural daughter a primly respectable attitude, and a modesty quite Calvinistic. He was as careful to avoid the occasions of meeting her, as Claire herself was eager to provoke them. The more she overwhelmed him with little presents, worked by her own fingers, tender evidences of an unconquerable affection, the more indifferent and discourteous he showed himself, forgetting to pay her monthly allowance, forgetting to give her New Year's presents, forgetting even to keep his appointments with her, leaving her to wait patiently in the cold studio of Rue de l'Abbaye while he played the gallant on the boulevard.

He had, nevertheless, permitted the girl to make the acquaintance of his legitimate children, and had gone so far as to put his youngest child, Charlotte Pradier, at the same school, when he sent his two sons to Auteuil to a boarding-school. In the month of May, 1845, Claire, with an impulse natural in a girl of nineteen, wished to give the two school-boys the pleasure of a sisterly letter; she got Charlotte to write also. The sculptor heard of it and this is how he treated her trivial indiscretion:

"MY DEAR BIG CLAIRE,

"I have seen the headmaster of ... who has informed me that you and Charlotte have written to J....[41] Pray write as seldom as possible. I do not think young girls should use their pens to reveal their sentiments. Such a habit is too easily acquired; they should know how, yet not do it. Besides, the children see each other every fortnight, and that is enough. Please do not sign yourself *Pradier* to them any more. Such a thing becomes known and might cause gossip. You do not need the name, to be loved and respected. Be frank and fear nothing. Your good time will come some day. You must be prudent in all respects. The children must accustom themselves to your position as it is; they will take more interest in you later. Also, as I am on these subjects, pray use some other formulæ in your letters to me than 'adored father,' or 'beloved.' I am not accustomed to them. Such epithets are only appropriate to a god. Call me anything else that comes natural to you. It is unnecessary that I should prompt you; your feelings will be your best guide. Please write more legibly, for I receive your letters at night; and, above all, write only when you have something special to say. You must not become a scribbler about nothing—I mean for the mere pleasure of using your pen."[42]

How such a letter must have wounded the heart which once beat so tenderly for Pradier! Neither the caresses of Juliette nor the soothing words of Victor Hugo were able to comfort Claire.[43] One month after her father had thus disowned her, she went up for her examination, and, partly through grief, partly through timidity, failed utterly. It was the last stroke.

Not that her constitution showed any immediate sign of the shock it had sustained, or broke down at once. Her physical appearance remained unchanged, but death entered her soul and lurked there henceforward, as sometimes it lies under the depths of waters which flow calmly to outward seeming. She made her will.

From that moment Claire Pradier lived like those resigned invalids who, raising their gaze to the heaven above them, no longer heed the passing of the hours, while they await the supreme summons. She waited. Her mother, seeing her still apparently healthy, failed to realise her condition, and took the beginning of this mute colloquy with death for a mere return of her daughter's former depression. Nevertheless, an incident which happened in the month of February 1846 gave to Juliette also one of those presentiments which cannot deceive. Like Claire, she waited.

CLAIRE PRADIER ON HER DEATHBED.
Drawing by Pradier (Victor Hugo Museum).

It was not for long. On March 21st, 1846, having gone to St. Mandé to see the young assistant mistress, she took with her the design and material for a piece of work Victor Hugo had asked for. The idea was to embroider his family coat of arms on coarse canvas, in colours selected by himself. This complicated heraldic work was to adorn the backs of two Gothic arm-chairs in his rooms in the Place Royale.

Contrary to her usual habit, Claire showed very little interest in the poet's plans; she listened absently and spoke very little. A dry cough shook her frame from time to time, her cheeks burned with fever. Juliette walked home by way of the Avenue de Bel-Air, the Barrière du Trône, and the Faubourg St. Antoine. Victor Hugo, who was always anxious about her, was to meet her half-way. He did so; she was walking slowly, with bent head, and when he asked for news of his embroidery, she burst into tears. The poet understood in an instant. By his instructions, Claire was removed to Rue St. Anastase the very next day; Triger, her mother's doctor, was instructed to visit her daily. Not venturing to pronounce at once the dread name of consumption, he spoke of a chill and chlorosis. Claire scarcely heeded, and indicated by a feeble gesture that she was too spent to care. The head she tried to raise from the pillow, fell back as if too heavy for the frail neck. Her large dark eyes gazed through space at some melancholy vision. Her hands upon the white sheets hardly retained strength to clasp themselves in a caress or a prayer.

She begged that Pradier might be informed of her illness. He wrote first, and then came. He demonstrated his affection by theatrical gestures and well-chosen words. Then he placed a villa, which he said he possessed at Auteuil, at the disposal of the invalid and her mother. The so-called villa proved to be one floor in a tenement house, 57, Rue de La Fontaine. Claire was taken there in the early part of May. Her mother accompanied her. Victor Hugo visited them nearly every day, but neither the compliments of "Monsieur Toto" nor the roses he brought his ex-pupil, nor the exhortations of Doctor Louis, whom he brought with him one day, were successful in restoring colour to the countenance of one whose blood-spitting left her every day paler and more exhausted. Claire hardly dared raise herself in bed; icy sweats drenched her, and she moaned continuously, in a manner terribly painful to those who were forced to stand by, helpless.

On June 6th, she asked to see the Vicar of St. Mandé, her confessor. On the 16th, she received the Last Sacraments. On the 18th, delirium supervened, and she expired on the 21st. They buried the girl in the first place at Auteuil, but when her will was read, in which she had written, "I desire to be buried in the cemetery of Saint-Mandé. I also beg that Monsieur l'Abbé Chaussotte should celebrate my funeral Mass, and that green grass should be grown on my grave," Victor Hugo and Pradier agreed to have the coffin exhumed. The ceremony took place on July 11th. Juliette, who was more dead than alive, was not present; but Victor Hugo and Pradier walked together behind the funeral car, leading the white procession of Claire's young pupils and companions. The sculptor, always full of intentions, plans, and chatter, discoursed in a low voice of the magnificent tomb he would raise with his own hands to the memory of his daughter. It should be, he said, "a sacred debt; I shall execute it with so much love that my chisel will never before have fashioned anything so chaste or so beautiful."

After the long, slow journey through Paris in the sunshine, they reached the cemetery of Saint Mandé. Near the tomb of the poet's friend, Armand Carel, a freshly dug grave yawned, gloomy and covetous. There was some singing, some blessing, the turmoil of a congested crowd; then they separated, but not without a renewal of Pradier's promise.

Eight years later he died himself, without having discharged his "sacred debt." One more resolve had fizzled out in empty words. Victor Hugo was then living precariously in exile, but as soon as he heard of the sculptor's end, he wrote off and ordered a decent headstone for Claire, and directed that the grave should be sown with green grass. Upon the tomb were carved four of the lines he had erstwhile written for Juliette's consolation, and he set about composing others. Thus it came about that, to the very last, Claire Pradier was protected by the father of Léopoldine against two of the fears that had most alarmed her youthful imagination, "a neglected grave in some distant cemetery, and a faded memory in the hearts of men."

CHAPTER VI

"ON AN ISLAND"

I

Juliette relates that when she had occasion to admonish her maid, or find fault with a tradesman during her residence in Jersey and Guernsey, the answer she invariably received was: "It cannot be helped, Madame; we are on an island...."

The phrase tickled her fancy, and she adopted it and made use of it on many occasions.

The reader of the following chapters must likewise accept the axiom that, "on an island," things are not quite the same as on the mainland; for, only by so doing, will he be enabled to peruse without undue astonishment the extraordinary narration of the life led in common by Victor Hugo, his wife, sons, friends, and mistress, between 1851 and 1872.

Its beginning dates from the poet's sojourn in Belgium without Madame Victor Hugo, at the beginning of his exile[44]; that is to say, in the last weeks of the year 1851 and the first half of 1852. Not that his precarious circumstances and prudent, somewhat middle-class habits, permitted him to house Juliette under his own roof: indeed, their *liaison* was never more secret. But, at Brussels, the problem of the relations henceforth to exist between the sons of Victor Hugo and she whom they already called "our friend, Madame Drouet," first came up for solution. It was at Brussels also, that Juliette set herself to simplify it, if not settle it, by her devotion, unselfishness, and unremitting attentions.

At his first arrival on December 14th the poet had taken rooms at the Hôtel de la Porte Verte in the narrow street of the same name. He remained there barely three weeks, and on January 5th, 1852, took a small room on the first floor of No. 27, Grand' Place. It was "furnished with a black horsehair couch, convertible into a bed, a round table, which served indifferently for work and for relaxation, and an old mirror, over the chimney which contained the pipe of the stove."[45]

Juliette never went there, but we learn from the poet's complaints to her, that the couch was too short for a man, the mattresses hard, and offensive to the olfactory nerve, and that sleep was difficult to obtain, on account of the noises in the street. But with the first streak of dawn outside the lofty window, the "great façade of the Hôtel de Ville entered the tiny chamber and took superb possession of it"[46]; the atmosphere became impregnated with art and history. The poet's fine imagination and ardour for work did the rest. Hence the tone of his letters to his wife, who had remained behind in France, was almost joyous. It was full of masculine courage. Hence, also, that air of "simple dignity and calm resignation," which characterised his bearing in exile, "adding to his inherent nobility and charm," and drawing from Juliette the enthusiastic exclamation: "Would that I were you, that I might praise you as you deserve!"[47]

Truth to tell, she merited a rich share of the praise herself. The little comfort Victor Hugo was able to enjoy, and the moral support he needed more than ever, came to him solely through her.

She lodged almost next door, at No. 10, Passage du Prince,[48] with Madame Luthereau, a friend of her youth, married to a political pamphlet writer. For the modest sum of 150 frs. a month, of which 25 were paid to her servant, Juliette obtained food, shelter, and sincere affection. But what she appreciated more than all these, was the liberty she enjoyed of superintending from afar the poet's domestic arrangements, and preparing under the shadow of the galleries the dishes and sweetmeats he partook of in the publicity of the Grand' Place. Every morning at eight o'clock her maid, Suzanne, conveyed to Victor Hugo a pot of chocolate made by Juliette, linen freshly ironed and mended, and sometimes even the modicum of coal the great man either forgot, or did not trouble, to order.

When Suzanne had swept and cleaned the room which Charras, Hetzel, Lamoricière, Émile Deschanel, Dr. Yvan, Schoelcher and sometimes Dumas *père* daily enlivened with their wit and littered with the ashes from their pipes, she returned at about two o'clock. She found her mistress busy preparing the master's luncheon—a cutlet generally, which Juliette took the trouble to select herself, in order to make certain that the butcher cut it near the loin! Suzanne started off again bearing the cutlet, the bread, the plates and dishes, and even the cup of coffee! Obedient to her mistress's injunction, she hurried through the street, for, at any cost, the luncheon must not be allowed to get cold.

When Charles Hugo joined his father in February 1852, it might be supposed that Juliette would relinquish her rôle of *cordon bleu*; but nothing was further from her intention. She merely proceeded to supplement the daily cutlet with a dish of scrambled eggs, in honour of the young man. Hugo having opened the necessary credit, she continued the task she had undertaken, and prepared two luncheons instead of one. Again, when on May 24th Madame Victor Hugo came for the second time to visit her husband in Brussels, it was Juliette who undertook to cook a little feast for her. In the agitation caused by such a high honour, she forgot to add an extra fork. She worried for the rest of the day over the omission, and apologised in successive letters to the poet, in the terms a *dévote* might employ to confess a mortal sin.[49]

But these occupations did not prevent the afternoons from hanging heavy on her hands. Victor Hugo spent them in writing *Napoléon le Petit*; or he organised expeditions to Malines, Louvain, Anvers, with friends; or he yielded to the material pleasures of Flemish life, and accepted invitations to dine at some of those culinary institutes on which Brussels so prides herself.

But none of these resources were open to Juliette. Confined within the four walls of her narrow chamber, her only view was of roofs, and a dull wall, pierced by a single dirty window; she spent whole hours watching a canary in its cage, through the thick panes. She likened her condition to that of the tiny captive. At other times, she allowed her thoughts to roam among past events, and brooded over the packet of letters so cruelly sent to her the year before[50]; she dwelt upon the grief she had endured for many months, the choice the poet had finally made in her favour, and their joint excursion to Fontainebleau to celebrate the reconciliation. Under the depressing influence of the grey Belgian sky, always partially obscured by thick smoke, she realised that her splendid vitality and her love for novelty had departed for ever. Then she allowed jealousy to resume its sway over her, more powerfully than ever.

In this mood, she once more resolved to set Victor Hugo free: "If you tell me to go," she wrote on January 25th, 1852, "I will do so without even turning my head to look at you." But again he bade her stay.

Gravely, then, without showing any symptom of her former coyness, she proposed to discontinue her letters.

JULIETTE DROUET IN JERSEY.

Fortunately, at this very juncture, the unwelcome attentions of the Belgian police, who were nervous about the forthcoming publication of *Napoléon le Petit*, had decided Victor Hugo to leave Brussels and go to Jersey. Juliette was to go also, either in the steamer with him, or in one starting a few hours later. Naturally he urged her to go on writing, if only to bridge over the short separation. She admits that when she landed at St. Helier, on August 6th, 1852, hope had once more gained the ascendant within her breast. For the first time in her life, she was about to enjoy the society of her "dear little exile," her "sublime outlaw," all by herself, far from the madding crowd.

II

Victor Hugo resided at first in an hotel at St. Helier, called La Pomme d'Or. Later he settled on the sea-front at Marine Terrace, Georgetown, in an enormous house which, owing to its square shape and skylights, resembled a prison.

Juliette had intended to put up at the Auberge du Commerce, but for twenty years she had never sat at a table d'hôte without the protection of the poet. The proximity of tradespeople and farmers proved insupportable to her. On August 11th she began a search for a suitable boarding-house, and presently concluded a bargain with the proprietress of Nelson Hall, Hâvres-des-Pas, for lodging at eight shillings a week, and board at two shillings a day. This made a monthly expenditure of about a hundred and fifteen francs, to which was added twenty-five francs, the wages of Suzanne, her maid.

Like Marine Terrace, Nelson Hall's chief claim to maritime advantages was its name. At Victor Hugo's house there were no large windows overlooking the sea, and in Juliette's ground-floor rooms, a high paling screened the topmost crest of the highest wave.

Our heroine tried to console herself by listening to the surge of the ocean, and copying the nearly completed manuscript of *L'Histoire d'un crime*, or the poems the poet intended to add to the volume of *Les Châtiments*. At the end of September she moved upstairs to a large room on the first floor of the house, whence a wide view could be had of the barren scenery of Hâvres-des-Pas, from the battery of Fort Regent on the right, to the rocks of St. Clément on the left; but Juliette's peaceful contemplation was constantly disturbed by the violence of the proprietress, a drunkard, who was renowned all over the island for the vigour with which she beat her husband when in her cups.

A further removal was therefore decided upon in January 1853, and carried out on February 6th. Juliette went to live in furnished apartments next door, consisting, as in Paris, of a bedroom, drawing-room, dining-room, and kitchen, on the first floor. They overlooked a vast stretch of sand and shingle, rocks and seaweed.

At first Victor Hugo seldom went to his friend's house, but met her each day at the outset of his walk and took her with him along roads where the magic of summer glorified every blade of grass. From end to end of the island, Dame Nature had transformed herself into a garden, where all was perfumed, gay, and smiling. Juliette, walking arm in arm with her lover, could feel the glad beating of his heart; her upraised eyes noted that his dear face seemed less worried. With the ingenuity of a twenty-year-old sweetheart, she entertained him of his own country, and invoked memories of the journeys they had made together in former days to the Rhine, the Alps, the Pyrenees. The exile remembered, not the rain, nor the omnibuses, nor the thousand trifles recalled by Juliette, but France ... his own beautiful France.... Under the influence of that voice which had once made him free of the realm of love, his country was restored to him for a fleeting moment.

The lovers were unpleasantly surprised by the week of tempests which ushered in the equinox, and was followed without a pause by the setting in of winter. "Everything became sombre, grey, violent, terrible, stormy, severe." Day and night rain fell, and "the drops chased each other down the window-panes like silver hairs."[51] Amidst the uproar to which frenzied Nature suddenly delivered herself, the daily tramps were perforce discontinued. Fortunately for Juliette, Victor Hugo found Nelson House warmer than his house at Marine Terrace. His wife had recently joined him, but had brought with her neither comfort nor the serene atmosphere propitious for an author's labours. As in the old days of the Rue St. Anastase, therefore, he set up a writing-table near the fire in Juliette's sitting-room, with a few volumes of Michelet and Quinet, and a novel or two by Georges Sand; and every day, after lunching with his own family, the poet came to work in his friend's room. Juliette determined to "find the way back to his heart through his appetite,"[52] as she wrote to him, so she insisted upon his dining with her. She appealed to his greediness as well as to his hospitable instincts, assuring him that nowhere else could he so successfully entertain his new companions, the exiles, as at her abode. Soon she gave two "exiles' dinners" a week, then three, then four; finally, she had one every day.

With the assistance of his two sons, whom he had at length presented to Juliette, Victor Hugo presided at these feasts with an affability born in part of a desire for popularity. Juliette showed herself more reserved, more severe. Accustomed to treat the poet as a divinity, she could not tolerate the familiarity of these petty folk. "A brotherly cobbler is not to my taste," she said harshly. "I cannot resign myself to this consorting of vulgar mediocrity with your genius."

Her sweetness to the two sons of the poet was as marked as the haughtiness of her manner towards the victims of the *Coup d'État*. For twenty years she had longed to be friends with them. As far back as 1839, on the occasion of a distribution of prizes at which Charles and François Victor were to cover themselves with honours, she wrote: "What a pity I cannot witness their triumph! I love them with all my heart, and would give my life for them; but that is not enough. I will avenge myself by praying that they may remain always as they are at present: charming and good."

Later we find her treasuring their portraits, anxious about their little childish ailments, pleading for them when they incurred punishment, and overwhelming them with little presents manufactured by her pen or needle, whenever she received the master's sanction to do so.

What joy it must have given her to receive officially at her table these children grown to manhood! As soon as she became acquainted with them, she raised the young men to the level of Victor Hugo in the order of her preoccupations, and resolved to do nothing for the father, in the way of spoiling and cherishing, that she did not do also for the sons. If she copied *Les Contemplations*, she protested that she must also write out François Victor's translation of Shakespeare. If she sent Suzanne to Marine Terrace with a herb soup for the master, she bade her carry six lilac shirts for Charles.

Even young Adèle and Madame Victor Hugo accepted her good offices without demur. For Adèle, Juliette picked the earliest strawberries and the first roses of the Nelson Hall garden; she embroidered handkerchiefs on which Charles had designed the monogram, and bound together the serial stories of Madame Sand, cut from magazines. For Madame Victor Hugo she prepared a certain soup made of goose, which, she said, was most succulent. She lent her Suzanne, her own servant, for the whole time Marine Terrace was without a cook, and meanwhile went without a servant herself, and did her own cooking. She spoilt her skin and wore down her nails, but she took a pride in her devotion and self-abnegation, and resolved to carry them even further. She dreamt of entering Victor Hugo's household for good, to assume in all humility the position of an ex-mistress become housekeeper.

However numerous may have been the wrongs Victor Hugo inflicted upon this woman, whose jealousy he never ceased to excite, one must admit that he felt and appreciated the greatness of her love. Like a great many men, the artist in him recognised a moral worth that no longer satisfied his needs as a lover; he experienced generous revulsions, under the influence of which he paid her carefully studied attentions, which bore a semblance of impulse and spontaneity gratifying to her feelings.

III

The young queen, Victoria, having paid France, in the person of Napoleon III, the gracious compliment of a visit in August 1855, the exiles of Jersey dared address an insolent letter to her, which was published by their quaintly-named journal, *L'Homme*. True to his native chivalry, Victor Hugo declined to sign this manifesto[53]; but he was indignant when the authorities of Jersey marked their disapproval by expelling its three authors. He protested vigorously against their punishment, and was in his turn driven from the island on August 31st.

He went to Guernsey, a neighbouring island, bleaker and less temperate in climate. He settled at first at No. 20, Rue Hauteville, St. Pierre Port. On May 16th, 1856, he bought a roomy, substantial house built on the shore at some former period by an English pirate. It only required restoration, to make it a suitable residence. It was called Hauteville House.

Here again, Juliette lived successively at the inn, and at a boarding-house kept by a Frenchwoman, Mademoiselle Leboutellier. But when she found that Victor Hugo could no longer content himself with a temporary house, and intended to send for the furniture and art-collection he had stored at the rooms in Paris,[54] she begged him to include her in his plans, and let her have her own things also. She was tired of so-called English comfort, with its hard beds, narrow sheets, straight-backed chairs, and tiny wardrobes.

Victor Hugo gave a generous assent to her request. He took a little house for her, called La Pallue, close to, and overlooking, Hauteville House. The faithful Suzanne was despatched to France to pack and send to Guernsey all the Hugo family's and Juliette's possessions. She returned on August 9th. The furniture and art-collection arrived on the 20th of the same month.

A busy time followed, for the lovers. They threw themselves feverishly into the excitements of removal, decoration, and treasure-hunting. Victor Hugo dropped spiritualism and photography, which had been his recreations in Jersey, to become architect, cabinet-maker, and joiner. He undertook the supervision of Juliette's arrangements as well as his own, bought antique Norman furniture, which he turned to various uses, manufactured carpets and curtains out of Juliette's old theatre frocks, designed panels and mantelpieces, and the many incongruous articles which now decorate the Musée Victor Hugo, and which his friend aptly called "a poetical pot-pourri of art."

In this wise, the fitting up of the two houses lasted over a considerable period. We learn from Juliette that the poet was still busy with his dining-room on April 2nd, 1857, and on May 28th, 1858, he wrote to Georges Sand: "My house is still only a shell. The worthy Guernseyites have taken possession of it, and, assuming that I am a rich man, are making the most of the French gentleman, and spinning out the work."

Juliette, whose dwelling was more modest, had the enjoyment of it sooner. She settled into La Pallue at the beginning of November 1856, and had the happiness henceforth of seeing her friend many times a day. He had constructed on the roof of Hauteville House a room that he somewhat pretentiously named his "crystal drawing-room," and that we should call a belvedere; it was roofed and covered in with glass on all sides. His bedroom opened out of it.

Every morning he sat and worked there, at a flap-table affixed to the wall, when the cold did not drive him to some warmer part of the house. Beneath his gaze spread the low town, the port, the group of Anglo-Norman islands, and, in clear weather, the coast of Cotentin. At his back, and slightly higher up, Juliette, from her little house, kept watch and ward over him. From that moment it may be said that, though Juliette's body was at La Pallue, her heart and mind inhabited Hauteville House.

Unfortunately, as winter progressed, the storms grew worse, and a darkness reigned that made reading and copying difficult. "Like a great lake turned upside down," the sky hung lowering above the gloomy houses, and only allowed the pale rays of a leaden sun to pierce through it, at infrequent intervals. The rest of the time the atmosphere remained charged with rheumatic-dealing clamminess.

VICTOR HUGO IN JERSEY.

Juliette, just entering her fiftieth year, bore the rigours of the climate with difficulty. She would have died of it, she declared, had she not been upheld by the influence of love. She was a martyr to gout, and greatly dreaded being crippled by it. She brooded long and often upon death and the dead. Whether under the influence of a priest, or in response to some inward prompting we cannot tell, but she reverted for a time to her former religious practices.

IV

In April 1863, when Juliette was slowly recovering from another attack of gout, Victor Hugo realised the extreme humidity of La Pallue. On the advice of his sons, who seem to have been of one mind with him on the subject, he decided that Juju, as he called her, should move as quickly as possible, and that he should for the second time assume the functions of architect, upholsterer, and decorator of her new dwelling.

Juliette offered a prolonged and strenuous resistance to the plan, for the house chosen for her possessed the grave inconvenience of being at some distance from Hauteville House. The idea that she would no longer be able to watch every movement of her lover, drew from our heroine lamentations and loving reproaches. But Victor Hugo was adamant, and on February 2nd, 1864, the anniversary of the first performance of *Lucrèce Borgia*, "Princesse Négroni" took up her abode in the new house, which she named Hauteville Féerie.

There again the poet had arranged everything himself. Remembering Juliette's attachment for her rooms in Rue St. Anastase, he had endeavoured to reconstitute faithfully its curtain of crimson and gold, its peacocks embroidered on panels, its china, the porcelain dragons which adorned the dresser, and especially the numerous mirrors that reflected and multiplied the furniture, knick-knacks, and embroideries.

When Juliette was shown this "marvel," she said she had no words to express her admiration and gratitude. Then, knowing how often Madame Victor Hugo was away on the Continent, and how uncomfortable the poet was at home, she offered to act in turn as hostess and housekeeper to him.

In 1863 we find her assuming Madame Victor Hugo's duties during the short absence of the latter, and at the end of 1864, during a further one which lasted until February 1867, she divided her time equally between Hauteville House and Hauteville Féerie.

But there is a difference in her methods of ruling the two establishments. At Hauteville House she governs without obtruding herself, wisely, discreetly, somewhat mysteriously. She directs the servants, reproves them if necessary, superintends the accounts, and keeps down expenses. But she carries out her task from her place in the background. Officially, the poet lives alone with his sons and his sister-in-law, Madame Julie

Chenay; when he entertains friends from Paris, Juliette's name is not mentioned.

At Hauteville Féerie, on the contrary, our heroine is at home. It behoves her to comport herself as the mistress of the house, and expend her gifts of mind, as well as her talents as a manager. As she says, "she must be both lady and housekeeper."

In this double rôle it might be supposed that she would be reluctant to receive the exiles presented to her by Victor Hugo, whose society is so distasteful to her. Not so. Once more Juliette accepts, through duty and devotion, that which she never would have tolerated on her own account.

The poet was bored, alas! Though he was composing splendid poetry, his long dialogue with Mother Nature was beginning to pall upon him. His somewhat theatrical genius demanded more than a fine stage; it required a public. Without it, the author of *Les Châtiments* was but the shadow of the poet of *Ruy Blas*. No doubt the bronzing of his skin by the salt breath of the sea, and the virulence of his spite against Napoleon III, lent him a fictitious appearance of spring and vigour; but there were times when he flagged sadly, and when despondency and fatigue expressed themselves in the droop of his lips, the sagging of his ill-shaved cheeks, the wrinkles on his brow, and, especially, the heavy pockets beneath his eyes. His attire betrayed his complete neglect of himself. When he walked through the Place de Hauteville in his Girondin hat all battered by the wind, his cashmere neckcloth carelessly knotted under an untidy collar, his open coat revealing a buttonless shirt in summer, and in winter, a faded scarlet waistcoat which Robespierre himself would have despised, the little children he so loved ran from him as if he were accursed.[55]

Juliette grasped these mute warnings, and, as soon as she was established in the vast frame of Hauteville Féerie, she attempted to reconstitute the society she had once presided over at Jersey. She even endeavoured to enlarge the circle and admit a few new-comers.

Juliette was able to maintain the simple dignity to which she attached so much importance, and from which she departed only in favour of her poet, in the most delicate circumstance of her life, namely, when Madame Victor Hugo offered her her friendship. She did not decline it, but, where many might have erred by an excess of satisfaction and familiarity, she showed a discreet reserve highly creditable to her. Since their exile, the relations of the two women had undergone a great change. On the one hand, Madame Victor Hugo's perpetual pursuit of pleasure, her constant fatigue, her laziness, and her incapacity to manage a house, had gradually involved her in the network of attentions, civilities, and petting, Juliette lavished upon her and hers. The reports brought to her by her sons and servants of the doings at Hauteville Féerie, had given her a good opinion of our heroine; her natural kindliness did the rest, and she showed herself disposed to treat in neighbourly, and even friendly, fashion one whom she might justly have hated as a rival.

On the other hand, Juliette no longer felt that jealousy of the mistress against the legitimate wife, that she had experienced at the beginning of her love-story. But actual friendship between Madame Victor Hugo and Juliette was hindered for a long time, by the fear of English criticism, and of those Guernseyites of whom Victor Hugo wrote, that they made even the scenery of the island look prim. Juliette dreaded the unkind tittle-tattle the exiles would not fail to retail to her, if she accepted the advances from Hauteville House. Therefore, during the first ten years at Guernsey, she only set foot in her friend's house once, in 1858, to inspect the treasures the master had collected in it. Madame Victor Hugo was absent that day.

At the end of 1864, the wife of the poet became more urgent in her invitations. She was about to depart to the Continent, to undergo treatment for her eyes; her absence might be, and indeed was, indefinitely prolonged. However careless she might be in housekeeping matters, she was probably loath to commit her husband to the tender mercies of her sister, Madame Julie Chenay, who boasted of possessing neither aptitude for business nor a head for figures. She saw the use that might be made of the poet's friend, and opened negotiations by inviting her to dinner. But Juliette declined. This policy of self-effacement was continued by her even during the long absence of Madame Victor Hugo in 1865 and 1866. When Victor Hugo pressed her to dine with him, in secret if necessary, she wrote: "Permit me to refuse the honour you offer me, for the sake of the thirty years of discretion and respect I have observed towards your house."

In the end, however, Madame Victor Hugo gained the day, and overcame this dignified reticence. On her return to Guernsey on January 15th, 1867, she declared her intention of paying Juliette a visit. The diplomatic abilities of the poet were taxed to the uttermost in the regulation of the details of this important event. The visit took place on January 22nd. It was impossible to avoid returning it. Juliette did so on the 24th, and thenceforth, no longer hesitated to cross the threshold of Hauteville House. She went there almost every day, to revise the manuscript and the copies of *Les Misérables* with the help of Madame Chenay; in 1868, she spent the whole month of May under its roof, while her faithful Suzanne was in France.

Similarly, she no longer minded being seen in public with Victor Hugo and his sons, and even his wife, during the journeys they made together. Whereas in 1861, for instance, on a journey to Waterloo and Mont

St. Jean, we still find her dining apart, and seeming to ignore Charles Hugo, in 1867, she is constantly at the latter's house in Brussels, attending the family dinners and enjoying the charm of what she calls "a delicate and discreet rehabilitation" by Madame Hugo and her daughter-in-law. She took her share in their joys as in their sorrows.

It was at Brussels that the three grandchildren of the poet were born, and there also that he lost successively, in April and August 1868, his eldest grandchild and his wife. He mourned the latter with the sorrow of a man from whom the memory of his early love has not faded. As for Juliette, her regret was thoroughly sincere. She did not venture to attend the funeral, in deference to outside gossip; but when, a few days later, she went to the house and saw the empty arm-chair Madame Victor Hugo's indulgent personality had been wont to occupy, she could not restrain her tears.

Victor Hugo and his friend returned to Guernsey on October 6th, 1868. They continued to inhabit separate houses, but dined together at one or the other. They also resumed their sea-side walks, and their long talks, of which the chief topic was the second son of Charles Hugo, an infant who had been left behind at Brussels.

The infirmities of increasing age occasionally prevented our heroine from following her indefatigable companion. She would then remain at her chimney corner, reading the *Lives of the Saints* or some devotional book. She was more than ever prone to reflect upon death. She had been greatly shocked by the rapidity with which Madame Victor Hugo had succumbed, and she felt that her turn, and that of the poet, must soon come. She prayed ardently that she might be permitted to go first.

In August 1869 Victor Hugo took Juliette with him, first to Brussels, where Charles Hugo and Paul Meurice joined them, and then to the Rhine, which held so many sweet memories for both. On their return to Guernsey on November 6th, he proceeded to plan a journey to Italy for the following winter. He also made arrangements for the revival of *Lucrèce Borgia* at the Porte St. Martin. The journey to Italy was never carried out, but on February 2nd, 1870, on the anniversary of its first performance, *Lucrèce* had a brilliant success.

The old poet was enchanted.

Foreseeing the fall of the Empire, and guessing that the French were sick of a régime which, during the last eighteen years, had confused government with spying, and politics with police, he redoubled the activity of his propaganda, and indited letter after letter, manifesto after manifesto. The more Juliette confessed to the lassitude of age, the more he seemed to defy his years.

CHAPTER VII

"THAT WHICH BRINGS SATISFACTION TO THE HEART"

I

WHEN Victor Hugo grasped the full extent of the national disaster in August 1870, he started immediately for Belgium. On the proclamation of the Republic, he proceeded to the frontier, where a few official friends awaited him.

The scene that took place on his arrival was impressive, though somewhat theatrical. The "sublime outlaw" asked for the bread and wine of France. After he had eaten and drunk, he begged Juliette to preserve a fragment of the bread, and buried his face in his hands with the gesture of one who is dazzled by too much light. Juliette relates that big tears flowed through his clenched fingers. The bystanders stood in silence, awed by his emotion....

The poet and our heroine stayed with Paul Meurice at Avenue Frochot for a time, and then went to the Hôtel du Pavillon de Rohan. Finally they settled, he in a small furnished apartment at 66, Rue de la Rochefoucauld, and she close by, in a fairly spacious *entresol* rented at fourteen hundred francs, at 55, Rue Pigalle.

VICTOR HUGO, HIS FAMILY, AND JULIETTE DROUET AT HAUTEVILLE HOUSE.

But hardly had they resumed the peaceful tenor of their ways when they were forced to uproot again. On February 8th, 1871, Victor Hugo was elected a member of the Assemblée Nationale, and, as he could not bear to be parted any longer from his grandchildren, he removed his whole household to Bordeaux, including his son Charles, his mistress Juliette, and the little heroes of *L'Art d'être grandpère*. They started on February 13th, and the poet took his seat on the 15th. On March 8th he felt it his duty to resign, on account of the refusal of his colleagues to allow Garibaldi to be naturalised a Frenchman. He was about to leave, when a fresh sorrow struck him down: this was the sudden death of Charles Hugo, on March 13th.

The body of the unfortunate and charming young man was taken back to Paris, and the funeral took place on the 18th, in the sinister scenario of the rising insurrection. On the 21st, Victor Hugo went to Belgium to make arrangements for his grandchildren's future. Two months and a half later, he was expelled from Brussels, for rewarding its hospitality by throwing his house open as a refuge to the political miscreants who had just fired Paris and shed the blood of their compatriots. He was the object of a violently hostile demonstration on May 27th, 1871, and afterwards received the decree of expulsion. He went to Vianden, in the Grand Duchy of Luxembourg, and returned definitely to Paris in September 1871. Juliette had accompanied him everywhere.

No sooner was the luggage unpacked, than she bravely undertook to amuse him, by forming a small circle of his friends and admirers, in her drawing-room at Rue Pigalle. But the undertaking was beyond her powers. Her long sojourn in a solitary island and her complete absorption in one sole object, had resulted in the loss of what might be termed her social talent. In France, and especially in Paris, everything was new to her, everything caused her agitation.

The state of her health was not such as to restore her equanimity. She suffered from gout and heart-disease, was growing stout, walked with difficulty, slept badly, and was terribly weary: "I am so tired," she writes, "that I feel as if even eternity would fail to rest me."

Victor Hugo, therefore, gave up the entertainments at Rue Pigalle; the boxes were repacked, and on August 14th, 1872, the party returned to that island where everything spoke to the exile of former joys, from the anemones he loved, to the cherry-tree he had planted himself.

In the mornings, at half-past eleven, Victor Hugo used to make his joyous appearance at Hauteville Féerie, and escort his friend to Hauteville House, where the luncheon-table was proudly attended by Georges and Jeanne. In the afternoon, a family drive was organised. The largest carriage on the island was hardly big enough to contain the dear beings by whom he loved to be surrounded. The hours drifted peacefully towards dusk.

While our heroine lived on future hopes and past memories, Victor Hugo enjoyed the present more than ever. Every one knows of his gallantry, and the bold front he offered to advancing age. Amongst other comforting illusions, he chose to believe that women prefer old men, and he gloried in proving his theory. With more sense than she has been credited with, Juliette sometimes managed to close her eyes and ears; at other times she gently rallied him, congratulating him on the success of his most recent exploit. But more often it must be admitted that her temper was not equal to the nobility of her nature. To jealousy was presently added the pain of humiliation and offended dignity, caused by a vulgar intrigue, conducted under her very eyes, at her own fireside.

At last, at the end of the visit to Guernsey, which had turned out so differently from her expectations, Juliette came to a grave decision. She resolved to abandon the field to the frail beauties whom chance, desire, or self-interest, gathered around her poet, and to retire to live at Brest with her sister, or at Brussels with her friends the Luthereau.

Having borrowed 200 frs. from some one, Juliette actually started on September 23rd, 1873, without leaving the smallest note of farewell for Victor Hugo. But he lost no time in despatching a letter of recall, and he couched it in terms so eloquent, and so pathetic, that once more the poor woman was fain to overlook the past. She returned to Rue Pigalle on

September 27th. She subsequently wrote to the kind hosts with whom she had taken refuge: "I have been very foolish, very cruel, very stupid; but I am rewarded. If one could hope for a second resurrection like this, one might be almost tempted to go through it all again."

II

Shortly after Juliette's act of defiance, her friend imposed the fatigue of a new removal upon her. The author of *L'Art d'être grandpère* had just lost his son, François Victor. More than ever he turned to his little grandchildren for consolation, and at the end of 1873, he decided to join households with them and their mother. For a rental of 6,000 frs. a year, he took two apartments, one above the other, at 21, Rue de Clichy. On April 28th, 1874, Juliette took possession of the third floor with her maid, while Madame Charles Hugo, her children, and the poet, settled in the fourth.

The receptions and dinners began again almost at once. At first they were weekly, then bi-weekly, and finally daily. The table was large and well attended. In addition to the five people forming the family party, including Juliette, there were rarely fewer than seven guests. Our heroine, in her capacity of chief steward, usually provided for twelve. She liked the fare to be simple and substantial: *sole Normande, côtelettes Soubise,* and *poulets au cresson* were the chief items of the repast.

Housekeeping on this scale demanded a staff of competent servants. Juliette had five, for whom she was responsible. She superintended their expenditure, their purchases, and the use to which they put the provisions; she commended good work and reproved faults, and in fact fulfilled the functions of a majordomo in a situation where the daily expenditure exceeded £4 for food, and approximated £2 for wines and spirits. She also had to supervise the department of the invitations, draw up lists, and sort the guests of each day, so as to temper the solemnity of a Schœlcher or a Renan, with the wit and froth of a Flaubert or a Monselet. Juliette assumed this charge, submitted the names to Victor Hugo, wrote the letters, opened the answers, and classified them. If anybody failed at the last moment, she telegraphed to some one on the "subsidiary list," as she called it, and only ceased her efforts when she was assured of being able to offer to the gratified master a full table and a numerous and docile court.

She was now at the head of that court, but it must not be supposed that it was by her own desire. On the contrary, she practised the most severe self-effacement. Clad in black, wearing as her only jewel a cameo set in gold, representing Madame Victor Hugo, and bequeathed to her in the latter's will, she usually sat at the chimney-corner in a large arm-chair. Fatigued by her laborious preparations, it frequently happened that she fell asleep in the drawing-room, as Madame Victor Hugo had been wont to do.

This lapse of manners so covered her with confusion, that she made a vow either to bring her health up to the level of her devotion or else to disappear from view. She did, in fact, redouble her activities, to an extent astonishing in a septuagenarian. She undertook to follow the aged poet whenever he mingled with crowds. At Quinet's and Frédéric Lemaître's funerals, she was present in the throng, an infirm old woman, watching from a distance, over a Victor Hugo, upright as a dart, and full of vitality. Did he wish to make an ascent in a balloon, she was there; when he conducted a rehearsal, or read one of his early dramas to his modern interpreters, it was she who led the applause, declared that the voice of Olympio had retained all its strength and beauty, and that he had never read better.

In the period between 1874 and 1878 it must be conceded that Victor Hugo did his best to secure to his friend a greater degree of mental tranquillity than she had ever enjoyed before. He was careful to conceal his infidelities from her, and often succeeded in averting scenes and reproaches; or, if denial seemed impossible, he tried to palliate his fault and gain indulgence by addressing to her one of those poetical odes in which he excelled, and from which she derived such pride and joy.

But these were only passing revivals of youthful emotions, in the poet as well as in his friend. They resemble those bonfires of dead leaves, lighted by labourers in autumn on the summit of bare hills—their flame can ill withstand the slightest puff of wind. Such a puff blew upon the old couple in the course of the year 1878.

Juliette was greatly troubled about the state of her health. She wrote to the poet, on January 8th: "I feel that everything is going from me and crumbling in my grasp: my sight, my memory, my strength, my courage."

On June 28th of the same year, at one of those copious banquets to which he still did full justice, and in the midst of an argument with Louis Blanc concerning Voltaire and Rousseau, Victor Hugo had a cerebral attack which alarmed his friends exceedingly. His speech faltered, he gesticulated feebly. Two doctors summoned in haste failed to give reassurance, and prescribed absolute rest in the country. On July 4th, the poet was escorted to Guernsey by a large retinue consisting of his grandchildren, the Meurice family, Juliette, Monsieur and Madame Lockroy, Richard Lesclide, and another friend, Pelleport. But no sooner had they reached the island, than Victor Hugo began to show symptoms of agitation. It could not be on account of his illness, for he was living quietly and comfortably, rejoicing at the amusement the season afforded his friends, and taking his own share of it. But, according to the testimony of one who has published a book concerning the master as witty as it is frank,[56] the reason was that he had left behind him in Paris the heroines of several intrigues; amongst others, the young person whose behaviour had occasioned Juliette's fit of anger and departure for Brest,[57] and he was fearful lest the post should convey to Guernsey the forlorn cooings of the deserted doves, and that some echo of them should reach Juliette.

Our heroine was certainly informed of some of the circumstances, for on August 20th, 1878, while still at Guernsey, she wrote the old man a letter which is a revelation of the changed character of their intercourse. Victor Hugo answered somewhat crossly and contemptuously, and nicknamed Juliette "the schoolmistress."

On his return to Paris on November 10th, he consented to remove to the little house at Avenue d'Eylau where he ended his days, and which was then almost in the country. Juliette took the first floor, and he occupied the second. But presently she arranged to spend the nights in a spare room next to his, so that she might be at hand to attend upon him if necessary.

From that moment it may be said that her life declined into uninterrupted sadness and servitude. She was suffering from an internal cancer, and knew that she was condemned to die of slow starvation! Nevertheless, she played her part of sick nurse with a devotion and a minute attention to detail to which all witnesses tender their homage. She it was who entered the poet's chamber each morning, and woke him with a kiss; she, who put a match to the fire ready laid on the hearth, and prepared the eggs for his breakfast; she, who waited on the old man while he ate, opened his letters, made extracts from them when necessary, and answered the most important. It was she, again, who undertook to keep her beloved friend company until midday, and to amuse him, and acquaint him with the current political and literary news.

The task was heavy enough to weary a much younger brain. Juliette found it almost beyond her strength. In 1880 she was so overwrought that she had become nervous, irritable, and restless. At night, when her offices of reader and sick nurse were over, it must not be supposed that she was able to sleep. From her bed in the adjoining room, with eyes fixed, and ear on the stretch, she watched the slumber of her dear neighbour, under the great Renaissance baldachino, with its crimson damask curtains. Did he cough, she rose hurriedly and administered a soothing drink; but if she coughed herself, and thus ran the risk of awaking him, she was furious, longed for a gag, and tried to suppress the labouring of her suffering breast. She cursed the years that had made her love a burden to its object, and chid her body for a bad servant no longer subservient to her will.

Severe as were the physical sufferings she bore so patiently under shadow of the night, Juliette preferred them to the sadness she endured during the long, solitary afternoons, while her former companion was at the Senate, at the Académie, or elsewhere.

JULIETTE DROUET IN 1883.
From the picture by Bastien Lepage.

We must picture her at that period, not as Théodore de Banville represents her in his formal description, but as Bastien Lepage painted her with more truth, about the same time. Disease has made cruel inroads on the grave, serene, once goddess-like features. Her poor countenance is worn and wasted, covered with a fine network of wrinkles, each one of which tells its tale of suffering. Her hair, whose sheen was formerly likened by poets to the satin petals of a lily, and which once fell naturally into crown-like waves, is roughened and harsh, and has assumed that yellowish tinge which so often presages death. Her lips, no longer revived by kisses, are pale, her eyes heavy and anguished, her smile faded.

Seated by the fire in winter, and at the open window overlooking the Avenue d'Eylau in summer, she who was the "Princesse Négroni," now presents the woeful appearance of a grandmother without grandchildren.

Sometimes she tries to pray. She calls death to her aid, she complains of the slowness with which the bonds of the soul loose those of the body.

In September 1882, she made a short journey with Victor Hugo to Veules, to stay with Paul Meurice, and to Villequier, to stay with Auguste Vacquerie. She took to her bed immediately on her return. By a great effort of will, she got up once more, to attend the revival of *Le Roi s'amuse* on November 25th; then she finally returned to her chamber and never left it again.

Neither her body nor her mind was capable of assimilating nourishment. She waved happy memories aside.

Every afternoon the old poet paid her a visit. He disliked any mention of death, and could not bear the sight of suffering. If we are to believe Juliette, he had made a rule that every one must forswear melancholy, and shake off sad thoughts, before appearing in his presence. Docile as ever, the sick woman endeavoured to smile when he entered her room. She listened submissively to the arguments by which he sought to persuade her that she did not really suffer, that there is no such thing as suffering. Up till May 11th, 1883, the very day of her death, there remained thus about one hour of the day during which she still had to play her part, restrain her moans, and look cheerful. She did it to the best of her power, and doubtless, in the triumph of that daily victory gained over torture by her indomitable spirit, she found at last the answer that the poet should have put into the mouth of Maffio—she discovered that "That which brings satisfaction to the heart" is neither desire, nor caresses, nor even love: it is self-sacrifice.[58]

PART II

LETTERS

Sunday, 8.30 p.m. (1833).

Before beginning to copy or count words,[59] I must write you one line of love, my dear little lunatic. I love you—do you understand, I love you! This is a profession of faith which comprises all my duty and integrity. I love you, *ergo,* I am faithful to you, I see only you, think only of you, speak only to you, touch only you, breathe you, desire you, dream of you; in a word, I love you! that means everything.

Do not therefore give way any more to melancholy; permit yourself to be loved and to be happy. Fear nothing from me, never doubt me, and we shall be blissful beyond words.

I am expecting you shortly, and am ready with warm and tender caresses which, I hope, will cheer you.

Your JUJU.

(1833).

Since you left me I carry death in my heart. If you go to the ball to-night, it must be at the cost of a definite rupture between us. The pain I suffer at imagining you moving among that throng of fascinating, careless women, is too great for you to be able to inflict it without incurring guilt towards me. Write to me "Care of Madame K...." If I do not hear from you before midnight, I shall understand that you care very little for me ... that all is over between us ... and for ever.

J.

Wednesday, 2.30 p.m. (1833).

I cannot refrain, dearly beloved, from commenting upon the profound melancholy you were in this morning, and upon the doubt you manifest on every occasion as to the sincerity of my love. This unjustifiable suspicion on your part disheartens me beyond all expression. It intimidates me and makes me fear to confide to you the incidents my dubious position exposes me to. To-day, for instance, I concealed from you the visit of a creditor, who presented himself to the porter, but was not shown up. I paid him out of my own resources, without your knowledge, because you are always telling me *I do not love you.* This expression from you makes me feel that you hold a shameful opinion of me and my character, rendered possible perhaps by my situation, but none the less false, unjust, and cruel.

I love you *because* I love you, because it would be impossible for me not to love you. I love you without question, without calculation, without reason good or bad, faithfully, with all my heart and soul, and every faculty. Believe it, for it is true. If you cannot believe, I being at your side, I will make a drastic effort to force you to do so. I shall have the mournful satisfaction of sacrificing myself utterly to a distrust as absurd as it is unfounded.

Meanwhile, I ask your pardon for the guilty thought that came to me this morning, and which may possibly recur, if you continue to see in my love only a mean-spirited compliance and an unworthy speculation. This letter is very lengthy, and very sad to write. I trust with all my soul, that I may never have to reiterate its sentiments.

I love you. Indeed I love you. Believe in me.

JULIETTE.

Wednesday, 8.15 p.m. (1833).

Here is a second letter. Forgive my epistolary extravagance. Honestly, I imagine you must soon tire, to put it as mildly as possible, of this superabundance of letters.

The reason of my writing again is no novel one: it is merely to repeat that I love you every day and every instant more and more; that I feel convinced you are only too eager to return my sentiments, but that between your desire and your capacity there stands a wall a hundred feet high, entitled "suspicion." Suspicion leads to contempt, and when that exists, no real love is possible. There is no answer to what I have just stated. I feel it, and am crushed by my sorrow. I know not what to do, where to go, what plans to make. I can only suffer, just as I can only love you.

JULIETTE.

If ever this letter is found, it will be seen that my love was insufficient in your eyes to atone for my past.

2 a.m. (1833).

MY VICTOR,

I love you truly, and neither know, nor can conceive, any personality more deserving of devotion than yourself.

I look up to you as a faithful, reliable friend, as the noblest and most estimable of men.

It hurts me to feel that my past life must be an obstacle to your confidence. Before I cared for you, I felt no shame for it, I made no attempt to conceal or alter it; but, since I have known you, this attitude of mind has changed in every respect. I blush for myself, and dread lest my love have not the strength to erase the stains of the past. I fear it even more, when you suspect me unjustly.

My Victor, it is for your love to sanctify me, for your esteem to renew in me all that once was good and pure.

I care for you so much that all this is possible. I will become worthy of you, if you will only help me.

Farewell. You are my soul, my life, my religion; I love you.

JULIETTE.

Your appreciation of my letters is one of the best proofs of love you have yet given me. I will set to work to reconstruct them. Nothing has happened since you left me yesterday, except that my love for you has increased.

(1833.)

Before reading this letter, look upon me once more with affection.

My poor friend, I am about to grieve and surprise you greatly. Yet it has to be done. I no longer have the courage to bear up against your unjust and suspicious jealousy, and your continued mistrust of a sentiment as pure and true as that which one cherishes towards God. They wear me out and make me wretched to the last degree. I would rather leave you, than expose myself to fresh grief, which might end in destroying either my reason or my love. This resolve is dictated by the excess of my affection. Even if you suffer, forgive me, and bless me before you leave me for ever. I love you.

J.

(1833.)

Since you insist upon a denial of offences which exist only in your imagination, I owe it to you to make it comprehensive and without restriction. It is not true that I have tried to offend you by reproaches unworthy of yourself and of me. It is not true that I have ever held any opinion of you, but this one, that I esteem you above all men.

The real and irrevocable cause of our estrangement, is the certainty that your love for me is incomplete. I am more persuaded of it every day, and particularly to-day, when you have actually told me that you thought I had misled you as to the state of my affections.

This is a grave offence towards a woman who has never deceived you on the subject of her heart, and whose only fault is to love you too much; for her very excess in this respect, has given her the sad courage to risk losing your esteem, in order to preserve your love one day longer.

But I am unwilling to think you intended to hurt me by allowing me to see the canker in your heart. I prefer to believe that we are equally the victims of a calamity, under which our only resource, is to separate from one another. Possibly our wounds will heal when they are no longer exposed to the continual friction of carping suspicion.

Good-bye. Forgive me if I have offended you. I am loath to hurt you.

J.

I beg you not to attempt to see me again. This is the last sacrifice I will ask of you.[60]

(June 1833.)

MY DEAR VICTOR, MY BELOVED,

Do not be anxious! I am as well as a poor woman, who has lost her happiness and the sole joy of her existence, can expect to be. If I could let you know my place of refuge without exposing us both, but more particularly myself, to useless wretchedness, I would do so. Confidence, the indispensable ingredient in a union such as ours, no longer exists in your mind. God is my witness that I have never once deceived you in matters of love, during the past four months. Any concealment I have been guilty of, has only been with the intention of sparing us both unnecessary worry, in view of the attitude of mind we have been in lately.

I may have been wrong; the purity of my intention must be my excuse.

CLAIRE PRADIER.
From an unpublished drawing by Pradier.

9.45 p.m. Saturday, August 13th (1833).

While you are on your travels, dearest, my thoughts follow you in all love. Though I still feel somewhat sore, I will strive to control myself, and speak only those gentle words you like to hear.

It was dear of you to allow me to come to your house.[61] It was far more than a satisfaction to my curiosity, and I thank you for having admitted me to the spot where you live, love, and work. Yet, to be entirely frank with you, my adored, I must tell you that the visit filled me with sadness and dejection. I realise more than ever, the depth of the chasm that gapes between your life and mine. It is no fault of yours, beloved, nor of mine; but so it is. It would be unreasonable of me to call you to account for more than you are responsible for, yet I may surely tell you, dearly beloved, that I am the most miserable of women.

If you have any pity for me, dear love, you will assist me to rise superior to the lowly and humble position which tortures my spirit as well as my body.

Help me, my good angel, that I may believe in you and in the future.

I beg and implore you.

J.
(1833.)

It is not quite six o'clock in the evening. I have just finished copying the verses you gave me yesterday. I am not very familiar with the forms of compliment in usage in fashionable society. All I can tell you is that I wept and admired when I heard you read them, that I wept and admired when I read them to myself, and that once more I weep and admire in recalling them. I thank you from the bottom of my heart for having thought of me when you were writing them. Thank you, my beloved, for the benign sentiments that inspired you. Your beautiful lines have had the effect you anticipated, for they have acted both as a cordial and a sedative to my sick spirit. Thank you! thank you! and again, thank you! You are not only sublime—you are kind, and, what is better still, you are indulgent, you who have so much right to be severe.

I love you. My heart melts in admiration and adoration. There is more rapture of love in my poor bosom than it is capable of containing. Come then, and receive the superabundance of my ecstasy.

If you only knew how I long for you, and desire you! If you knew *more still*, you would come, I am very sure! Come, come, I beg you, come! You shall have a kiss for every step, a recompense for every effort, more smiles, and more joy, than you will encounter fog and cold.

JULIETTE.

I am writing this a little later because, before turning to business, I had to unburthen my heart. I came home yesterday, read your poetry, dined, did my accounts, and went to bed. I read the newspapers you sent, went to sleep, dreamed of you, and woke up this morning at 8 o'clock. I rose almost immediately, did some housework, and mended yesterday's frock. In the middle of breakfast Lanvin arrived, bringing the newspapers and a letter from M. Pradier and some of Mademoiselle Watteville's luggage. He asked whether we should want him to see us off. He left again at 1 p.m., taking Claire's things with him and some of his wife's. When he had gone, I washed and did my hair, did the same for Claire, and at 2.30 I sat down to copy, and now I am writing to you. This, Colonel, is my report. Are you satisfied? Then, so is the Corporal of the Guard! After dinner I shall hear the children their lessons, and count the lines of *Feuilles d'Automne*.

After dinner.

I have heard the children's lessons, and been obliged to punish your *protégée*, Claire, who is the laziest and idlest of all the pupils. I have just read your poem to Madame Lanvin; she was deeply moved. The poor thing understands you, therefore I need not explain that she loves you. Good-night, until to-morrow, I hope.

I suppose you did not come to-day because you had arrangements to make for our journey; that is why I am able to possess my soul in patience.

J.

Sunday, 4 p.m. (1833).

I have just come in sad and depressed. I suffer, I weep, I wail aloud and moan under my breath, to God and to you. I long to die, that I might put an end once and for all, to this misery and disappointment and sorrow. It really seems as if my happiness had disappeared with the fine weather. It would be folly to expect to see either again. The season is too far advanced for fine weather or for happy days. You poor silly, who wonder that I should deplore so bitterly the loss of one day's happiness, it is easy to see that you had not to wait for the privilege of loving and being loved till you were twenty-six years old! You poet, who wrote *Les Feuilles d'Automne* in an atmosphere of love, laughter of children, eyes azure and black, locks brown and gold, happiness in full measure! You have had no cause to notice how one day of gloom and rain, like this, can make the greenest of leaves wither and fall to the ground. You cannot therefore know how twenty-four hours robbed of bliss can undermine one's self-confidence and strength for the future. It is evident that you do not, for you wonder when I weep; you are almost annoyed at my grief. You see, therefore, that you do not realise the measure of my devotion. Surely I have good reason for regretting that I love you so ardently, when I see that love uncalled for and unwelcome! Oh, yes, I love you, it is true! I love you in spite of myself, in spite of you, in spite of the whole world, in spite of God, in spite even of the Devil, who mixes himself up in it.

I love you, I love you, I love you, happy or unhappy, merry or sad. I love you! Do with me what you will, I still shall love you.

J.

Monday, 1.50 a.m., 1833.

I have been standing at the window all this time, my soul stretched towards you, my ear attentive to every sound, fearing always lest your courage should fail you before the end of your weary walk. It is half an hour since you left; I have listened hard, but no sound has reached me that could make me apprehend you had not the strength to reach your own house. I trust that while I am penning these lines, you are already experiencing the relief that bed and repose will bring to your suffering. No words of mine can suffice to express to you my regret, my sorrow, my despair, for what happened to-night. I do not acquit you altogether of guilt, but I ask you to pardon your own, as well as mine. Forgive me for having yielded to you after what had passed between us. I ought to have foreseen what would happen, and what did happen. God knows, I had resisted as long as I could, and had given way only upon the solemn promise you made me, never to refer to the stains of my former life, so long as my conduct towards you should remain honest and pure.

The last seven months of my life have been absolutely honest and pure! Yet, have you kept your word?

If I were the only one to suffer I should be more resigned, but you are as unhappy as I; you are as ashamed of the insults you heap upon me, as I am, of receiving them.

Now that I perceive fully the canker that lies at the root of our position, it is my part to arrest the progress of the evil by cutting out my soul and my life, to preserve what can still be saved of yours and mine.

Listen, Victor, I urge you not to refuse me your assistance in carrying out the plan I think indispensable for the honour of us both.

If anything can give you courage it must be the knowledge that I have been faithful to you alone, these seven months. Ah, truly I have never deceived you! Truly! truly! Yet in the course of these same months, how many mortifying scenes such as that of to-night have taken place!

Surely you can see that we must no longer hesitate! I will go away by the first Saumur omnibus. The health of my little girl can serve as a pretext. When I am with her, I shall be able to reflect upon my position, and see what I can do in order to render it tolerable. If, as probably may be necessary, I were to leave the theatre, the furniture would cover my debt to Jourdain, and if you were unwilling to be worried, I could request any man of business to sell it, up to the amount of my bill to Jourdain, which is the only one for which you are responsible.

I shall go abroad. Such as I am, I am still capable of earning my living, which is all that is necessary.

But all this is beside the question. The important point is that I ought to start as soon as possible, to-day even, in order to protect us both from ourselves.

Before going, I hope to see you once more, unless your condition should become worse—which is a horrifying thought when I consider that I am the cause of it.

But whether I see you or not, whether you are the victim of my temper or not, I leave with you all my love and all my happiness. I do not reserve even hope; I give into your keeping my soul, my thoughts, my life. I take only with me my body, which you have no cause to regret.

JULIETTE.

(December 20th, 1833.)

MY BELOVED VICTOR,

I have been very unjust to you. You have had cause to call me ungrateful and unworthy. You will soon hate me—soon also, you will have forgotten me. I feel it. You see, there can be no thought or sentiment of yours that I do not understand and apprehend. At this moment, even while I am writing to you, you are blaming me for suffering. You are annoyed with me for idolising you with an extravagance which renders me mad and jealous. You are tired of my love. It cramps you, fatigues you. You meditate flying from me. My bad luck frightens you; you fear to share it longer. You dread the responsibility—say, rather, you love me less, perhaps not at all. Oh, what suffering that fear gives me! My head is aching. I wish I could die. It must be my fault. I have been wrong to show you the hideous wound in my heart, the jealousy which lacerates and destroys it. Yes, I ought to have concealed my sufferings from you. I ought never to fly into those rages that betray the depth of my love and grief.

My Victor, do not leave me! I beg you on my knees, not to be daunted before a public responsibility. Who has the right to demand from you an account of the measure of the sacrifices you have made for me? What does it matter if you are denied the justice you deserve? What matter that you should be held responsible in part for my troubles? The point to be considered before all others, is your private relations with me. The responsibility you must accept is towards me only; it concerns only our two selves. If you repudiate it, it will kill me, for my whole life is wrapped up in you and your presence. I breathe only through your lips, see only with your eyes, live only in your heart. If you withdraw yourself from me, I must die.

Reflect! This is not a threat, to keep you near me. I am not exaggerating the extent to which you are necessary to my very existence—I am only telling you what I feel. It is the truth, but the truth under restriction, for I hardly dare acknowledge it in its entirety, even to myself. *I need you! Only you! I cannot exist without you.* Think of it. Try to love me enough to accept the charge of my life, with all its attendant bad luck.

JULIETTE.

2 a.m., January 1st, 1834.

TO THEE, MY VICTOR!

I dare not say anything. Guess what I am feeling and do with me what you will!

I love you ... the memory of what has gone before, and my fears for the future, prevent me from describing my emotions as freely as formerly. Forget the past, take the future into your own hands, and I shall regain the faculty of saying "I love you," as earnestly as I mean it.

I love you.... JULIETTE.

Saturday morning, 1834.

TO MONSIEUR VICTOR HUGO,

IN TOWN.

JULIETTE DROUET ABOUT 1830.
From Champmartin's picture (Victor Hugo Museum).

It is a quarter to one. I have been to your printing-works, numbers 16 and 19; you had not been seen. I went on to your house; you had not come in. I wrote you a line; I waited for you.... At last I came home hoping to find you; but you had not been here. My thanks to you for treating me like a vagrant dog. You had informed me that you were going to the printing-works, that you might go back to your house, that you would certainly go to mine.

You forgot your promises at once, and you apparently hold my love very cheap.

If you, indifferent though you may be, could see me in imagination, as I sit writing to you, you would be horrified at the condition your injustice and disdain have reduced me to.

It is evident that you no longer love me, and that you are only bound to me by the fear of causing some great calamity if you desert me. It is indeed grievous that this should be the only sentiment which links you to me, and I am unwilling to accept a devotion so hollow and humiliating. I give you back your freedom. From this moment you have no responsibility towards me, although my heart is broken, although my soul is still fuller of love than it is able to contain, although my eyes, as I write, are drenched with bitter tears. I shall still have the courage necessary to bear my life as it will be, when bereft of happiness and laughter.

You have been very cruel to me. I forgive you. Forgive also my tempests of rage. I am ashamed of them, and thoroughly wretched. I swear to you by that which I hold most sacred in life, namely my child, that I am unable to explain how I can have been guilty yesterday of a thing I utterly disapprove of, and which seems to me the acme of effrontery. I swear I never saw those men. I am innocent of any crime. I can say no more. You have crushed me by referring again to my past life, and even while I am assuring you of my love and repentance, and while I still hope for a reconciliation, I tremble to feel that you can suspect me so unjustly. My heart shrinks from the sorrow still in store for it ... my pen fails me ...

Farewell! May you enjoy greater tranquillity and happiness than will fall to my lot. Do not forget that, for a whole year, we were happy solely by means of our love.

Good-bye! I have indeed received my full meed of punishment for the imaginary crime of yesterday.

Farewell. Think of me without bitterness.

JULIETTE.

Monday, 2 a.m. (1834).

I returned from the Place Royale about two hours ago. It was ten o'clock when I arrived there, and I left at about midnight. I had hoped to bring you back with me, or, failing to do so, to catch at least a glimpse of you. I waited patiently all that time, hoping that you would become aware of my presence, and reward me for it by one glance. But everything remained dark and gloomy for me, though it was easy to see the lights through the drawn blinds, and the shadows of many people moving about.

It will not be the last time, in all probability, that I shall have the opportunity of seeing that, while I suffer and weep, you make merry. Forgive me, my Victor, forgive me for this comparison of our respective lots. It is the last time I shall make it, perhaps even the last time I shall write to you, for you have said that you will not read any more of my letters for a long time ... a long time signifies "for ever," for you will forget me and I shall die. Your love was my whole life. To-night I feel as miserable as I should be if you no longer loved me. God, how sorely I need pity!

I have just obeyed your wishes by putting all your works away carefully. As for my own relics of you, I have collected them in an English desk, under lock and key, and hidden them under my bolster, where they shall always remain.

Farewell, the performance of this duty has been a mournful satisfaction to me.

Saturday, 6 p.m., 1834.

TO THEE, MY BELOVED.

You promised that as soon as your work was finished, you would devote all your time to me; you also said, when you were leaving me yesterday, that you would come early this morning. Neither of these promises have you kept; yet I have never longed for your presence and your love more than at this moment, when anxiety seems to have taken up its abode with me. I have been so worried that I do not know whether I could endure another day like this.

I am thankful to leave this house; it is so haunted by ill-luck and sadness, that to be quit of it will be a relief.

My Victor, what is going to become of us? What can we do to avert the misfortune that threatens us?[62] Can you think of any way out of the trouble? Do you love me? I love you so! in prosperity, and still more in adversity. Oh, God be merciful to me! Without your help I am done.

JULIETTE.

I have no other refuge or I should not go to Madame K. I cannot wander about alone, for that would make you anxious; yet I cannot stay here, I am too miserable. I will wait for you at Madame K.'s house until nine o'clock. I hardly know what I am writing, or have written. My reason and will are in abeyance this morning.

I write because I am wretched, because I must make moan to someone or something. I write because I shall soon be dead. These lines will be the cold remains of my soul and thoughts and love, as my body will be the corpse of my warm flesh and blood.

I write to declare my faith, to obtain pardon of my sins, to weep, because my tears strangle me and will put an end to me.

I shall be in the street to-night. I shall remain there as long as my strength holds out, without hope, but still, near you....

Midnight, Saturday, August 2nd, 1834.

TO VICTOR.

Farewell for ever. You have decreed it thus. Farewell then, and may you be as happy and admired as I shall be hapless and forlorn.

Farewell! This word comprises my whole life, and joy, and happiness.

JULIETTE.

I am going away with my child. I am just going out to fetch her and take our places. The Comédie Française management has no claim on my services until it has assigned me my parts. My maid has orders to open my letters. If there should be one from the Comédie Française she would let me know at once and everything could be arranged. I need not, therefore, worry about it at present.

(1834.)

MADEMOISELLE MARIE,
  C/O MADAME DROUET,
  No. 4 bis, Rue de Paradis au Marais, Paris.

Enclosed is a letter for Monsieur Victor Hugo. If he should not come to the house, try and manage to let him know that there is one awaiting him at No. 4, Rue de Paradis au Marais, from Madame Krafft. If he is still in Paris I expect he will understand what you mean, and will either send for it or fetch it himself. In any case, write to me by every post and tell me about Monsieur Victor Hugo: whether you have seen him, what he has said to you, whether he is still in Paris, or whether he has left; in fact, tell me everything you can find out concerning him.

I am writing from Rennes, where I arrived very ill, with my child. I hope, however, to be able to leave to-morrow and go to my sister. Write to me there and address thus:

MADAME DROUET,
C/O M. LOUIS KOCK,
Saint Renan,
By Brest.

Please take good care of the house.

J. DROUET.

(ENCLOSURE)

RENNES,
2.30 p.m., Monday (1834).

MY DEAR VICTOR,

I am writing this letter on the chance of its reaching you, but with the sad premonition that you will never read it.

My beloved, I love you more than ever. I cannot do without you. I would willingly die for you, but I cannot consent to accept a devotion which might endanger your health and your life. I was forced to fly from you. It cost me much to resist your supplications and your wrathful glances. I suffered frightfully; and now, alas, I know that, were you with me, I could no longer withstand either your gentle pleading or your terrible anger. I am very wretched. I love and bless you. Be happy!

JULIETTE.

One portion of your curse has already come to pass. My soul and body have suffered severely. In addition, I have been harried to death by the idiotic authorities, who are suspicious of every woman without a passport. I have been at Rennes about half an hour. It is half-past two. I leave again for Brest to-morrow morning at four o'clock; I expect to arrive on Thursday at five in the evening. My Victor, I love you. I could do anything for you. Have pity upon me. I love you better than anything in life.

August 5th, 1834.

MADEMOISELLE MARIE,
Care of MADAME DROUET,
No. 4 bis, Rue de Paradis au Marais, Paris.

Here is another letter for Monsieur Victor Hugo. Try to get it to him. If he is in the country near Paris, let him know that there is something at my house in the name of Madame Krafft that will interest him.

I have spent a sad and sleepless night. I am afraid of falling really ill. Answer this at once.

(ENCLOSURE)

RENNES,
4 a.m., August 5th (1834).

Victor, I love you. Victor, I shall die of this separation. I need you, to be able to live. Since I told you everything, since the moment when my eyes could no longer rest upon yours, I have felt as if all my veins were being opened, and my life's blood slowly drained away. I feel myself dying, and I know that I love you the better for every pang. My Victor, can you forgive me? Do you still love me? Is it really true that you hate me, that I am odious in your sight, that you despise me, that you would grind my face to the pavement if I pressed my lips to your feet, pleading for forgiveness? Oh, if you still love me, if you still respect me, if you can forgive everything, only tell me so, and I will do all you wish! Everything, I swear! Will you take me back?

I am very ill.

J.

3 a.m. (1834).

FOR MY VICTOR.

While I was expecting to see you I could not sleep. Now that the hope is dead I still cannot sleep because I am unhappy. I grieve not to have seen you; I grieve because I was cross and ill-tempered when you were gentle and charming. I rehearse in imagination all the incidents of the evening, and the pain at my heart grows unbearable. It is wicked of me to torment you, yet I cannot help myself. My offence goes by the name of "jealousy." Much as I dread displeasing you, I yet cannot avoid giving way to that hideous passion. I make you miserable when I should like to saturate you with happiness. Oh, it is horribly wrong of me! I am much to be pitied, for I am jealous, and of whom? The most beautiful, the most gentle, the most perfect of women ... your wife! Heaven forgive me! My torment is surely sufficient expiation for my fault!

God, how I love you! how I love my Victor! All is contained in these words. You do forgive me, do you not? and you love me as much as ever? I hope so ... else, I should prefer to die.

JULIETTE.

Sunday, 3 p.m. (1834).

I have abandoned hope ... yet love remains. I no longer believe that any happiness is possible for me in the future, but *you* I love more every day; better than the first day, better than yesterday, better than this morning, better than a moment ago; and still I am not happy.

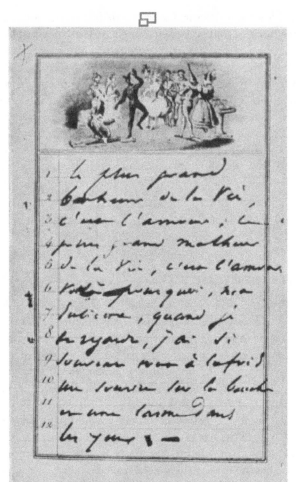

A PAGE OF JULIETTE DROUET'S NOTE-BOOK IN 1834.
The note-book belongs to M. Louis Barthou.

You remember what I used to say to you when *Marie Tudor* was in rehearsal? "Those wretches have robbed me of my self-confidence; I dare not, cannot rehearse any more; I feel paralysed."

To-day, it is not a theatrical part that is in question—it is my life. Now that calumny has crushed me, now that my mode of life has been condemned without my having a chance of self-defence, now that my health and reason have been expended in this struggle without profit or glory, now that I have been held up before the public as a woman without a future, I dare not, cannot live longer ... this is absolutely true ... I dare not live. This fear has brought me to the verge of suicide ... a peculiar suicide. I do not propose to kill myself like other people. I mean to sever myself from you, and, to me, such a severance signifies death. Death certainly. I have already made one experiment of the kind, therefore I am sure.

I am confirmed in this project by the reflection that you will thereby be restored to liberty; that you will be free to direct your life and your genius in the way best suited to your happiness; that I shall no longer be an obstacle in your path, but an object of pity and indulgence—pity for what I shall suffer, indulgence and forgiveness for such of my faults as have made you suffer.

If the excess of my love and grief should bring me back to your side, do not notice me ... shut your eyes, stop your ears, remain in your own house ... thus you may learn to forget, while I ... I ... shall die. I shall not suffer long. I shall soon be at rest.

It is raining hard at this moment, and I am in a raging fever. No matter, I shall go out. I do not know whether you propose coming to fetch me. If you do not, I cannot tell what time I shall return home. I don't care, I am mad! I am in torture such as I have never yet endured! yet I love you even more than I suffer. My love dominates my whole being. I love you!

JULIETTE.

5.30 (1834).

You wish me to write to you in your absence. I am always unwilling to accede to this desire, for when we are separated, my thoughts are so sad and painful that I should prefer to hide them from you if possible.

You see, my Victor, this sedentary, solitary life is killing me. I wear my soul out with longing. My days are spent in a room twelve feet square. What I desire is not the world, not empty pleasures, but *liberty—liberty* to act, liberty to employ my time and strength in household duties. What I want is a respite from suffering, for I endure a thousand deaths every moment. I ask for life—life like yours, like other people's. If you cannot understand this, and if I seem foolish or unjust in your eyes, leave me, do not worry about me any more. I hardly know what I am writing; my eyes are inflamed, my heart heavy. I want air, I am suffocating! Oh, Heaven, have pity upon me! What have I done to deserve such wretchedness? I love you, I adore you, my Victor; have pity upon me. Kill me with one blow, but do not let me suffer as many eternities as there are minutes in every one of your absences.

What am I saying? I am delirious, feverish. Oh God, have mercy on me!

JULIETTE.

November 4th, 8.30 p.m. (1834).

Yes, you are my support, the stable earth beneath my feet, my hope, my joy, my happiness, my all! I do not know how these halting words of mine can be expected to convey my thoughts to your mind, but this indeed is truly and sincerely meant: that you are to me the noblest, most sincere, most generous of men. I believe this, and have absolute confidence in your power to frustrate the evil fate which holds me in its grip.

My dearly beloved, you were quite charming just now, and you are perfectly right when you say that there is an element of vanity in your nobility of conduct; for nothing could be more becoming than the elegant and dignified manner in which you raised me just now from my knees. You were really great. You were a king!

My darling little Toto, *chéri!* I am going to bed now, because I am not certain that you will come early enough to take me out; and, after all, you are not the sort of man to be scandalised by finding a woman in bed, especially ...

JULIETTE.

1834.

MY DEARLY BELOVED,

I am always wishing I were a great actress, because, if my soul and intellect were equal to yours, another link would be forged between us; but I wish it still more at such a time as this, for I should then be able to relieve you of the annoyance of being at the mercy of an old woman, whose conceit has made her aggressive.[63]

I need not finish this letter, for here you are!

1835.

It is long after 11 o'clock. I am no longer expecting you for a walk, but I still hope to see you this evening. I write you these few lines as an apology for the disappointment I feel each time you fail me. I am miserable, but not angry; I shed tears, but do not reproach you; I am often much to be pitied, but I never cease loving you to distraction. If only you would believe this, I think I could bear my invidious position with more resignation. I am afraid you misapprehend my love, and this anxiety often makes the days seem long and sad.

But I must not forget that you are working and worn out, and that you have neither strength nor leisure to listen, that is to say, to read of my worries.

11.30 *p.m.*

Here you are! I am finishing this letter more untidily even than usual. Luckily one's character, and, more important still, one's heart, are not exclusively interpreted by one's handwriting.

JULIETTE.

Saturday, 3.15 p.m. (1835).

MY POOR, DEAR, BELOVED TOTO,

When I see you so preoccupied with important business I am ashamed to add to your fatigues by the reiteration of my devotion, which you already know by heart. Did I not fear that you would misunderstand my silence, I should put an end to these letters, which, after all, are only a cold skeleton, a dull narrative of the generous, tender, passionate feelings which fill my heart. I should stop them, I say, until after the production of your play, reserving to myself the privilege of taking my revenge afterwards by multiplying my words and caresses. This is what I should do if you felt only a quarter as much solicitude for your dear little person as I do.

It is nearly three o'clock. I hope by this time everything has gone off well at rehearsal. It is high time, my admired, beloved, adored poet, you left that wretched den they call the Théâtre Français. You will leave it with full credit to yourself, notwithstanding the ill-will of that jealous old wretch, and the stupidity, hatred, and malice of the cabal against you.

You will see, my splendid lion, whether those hideous crows will dare croak in face of your roaring. As for me, if anything could make me prouder and happier, it would be that I alone understand you.

JULIETTE.

Saturday, 1.30 p.m., April 11th (1835).

Why were you so smart just now? It makes me dreadfully anxious, especially in conjunction with your early morning walks to the Arsenal. Toto ... Toto ... you do not know what I am capable of; take care! I do not love you for nothing. If you deceived me the least bit in the world I should kill you. But no, seriously, I am jealous when I see you so fascinating. I do not feel as reassured as you would wish me to be. In fact, I insist upon attending these rehearsals. I do not choose to confide my dear lover to the discretion of nobody knows who. I wish to keep my lover to myself, in the face of the nation and of all French actresses.

That is my politic and literary resolve: I shall put it into execution, from to-morrow.

By the way, this is my birthday. You did not even know it—or, rather, I dare say you do not care whether I was ever born or not. Is it true that you do not mind one little bit? That is all the importance you attach to my love! And yet one thing is very certain: that I was created and put into the world solely to love you, and God knows with what ardour I fulfil my mission.

I love you—ah, yes, indeed, I love you—I love my Victor!

JULIETTE.

Saturday, 8 p.m. (1835).

I am more than ever resolved to separate our lives one from the other. What you say about Mlle. Mars's increasing age and the impossibility of obtaining a double success through her, literary as well as financial, and about the necessity of securing the services of Madame Dorval or some equally handsome and celebrated actress, makes me determined to sever our connection as speedily as possible, no matter where I may have to go, or under what pecuniary conditions. Your words to-night prove that you have had private intelligence about Mlle. Mars, Madame Dorval, and the theatre generally, that you have concealed from me, although it must completely revolutionise the plans made by you for the first play you were to give at this theatre. The secrecy you have maintained on the subject, contrary to all your promises to conceal nothing from me, grieves me more than the treachery of Monsieur Harel and Mlle. George, more even than the wicked animosity of your enemies and the perfidy of your intimate friends against myself. This silence is proof positive that I am a hindrance to your interests; you dread my ambition and my jealousy; you had already seen the propriety of giving a part to Madame Dorval, but you did not dare tell me so, for fear of encountering resistance and tears from me at this new distribution. You have only partially averted these. I will not attempt to thwart you, on the contrary; as for my tears, they are not worth wiping away, nor even restraining.[64] From this very night we cease our communion of dramatic interests. I go back to the position I ought never to have left: that of a hack actress, who is given any part, and badly paid at that. You resume your liberty without any impediment.

Let us hope this new resolution will conduce to our greater happiness.

JULIETTE.

Tuesday, April 28th, 1835.
Four hours before the production of "Angélo."

This is just to remind you of my love, and that it will only be purified and augmented by the ill-luck and perfidy to which you are more exposed than others, my noble poet, my king—king, indeed, of us all, though lover only of me: is that not so? I have nothing to fear from you, have I, my darling? You will take care of yourself and resist the advances of that shameless woman. Promise me this. I would not allude to it to-day, only I feel so uneasy at the thought of your spending the whole evening in her society, that I would give my life to prevent it. If you understood the greatness and quality of my love, you would appreciate my alarm.

Think of poor me, sitting at the back of a box to-night, enduring all the anguish of jealousy and love.

JULIETTE.

Madame Pierceau came at one o'clock, leaving Monsieur Verdier in a cab below. He was desperate at the loss of his stall, which, he hears, was taken from him by your orders. As I did not know what to say about it, I advised Madame Pierceau to send him to you. Monsieur Pasquier, as I anticipated, has not taken Madame Récamier's box. I wonder what you have done with it. Did it reach you in time?

Midnight, Tuesday, April 28th, 1835.
An hour after the triumph of "Angélo."

My cup is full. Bravo! bravo!! bravo!!! bravo!!!! bravo!!!!! For the first time I have been able to applaud you as much as I wished, for you were not there to prevent it.

Thank you, my beloved! Thank you for myself, whose happiness you increase with every second of my life, and thank you also for the crowd that was there, admiring, listening, and appreciating you.

AUTOGRAPH LETTER FROM JULIETTE DROUET TO HER DAUGHTER CLAIRE.

AUTOGRAPH LETTER FROM JULIETTE DROUET TO HER DAUGHTER CLAIRE (continued).

I saw and heard everything, and will tell you all about it; although if the applause, enthusiasm, and delirium could be measured by sheer weight, my load would indeed be heavy. I will give you full details of the performance, to-morrow, for I dare not hope to see you to-night; it would be too much happiness for one day, and you do not want me to go mad with joy!

Till to-morrow, then. If you knew how conscientiously I clapped Madame Dorval, you would hesitate to say or do anything to add to the soreness I already feel at the thought that another than I has been selected to interpret your noble sentiments. There, now I am giving way to sadness again, because you are with that woman!

Good-night, my beloved. Sleep well, my poet, if the sound of the great chorus of praise does not prevent it. To your laurels I add my tender caresses and thousands of kisses.

JULIETTE.

Friday, 8 p.m. (1835).

If I were a clever woman, my gorgeous bird, I could describe to you how you unite in yourself the beauties of form, plumage, and song! I would tell you that you are the greatest marvel of all ages, and I should only be speaking the simple truth. But to put all this into suitable words, my superb one, I should require a voice far more harmonious than that which is bestowed upon my species—for I am the humble owl that you mocked at only lately. Therefore, it cannot be. I will not tell you to what degree you are dazzling and resplendent. I leave that to the birds of sweet song who, as you know, are none the less beautiful and appreciative.

I am content to delegate to them the duty of watching, listening and admiring, while to myself I reserve the right of loving; this may be less attractive to the ear, but it is sweeter far to the heart. I love you, I love you, my Victor; I cannot reiterate it too often; I can never express it as much as I feel it.

I recognise *you* in all the beauty that surrounds me—in form, in colour, in perfume, in harmonious sound: all of these mean *you* to me. You are superior to them all. You are not only the solar spectrum with the seven luminous colours, but the sun himself, that illumines, warms, and revivifies the whole world! That is what you are, and I am the lowly woman who adores you.

JULIETTE.

If you are coming to fetch me, as you led me to expect, I shall see you very soon now. I have never longed more ardently for you. Lanvin has just come. I will tell you about it when I see you.

Thursday, 7.30 p.m. (1835).

TO MY DEAR ABSENT ONE.

I hardly saw you this morning. I have not seen you this evening, and God knows what time it will be before you come to take me to *Angélo*—for I do not admit the possibility of a single performance taking place without my presence: besides, I am not sorry to know exactly how much time you spend with these actresses of the sixteenth century, and those of the nineteenth, who are no less dangerous. There, I am nearly as cross as I am sad. I had vowed I would not write at length to-day, just to teach you not to throw my letters aside without reading them. Myself, my letters, forgotten! You certainly manage to be the most worshipped and the least attentive of lovers. Oh, you do not care!

Never mind, I am sad. I am longing for you to-night, as the poor prisoner hungers for his pittance at the hour he is accustomed to receive it.

But you are indifferent—you can calmly let my soul die of inanition—do you not love me, then? Tell me!

Well, I love *you*. I love you my Victor. I forgive you, because I hope it is not your fault, and also, because I cannot prevent myself from loving you.

JULIETTE.

Tuesday, 8 p.m., 1835.

You hurt me a little bit just now, my Toto. While I was sacrificing the happiness of being with you one moment longer, to your need of repose, you were worrying about trifles, and not giving me a thought or a farewell. In moments like these I am forced to realise that you do not care for me as I care for you, and I feel wretched in consequence.

Another thing I have observed is that you never allude to my letters. You neither notice the complaints I make nor the love I shower upon you with every word. You have turned my happiness and content into sadness. My Toto, *you do not love me as I love you.* You have exhausted your faculty of loving. I tell myself that the enthusiastic and passionate devotion you once cherished for me has degenerated into mere partiality—then I mourn and mope, like a woman betrayed.

If you knew how I love you, my Toto, you would understand the anguish of my eagerness, you would pity me, and, instead of leaving my letters unanswered, you would fly to me the moment you have read them, to reassure and comfort me if my fears are unfounded.

Never mind, I give you a thousand kisses. How many will you waste?

JULIETTE.

Tuesday, 12.30 p.m. (1835).

MY DEAR LITTLE TOTO,

You have written me a very charming letter. I cannot send you one as fascinating; all I can do is to give you my whole heart and thoughts and life.

You are quite right when you say that I shall soon give myself to you again, regardless of the sorrows that may follow. It is true, for I could sooner dispense with life than with your love.

But let me tell you again the joy, surprise, and happiness, your letter caused me. You are better than I, and you are right when you think me an old idiot. I am in the seventh heaven this morning. You have never given me so much happiness, my dear little Toto. I am so grateful! I cannot love you more in return, for that were impossible; but I can appreciate in a higher degree your worth and the depth of your affection for me.

You are my dear little man, my lover, my god, my adored tyrant! I love you, adore you, think of you, desire you, call upon you!

JULIETTE.

Which do you like best, quality or quantity?

Monday, 8.20 p.m. (1835).

I adore your jealousy when it gives me the pleasure of seeing you at an unaccustomed hour; but when it simply consists in suspecting me without advantage to ourselves, oh, how I detest it!

You were rather cross to-day, but you atoned so amply by coming as you did, that I would willingly see you a little bit unjust to me every day, if it entailed the pleasure of having you one minute longer in the evening.

If you only knew how true it is that I love you, you could never be jealous, or admit the possibility of my being unfaithful to you; and again, if you knew how much I love you, you would come every moment of the day and of the night, to surprise me in that occupation, and you would ever be welcomed with transports of joy.

Yes, yes, I love you! I do not say so to force you to believe it, but because I crave to repeat it with every breath, with every word, in every tone. I adore you much more than you can ever wish. I love you above all things.

JULIETTE.

You attach too little importance to my letters as a rule. You forget that fine unguents are contained in small boxes, great love in trivial words.

Friday, 2 p.m. (1835).

You want a huge long letter ... and yet another huge long letter ... you are not very modest in your requirements. What would you say if I asked as much?—you, who write to every one in the world except me. I have a great mind to treat you according to your deserts, and write only as much as you write, love you only as much as you love me. You would be nicely punished if I did this. But do not fear; I should never play you such a scurvy trick. I am too much in need of an outlet for the superabundance of my heart, to venture to close the issue. I am too anxious to tell you every day how much I adore you, to condemn myself to silence. I long too much to get near you, in thought at all events, to afford to cut off the way of communication. Now that you know why I write so often, I will begin my letter.

My dear little Toto, although it is not long since I left you, I desire you with all the impatience and all the inclination that comes of a long separation. I should like to know where you are and what you are doing. I should like to be wherever you are, and, above all, I should like to be in your heart and thoughts, as you are in mine. I should like to be you and you me, in respect of love. The rest becomes you and you only. You are admired; I need to be loved. Are you capable, I ask you, of loving me as much as I love you, or half as much? even that would be immeasurable. If you only knew the extent of my love, you would treasure me, only for that.

I love you, love you, love you, love you, love you!

This short little word, issuing from my heart, has impetus enough to mount right up to the heavens. I love you!

JULIETTE.

I have received a letter from my daughter. This, combined with the horrible weather, makes me quite happy.

Friday, 9 p.m. (1835).

You gave me a delicious afternoon. How delightfully you talked! I am not alluding to your wit; a fly does not seek to raise an ingot of gold! Neither do I speak of the happiness of leaning upon your arm, listening to your voice, gazing into your eyes, breathing your breath, measuring my steps by yours, feeling my heart beat in unison with yours.

There can be no happiness greater than that I enjoyed this afternoon with you, clasped in your arms, your voice mingling with mine, your eyes in mine, your heart upon my heart, our very souls welded together. For me, there is no man on this earth but you. The others I perceive only through your love. I enjoy nothing without you. You are the prism through which the sunshine, the green landscape, and life itself, appear to me. That is why I am idle, dejected, and indifferent, when you are not by my side. I do not know how to employ either my body or my soul, away from you. I only come to life again in your presence. I need your kisses upon my lips, your love in my soul.

JULIETTE.

Saturday, 11 a.m. (1835).

GOOD MORNING, MY VICTOR!

Let me first kiss you. Of all the promises I made you yesterday, when we separated, only one has been broken. I promised to love you as I loved you at that moment—that is to say, more than all the world; but I do not know how it happened, I have come to love you much more! and I feel it will be so as long as I shall live. I beg you, my dear little Toto, to make up your mind to this, as I have already done.

Do you know, my blessed Toto, you are a second little Tom Thumb, far more marvellous than your prototype; for, not merely with pebbles or crumbs of bread do you mark the roads along which you travel, but actually with jewels and precious stones. I shall always recognise the spot where you dropped an enormous ruby as big as a flint, yesterday, with as much indifference as if it had been a piece of grit from Fontainebleau.

What do you suppose must happen to an insignificant creature like myself in the presence of so much wealth, in the midst of the enchantments of your mind? Will she lose her reason? That is already done. As to her heart, you stole it from her very easily, and therefore nothing remains to the poor wight but what is already yours.

Her love, her admiration, her life, belong to you! My glances, words, caresses, kisses, all, are yours!

JULIETTE.

(1835.)

It seems to be always my turn to write to you now. In the old days your letters called forth my letters, your love mine—and it was meet that it should be so, for, as you have often said, the man should be the pursuer of the woman. It is always awkward when a change of *rôles* occurs, and I am acutely conscious of it. I feel that a caress from you gives me far more happiness and security than thousands of those elicited by me.

It is already half-past eleven and you have not arrived. Perhaps you are not coming, and the prohibition you laid upon me yesterday against seeking you at the printing works redoubles my anxiety and jealousy. I fear lest some untoward thing may have befallen you, or, worse still, some agreeable invitation reached you. My heart is crushed as in a vice; I think there is no greater suffering in this world than that of loving yet fearing. We arrange our lives very badly. Since you are not a free agent, and may be prevented from seeing me by thousands of circumstances we cannot foresee, you should at least allow me the opportunity of knowing what you are doing and where you are. It would satisfy me and keep me content. Instead of this, I have to wait for you, a prey to fears that tear at my heartstrings. Alas, I am to be pitied for loving you so intensely. It is a superabundance that will surely kill the body which bears it.

If you love me only moderately, I pray God to deprive me of one of two things: either my life, or my love.

JULIETTE.

Nearly midnight. What a night I have before me! God pity me!

AT METZ,
September 17th, Thursday, 8.15 a.m., 1835.

Good-morning, my Toto, good morning. It is magnificently fine, and we are going to be enormously happy. We are about to resume our bird-life, our life of love and freedom in the woods. I am enchanted. If only you were here, I should kiss you with all my might and main, as a reminder.

What sort of a night did you have? Did you love me? Have you been writing to me under the old chestnut-tree? I am sure you have not. You scamp, I am afraid I go on loving you in proportion to the decrease of your affection.

I was not able to read last night. I went to bed at a quarter past ten, and had horrid dreams. I trust they will not come true, but I confess I should be glad to get news of my poor little girl, whom we neglect far too much. If two more days go by without a letter, I shall write to Saumur, for I am really worried about her.

My dear little Toto, I am going to dress now, so as to get to you earlier. I love you, I love you with all my strength and all my soul. I kiss you! I adore you! Till this afternoon.

Your JULIETTE.

AT METZ,
September 24th, Thursday, 8.45 a.m.

Good-morning, my darling Victor. I love you and am happy, for we are going to be more absolutely together than was possible yesterday, or the day before, when an inconvenient third disturbed our privacy. Also the weather is glorious, and I am madly in love with you; so everything around me glows radiant and beautiful.

I stayed in bed until 8.30, although I woke up at seven o'clock; but I just rolled lazily about, thinking of you, and reading yesterday's newspapers. I reached home exactly at seven o'clock last night, undressed, tidied my things, dined, wrote to you, did my accounts, and read *Claude Gueux* till half-past ten. Then I put my hair into curl-papers, and got into bed at eleven o'clock. I went to you in spirit, and dreamt that I was kissing Baby Toto, and making big Toto jealous. This is the complete history of my morning up to date; now I shall dress, breakfast, and go for a walk in the meadows with the maid. Farewell, dearest, until this afternoon's happiness. Always yours in love and longing.

I love you with all my heart, I embrace you in spirit, I adore you with my whole soul, I admire you with every faculty of my mind. Think of me, come to me, come to me as soon as possible. My arms, my cheek, my whole being, await you.

J.

AT METZ,
Thursday, 8.45 p.m.

MY DEAR, GOOD TOTO,

I should have got back without adventure, had I not met an enormous and horrific toad in the road, which sent me flying home, shrieking as if the devil was at my heels. I was here by ten minutes past seven, began my dinner at five minutes past eight, and am now sitting writing to you, to thank you for all the bliss you lavish upon me. This day, drenched with rain though it was, has been one of the most beautiful and happiest of my whole life. If there had been rainbows in the sky, they would be reflected in our hearts, linking our souls together in thought and emotion.

I thank you for drawing my attention to so many lovely things I should never notice without your assistance and the touch of your dear white hand upon my brow; but there is one beauty greater and nobler than all the combined ones of heaven and earth, for the recognition of which I require no help—and that is yourself, my best beloved, your personality that I adore, your intellect that enchants and dazzles me. Would that I possessed the pen of a poet, to describe all I think and feel! But, alas, I am only a poor woman in love, and such a condition is not conducive to brilliancy of expression!

Good-night, my adored one; good-night, my darling. Sleep well. I send you a thousand kisses.

J.

Great indeed was our misfortune yesterday! I agree with you in that, my Victor, because I love you. For over a year I have suffered much; oftener than not, without complaint. I always trusted that my love and fidelity would engender in you feelings of esteem and confidence, but now that hope is for ever at an end; for, far from diminishing, your suspicion and contempt have grown to terrible dimensions. You love me, I know, and I worship you with all the strength of my being. *You are the only man I have ever loved, the only one to whom I have ever given this assurance.* Yet I now implore you on my knees to let me go. I cannot urge this too strongly. You see, my dear, I am so wretched, so humiliated, and I suffer so acutely, that I shall have to leave you, even against your will; so it would be kinder of you to give your consent, that I may at least have the sad satisfaction, if I must forsake you, of knowing that I have not disobeyed you.

Farewell, my joy; farewell, my life; farewell, my soul! I leave you, for the very sake of our love—I offer this sacrifice on behalf of us both. Later, you will understand. But before bidding you a last good-bye, I swear to you that, during the last year, I have not committed one single action I need blush for, nor harboured one guilty thought. I tell you this from the bottom of my heart. You may believe it.

I shall go to my child, for I am anxious about her since she has been at Saumur. Perhaps I may bring her back with me. I think I was very wrong to send her away. I mean to repair my fault if there is yet time. The pretext of her health will be sufficient before the world. My heart shall be dumb upon all that concerns you. I will keep everything to myself. I must get work. If you can do anything to help me find some, it will be good of you. I mention this for the first and last time, for, if you were to forget me, you know very well that I should be the last to venture to recall myself to you.

Good-bye again, my friend; good-bye, for ever! I have been copying your little book, hoping you would be generous enough to leave it with me. Good-bye! good-bye! Do not suffer, do not weep, do not think, do not accuse yourself! I love and forgive you.

JULIETTE.

You were in a great hurry to leave me to-night, my best-beloved. If consideration for me was your motive, it was high-handed and blundering of you, for I never enjoyed myself more than this evening, and, until the moment you left me so abruptly, I had never so savoured the happiness of being with you in the highways and byways.

I therefore returned home sadly and thoughtfully. I have begun my letter to-night with diminished joy and confidence in the future, for your hurry to leave me weighs upon me, and I cannot explain it satisfactorily to myself.

I came in at a quarter past six, suffering greatly from indigestion. The maid told me some one had called for the dog—two gentlemen, who seemed much attached to it. Poor brute, it was a wrong instinct that led it to follow us. I have no doubt it is expiating its offence in hunger and cold at this very moment. I am somehow unduly interested in the fate of the poor thing. I feel something beyond ordinary pity for it; it makes me think of the fate and future in store for a poor girl we both know. She also follows step by step a master who will have no scruple in casting her adrift when his duty to society proves as pressing and sacred as that which called him away to-night.

I am depressed, my dear friend, and unwell. The oppression on my chest is increasing. I hope your sore throat will diminish in proportion to what I am enduring. Providence is too just to allow such cumulation of suffering. Good-night—sleep well and think of me if you can. As for loving me, that is another question; one's emotions cannot grow to order. I love you.

J.

Sunday, 8 p.m., 1835.

My dear darling, I cannot describe to you the rapture with which I listened to the two sublime poems you recited to me, one on the first Revolution and the other on the two Napoleons.

But where can your equal be found on earth!... My dear little Toto, do not laugh at me. I feel so many things I cannot express, much less write. I love and revere you, and when I reflect upon what you are, I marvel! Since you left me, I have read again *Napoleon the Second*. I shall never tire of it. It is going to bed with me now.

You told me to wait for you till 9.30; after that hour I shall go to bed. If you should happen to come later, I will open the door to you myself, as you have forgotten the key. I want to do so, that I may not lose one second of the happiness of having you with me. Sleep well—good-night—do not suffer—do not work—sleep!

JULIETTE.

Wednesday, 8.30 p.m., 1835.

I am half afraid of taking too literally your request for a daily letter. Tell me seriously how I am to interpret it, so that I may not make myself ridiculous, by overwhelming you with letters you do not want. Tell me the truth once for all, so that I may know where I am, and may give myself up without restraint to the pleasure of telling you, and writing to you, that I love you with all my heart, and that you alone constitute my sole joy, my sole happiness, and my sole future. If you can experience only one quarter of the bliss in reading, that I shall feel in inditing my scribble, you shall receive some of my prose every day, but in limited quantities, calculated not to wear out your patience.

And, in order to demonstrate my powers of self-restraint, I will limit myself to six trillions of kisses for your beautiful mouth. Besides, here you come! I love you.

JULIETTE.

Wednesday, 8 p.m., December 2nd, 1835.

MY BELOVED,

When one is ill and feverish, everything tastes bitter to the lips and palate. I am in that position. I am abominably miserable, and all the sweet words you lavish upon me seem tainted. But I have enough sense left to realise that it is my condition that prevents me from relishing the full meed of happiness you are able to give me in one moment. Forgive me for suffering, and for not having the strength or generosity to conceal it from you; it is only because I suffer too much, and love you too much, which is the same thing.

I promise to be very cheerful to-night, and to disguise my feelings. I have read everything concerning you in the papers, and I cannot help suspecting that a passage about you and your work has been purposely cut out. If this is so, you had much better tell me, for I am quite equal to bearing the truth, and even to hearing lies; so I beg you to tell me what was in that newspaper, and thus spare me the trouble of procuring another copy. You must indeed be happy and proud on behalf of the person to whom you are supposed to have dedicated your sublime poem.

VICTOR HUGO.

The article by Monsieur F. Dugué seems singularly well-informed about your restoration to the *domestic hearth*. I am apparently not the only one who notices that for the last year you have been changing your habits and feelings, though I am probably the only one who will die of grief in consequence—but what matter, so long as the domestic hearth remains *cheerful* and the *family*, *happy*.

I hope you will do your best to come and see me to-morrow, during the intervals of the performance unless the salutations you have to make, and the compliments and admiration you must acknowledge should detain you against your will; in which case I hope I may be brave enough not to worry about such a trifle, and reasonable enough not to let the magnitude of my love depend upon so slight a pleasure.

You see, my dear angel, I bow to the arguments you impress on me. I am no longer sad, neither do I suffer. I love you; that is the truest word of all.

JULIETTE.

Of course, my darling, you did right to come back, whatever your reason might be; but the pleasure of your visit was quite spoilt by your inquiry as to how I spend my time, when it is self-evident that my conduct is irreproachable.

It may surprise you that I should have borne the inquisition you habitually subject me to, with less equanimity to-day than usual. I own, my poor angel, that I do not know why it should be so. Perhaps I am like the cripple, who feels pain in the leg which has been cut off, long after he has lost it. I often suffer over my past life, though the present is so widely different. I suffer, not from variations of temperature, but from the variations of your love, which seems to grow daily colder and more gloomy. If I am mistaken, forgive and pity me; but if, as I fear, I make no error, tell me so frankly, and I shall be grateful for your sincerity. You see, my poor friend, I cannot believe that your jealousy is other than an insulting mistrust of us both. I have watched you carefully for the last six months, and I can see quite well that, although your love is gradually waning, your supervision becomes ever more active and more fidgety. If I were absolutely sure of what I suspect, I should not say this to you—I should go away at once, and you would never hear of me again; but if by chance I were wrong, and you still care for me, such a course would entail frightful sorrow upon us both. Therefore I remain, preferring to incur your hatred and contempt, rather than run the risk of grieving you.

There, my poor angel, is the attitude of mind and heart in which you found me this evening; it will explain why I received your question so badly, although I was grateful for your presence. You see, my head and heart are weary. If you are not careful, some calamity, resulting from this condition, will overtake and crush you, at a moment when neither you nor I will be able to prevent it. I give you this warning in all sincerity, but with the intimate conviction that it will not affect you. As long as you feel I belong to you wholly and entirely, you are as indifferent to my sufferings as to my happiness.

J.

If I have grieved you, my beloved, I beg you to forgive me, for I know your position is awkward and demands much consideration, especially from me. Besides, why should I complain of my mode of life more to-day, than yesterday? I accept my position without regret; therefore there is no reason for questioning an arrangement which only you can alter.

I cannot help noticing that your love is not what it was. I may say I am sure of it, if I may judge by the impatient words you occasionally utter, half against your will, and by other signs it would take too long to commit to paper. I certainly possess a *devoted* Victor, but no longer the *lover* Victor of former days. If it is as I fear, it becomes your duty to leave me at once; for I have never wished to live with you otherwise than as an adored mistress— certainly not as a woman dependent upon a man whose passion is spent. I want no pension. I demand my place in your heart, apart from any feeling of duty or gratitude. That is what I desire, as earnestly as I long to be a faithful woman, submissive to your every whim, whether just or unjust.

If I have hurt your feelings, my dearly beloved, I plead for pardon from the bottom of my heart. If you have to acknowledge a decrease in your love, be brave enough to do so frankly, and do not leave to me the frightful task of guessing it; but if you care for me as much as ever, say it again and again, for I doubt it, alas, and, in love, doubt is more painful a thousand times than the most heartbreaking certainty. Farewell, I worship you.

J.

Wednesday, 8.15 p.m., February 17th, 1836.

You must think me either very cruel or very blind, my beloved. I think, perhaps, it would be best for you to accept the latter hypothesis. I love you, which means that I am jealous; but, as my jealousy is in proportion to my love, my doubts and frenzy are more vivid, more bitter, than those of ordinary women, who are only capable of an ordinary affection. Very well—I am cruel! So be it! I detest every woman upon whom your glances rest. I feel capable of hating all women, young or old, plain or handsome, if I suspect that they have dared raise their eyes to your splendid and noble features. I am jealous of the very pavement upon which you tread, and the air you breathe. The stars and sun alone are beyond my jealousy, because their radiance can be eclipsed by one single flash from your eyes.

I love you as the lioness loves her mate. I love you as a passionate woman, ready to yield up her life at your slightest gesture. I love you with the soul and intelligence God has lent His creatures to enable them to appreciate exceptional men like yourself. That is why, my glorious Victor, at one and the same moment, I can rage, weep, crawl, or stand erect; I bow my head and venerate you!

There are days when one can fix one's gaze upon the sun itself without being blinded: thus it is with me now. I see you, I am dazzled, entranced, and I grasp your beauty in all its splendour.

JULIETTE.

Thursday, 8 p.m., August 15th, 1836.

Since you leave me here all by myself, my beloved, I shall think only of you, and in proof of this, I will scribble all over this virgin sheet of white paper. It is barbarous of you to let me grow fatter than I already am, by leaving me to dawdle at my fireside, instead of taking me out to walk and get thin.

I am in love with you, but you do not care a bit. I am very sad not to have you with me, doubly so, when I think that it is on account of a play in which I am to have no part, after all the time I have waited and endured. When I reflect seriously upon this, my despair makes me long to fly to the uttermost ends of the world. It is so necessary that I should think of my future. I have wasted so much time waiting, that it almost spells ruin to me that you should produce a piece in which I may not play. You see, my dearest, I am not as generous as you thought. I am afraid I can no longer disguise from you the injury it does me to be three years out of the theatrical world, while you are bringing out plays. Forgive me, but I have a horror of poverty, and would do anything in reason to evade it. I love you.

JULIETTE.

Friday, 8.30 p.m., March 11th, 1836.

DEAR LITTLE SOUL,

You are quite happy, I hope, now that you possess the keys of Paradise. I had a few more difficulties to encounter after you went away, but they were of no consequence. Now that our little palace is nearly finished, my soul, I hope we shall celebrate the event in the usual way; but I must first rest a little, and nurse myself up, for I am really quite worn out with the dirt and litter. I am afraid to look at you or touch you in your beauty and purity and charm, while I am so ugly and untidy and exhausted that I hardly know myself as your Juju. But it will not last. My foulness will fall from me, and reveal me dressed, as in the fairy-tale, in garments of blue, bordered with golden stars, and a prince will marry me after tasting of my cooking. Splendid! But meanwhile you must graciously permit me to go on loving you, stains and all! Shut your eyes to the common lamp that guards the flame. If you will wait, you shall see that when we reach the heaven above us, I shall be as resplendent as yourself. Meanwhile, I drop a kiss upon your shoes, even if it entails your having them blacked again.

J.

Wednesday, 7.45 p.m., March 23rd, 1836.

No doubt, dear angel, I ought to disguise in your presence the sadness that overwhelms me when I have to wait too long for you; but the late hour at which you generally come, makes it difficult for me to forget the weary suspense I have already been through, and am to endure again shortly. I love you, my dear—indeed, I love you too much. We often say this lightly, but I assure you that this time I state it in full gravity and knowledge, for I feel it to the very marrow of my bones. I love you. I am jealous. I hate being poor and devoid of talent, for I fear that these deficiencies will cost me your love. Still, I am conscious of something within me, greater than either wealth or intellect; but is it powerful enough to rivet you to me for ever? I ask myself this question night and day, and you are not at hand to soothe my unrest; hence the sadness that wounds you, the jealousy that amazes you, the mental torment you are incapable of understanding.

But I love you all the same, and am happy in the midst of my pain. I smile through my tears, for I love you.

JULIETTE.

Saturday, 8 a.m., March 26th, 1836.

Good-morning, my little darling Toto.

I am up at cock-crow, though very tired; but I want to be ready to witness your new triumph—for, beloved Toto of mine, you are the *great* Toto, the greatest man on earth.

How I love you, my Victor! I am jealous. Even your success makes me uneasy with the dread that, amongst so much adulation, you may overlook the humble homage of your poor Juju. I fear that these universal acclamations may drown my lowly cry of—*I love you!* This apprehension becomes an obsession on such a day as this, when everything is at your feet, caresses, adoration, frenzy. Ah, why are you not insignificant and unknown like myself! I should then have no need to fear that the torch of my love will be eclipsed by that immense illumination.

Try, beloved, to keep a little place in your heart for the love and admiration of your poor mistress, who has loved you from the day she first set eyes upon you, and who will worship you as long as the breath remains in her body.

JULIETTE.

Saturday, 6.15 p.m., March 26th, 1836.

Let me tell you once again that I love you, my Victor. Presently, thousands of voices will be raised in a chorus of *praise*. I alone say: I *love* you. You are my joy, the light of my eyes, the treasure of my life, you are

YOU. This evening, my adored one, whatever you say or do, I must be jealous and wretched. Be merciful to me; do not let me suffer too cruelly. If you think of me when you are absent, I shall be conscious of it—if you love me, I shall feel it upon my heart like beneficent balm upon a raw wound.

Farewell, dear soul; *it is impossible to wish an increase of beauty to the man, or more glory to the genius; so, if you are happy, so am I.* Farewell, then, dearest; I cannot refrain from sending a word of love to the lover, before going to applaud the poet. The heart must have its due share.

Good-bye till later. For ever, for life and until death, love, nothing but love!

J.

Sunday, 7.45 p.m., March 27th, 1836.

I hardly dare speak to you to-night of love. I feel humiliated by my devotion, for all those women seem to be rivals, preferred before me. I suffer, but I do not hold you responsible. I feel worse even than usual this evening. I did not venture to ask what you had written to Madame Dorval, for I was afraid to discover some fresh reason for bitterness and jealousy; so I remained silent.

My dear treasure, you are very lucky not to be jealous: you have no competition to fear with any other celebrity, for there is none besides yourself, and *you* know that I love you with my whole heart, whereas all *I* can be sure of is, that I love you far too much to hope to be loved in proportion. In addition, I feel I shall never be capable of raising the heavy stone under which my intellect slumbers.

Forgive me, I am sad. I am worse than sad—I am ashamed, because I am jealous. I am an idiot, and consequently, I am in love!

JULIETTE.

Thursday, 8.30 p.m., April 14th, 1836.

I love you, my dear Victor, and you make me very unhappy when you seem to doubt it. It is still harder for me when you put your want of confidence into words, for I can only attribute it to the sacrifices you constantly make for me, and which probably cause you to think that an ignoble motive constrains me to remain under your protection. In addition to thus wounding me in the most sensitive part of my love, you exasperate me to a point I cannot describe, because it is true that I have not the wherewithal to live independently of you and your influence. Therefore, my poor angel, when you show your suspicions of my sincerity, I read into them more than jealousy and ill-will: I imagine a reproach against my dependent position. I feel an overwhelming need to prove to you, by any means, that you are mistaken in the woman and her love. *Remember your burnt letters!* You know what a doubt on your part led me to do on one occasion. Well, angel, I tell you honestly that when you question, not only my fidelity, but also my love, I long to fly to the other side of the world, there to exist as best I can, and never pronounce your name again for the rest of my life. This will be the last proof of love I can give you, and at least you will not be able to accuse me, then, of self-interest and self-love. You hurt me terribly to-night; you often do, and generally when I am most tender and demonstrative towards you.

Yet I love you.

J.

Tuesday, 8 p.m., April 19th, 1836.

Beloved, I am perfectly certain you will not come to fetch me to see *Lucrèce*, and I am already resigned. There is only one thing I shall never submit to, and that is, the loss of your love. I know you are devoted, that you lavish friendship upon me; but I feel that you have no more love to give me, and I cannot bear it. During the four months I have been alone, ill for the most part, I never knew whether the time would come when you would be impelled to say to me: *Take courage, for I love you.* I would have given life to find those words in your handwriting at my bedside in the morning, or on my pillow at night. I waited in vain, they never came; my sorrow grew, and now I am certain that you have ceased to care for me.

I know what you will say, Victor—you will tell me that you are hard at work, that you do everything for me, and do not let me want for anything. To that I reply that I have been just as busy or busier than you, yet have always found time to show you the outward signs of my inward love. I may also tell you that, without your love, I *do* want for *everything*, and that my life is utterly wretched without it. Lastly, I declare to you that if you continue to be so *reasonably* kind and attentive, I will release you from your self-imposed burden, at some moment when you least expect it, and for evermore. I must have true love or nothing.

JULIETTE.

Monday, 7.45 p.m., May 2nd, 1836.

MY DEAR LITTLE BELOVED,

I am sorry to find that you are not as convinced as I am, of the propriety of giving me your portrait.

I confess I feel the greatest disappointment when I realise, from your daily evasion of my request, that I shall probably never become the possessor of the picture which is so like you, nor even, perhaps, of a copy of the original. I am sad and dejected. I think you do not care enough for me, a poor disinherited creature, to do me the favour you have already bestowed upon another, who already has her full meed of the gifts of life. I am therefore greatly disappointed. I had counted upon having the portrait, and had anticipated much happiness from its possession. The contemplation of it would have so greatly contributed to my courage and resignation, that it is very grievous to have to renounce it thus suddenly, without any compensation.

If I wanted to speak of other things now, I could not; my heart is heavy, my eyes overflow with tears. I can only find bitter words for the expression of my wounded love.

I love you more to-day than I have ever done before, yet I am not happy.

JULIETTE.

Friday, 7.45 a.m., May 20th, 1836.

GOOD MORNING, MY DEAR LITTLE TOTO.

You failed me again last night, so I shall never count upon you again. I loved you with all my strength, and thought of you even in my sleep. This morning I love you with my whole soul, and heartily long for you, but I know you will not come, so I am cross and sad.

How fine the weather is, my Toto, and how happy we could be in the fresh air, on the high road, in a nice little carriage, with a month of happiness in prospect: it would be Paradise, but ... but ... I dare not set my heart upon it, for I should go crazy with grief if the treat were withheld. At all events, I am ready to start; my foot is well again, and we can set off to-night, or to-morrow morning, at whatever time suits you. I am quite ready, let us, therefore, seize our chance of the fine weather.

My adored one, I am dying to make this expedition.... Do try to get free at the earliest moment possible. I shall be so happy. I still love you, ever so much. I need you terribly. My heart is more than ready for the happiness you will give me during the whole time we shall be together.

JULIETTE.

Thursday, 12.45 p.m., July 21st, 1836.

Once more I am reduced to writing all that is in my heart, my adored one. It is but a slender satisfaction after the bliss we have been enjoying.

Nevertheless, we must take life as we find it, and it would be ungracious of me to complain. A month like the one we have just spent would compensate for a whole life-time of misfortune and worry. Poor angel, since you left me I feel lost and alone in the world. You cannot imagine the utter void, surrounded as you are at this moment by the affection of charming children and devoted friends, while I am alone with my love—that is to say alone in space—for my love has no limits. I seek what consolation I can, by speaking to you, and writing to you. Your handkerchief, breathing of you, lies by my side, with your adored name embroidered in the corner. I caress and talk to it, and we understand each other perfectly. For every kiss I press upon it, it exhales your sweet aroma; it is as if I scented your very soul. Then I weep, as one does in a beautiful dream from which one fears to awake. Heavens, how I love you! You are my life, my joy! I adore you!

JULIETTE.

Friday, 2.15 p.m., September 2nd, 1836.

My poor, beloved angel. The nearer the moment approaches, the more I dread the inevitable parting which must follow the few days of happiness you have just given me. I long for delay, but I know very well that, however Providence may interpose in my favour, the day must come when you will have to go to St. Prix. Lucky for me if it is not to-day. But, putting aside all considerations of love and Juju, it would really not be prudent for you to go to the country in this cold, foggy weather; even this morning, in the warmth and repose of home, you felt a warning twinge of rheumatism, which prescribes prudence on your part. I fear your natural desire to kiss Toto on his donkey, and watch the other little rogues at their holiday occupations, may draw you, in spite of rain, wind, and the good counsel of your old Juju, to St. Prix. At any rate, if you do this foolish thing, try to avoid chills, to think of me, and to come back to my care and caresses as quickly as possible.

JULIETTE.

Saturday, 6 p.m., 29th, 1836.

You torment me unjustly, as usual, my darling beloved. Yet you ought to begin to know me, and not suspect my every action, down to the drinking of a cup of coffee. The awkwardness of my position, the absolute solitude in which I am compelled to live, and the many insults I have to tolerate daily from you, exasperate me so, that I feel I would rather go out of your life, than continue to exist like a woman condemned and accursed.

It is your fault that I am so unhappy. Nobody else will ever love you so well, or be so entirely devoted to you. But one is not bound to put up with impossibilities, and I cannot live longer under a yoke which you make more crushing every day. What am I to do, beloved? Run away from you? I have scarcely enough money for my quiet Paris *routine*. Remain here? If you have not the courage to abstain from visiting me, I certainly shall never have enough to prevent you from coming.

The wound in my heart is raw and bleeding, thanks to the care you take to keep it in that condition. The slightest additional twinge becomes unbearable torture. I do not know what moral operation I would not consent to, to be cured of it.

For the last three years you have really given me too much pain. I implore you, from the bottom of my heart, to be less offensive with me, or else to leave me for good and all. You may guess from this what I am enduring.

JULIETTE.

Sunday, 2 p.m., January 1st, 1837.

Your darling, adorable letter has reached me. I have devoured it with caresses. Oh, how I love you! I have just sent my child out of the room, so that I might read it on my knees in front of your picture. These little pranks may seem foolish, but they contain a deeper, more sacred significance, like the devotion that inspires them.

When you come, you will find me joyous and radiant, as I was on that glorious day when you first revealed your love. My beloved, my heart, I am very happy. I am in heaven, for you love me, my Toto ... your dear letter has said it. Your eyes, your mouth, your soul, will tell me so still better, presently. Yes, indeed I am happy, I am surfeited. There is nothing left for me to desire or require—I have your love, a love which God Himself might envy were He a *woman*.

Thank you, adored one, thank you from my heart and soul. I am as good as gold, believe me.

JUJU.

Tuesday, 7.30 p.m., February 21st, 1837.

Do not grieve, my precious, do not lament. I will not attempt consolation, for you have better and more efficacious resources within your own self; but I share your affliction. Whatever saddens you saddens me: where you love, I love; when you mourn, I mourn. If I conjure you not to give way to your grief, it is not because I hesitate to bear my portion of it, but because I believe that your poor brother himself would not now desire a return to this life.[65] I look upon his death more as a blessing than a misfortune. Poor brother!

I love you, my adored Victor. In moments such as these, when sorrow brings you nearer to my level, I feel that my affection for you is absolutely true and purified from all dross. Try to come early this evening. I will lavish caresses upon you silently, with my eyes and my innermost self, without worrying you. You shall rest by my fireside, and lean your dear head upon my shoulder, and read, and I shall be glad.

I am jealous of that woman who has dared to *steal* your verses; such things are not *lost*. It was a two-fold wickedness on her part, for she caused *you* the trouble of rewriting them, and *me* the torment of jealousy. I will not have you see her again, ever! Do you hear?

Oh, I love you, I love you far too much.

JULIETTE.

Monday, 7.15 p.m., April 2nd, 1837.

CARICATURE OF MLLE. GEORGE, BY VICTOR HUGO. **PORTRAIT OF VICTOR HUGO BY HIMSELF.**
Victor Hugo Museum.

I have decided to get up, after all, thanks to the laundry-man; but for him, I should have remained in bed, nursing my depression. I am sad beyond everything, yet I cannot tell why—you are kind and affectionate, and I love you with my whole soul; but that does not seem enough. Esteem, the keystone of happiness, is lacking. I have worn myself out in the endeavour to gain it during the last four years, yet it cometh not, nor ever will come, now. I must turn my efforts in another direction. I must try to break with you, tactfully, as you say, by quitting Paris, and perhaps France. Will that be sufficient to stop the tongue of scandal? I wish to leave you before you abandon me, because I do not admit your right to inflict such a fearful blow upon me. There are people, capable of committing suicide, who yet recoil at the thought of being murdered—I am one. I can and will kill myself, but I shrink from the injury you might possibly inflict upon me before long. My courage does not outstrip your cruelty. I love you too much for happiness.

JULIETTE.

Tuesday, 10.15 a.m., May 2nd, 1837.

Good morning, my well-beloved. Did you have a good night? You looked overstrained and tired yesterday, and indeed there was enough to make you so, you poor dear. I do not know how you can put up with it all. Forgive me for adding to your burthen the exactions of a woman who loves, and fears to recognise in lassitude an evidence of coldness. Forgive me; if I did not occasionally doubt your love I should torment you less, and would show more consideration for your occupations and repose.

You hurt me very much last night by speaking as you did, yet I wanted to know your true opinion of me. I have long been tormented by a mournful curiosity on that point. Last night you satisfied it in full. I know now that you pity without despising me. I accept your compassion, for I need it, and ought to have it; but I should indignantly repudiate a contempt I do not deserve. My past history is sad, but not disgraceful. My life until I met you was the melancholy outcome of a poor girl's first fault; but at least it was never soiled by those hideous vices that deface the soul still more than the body. Even at the worst moments of my trouble, I cherished within me an inner sanctuary, whither I could betake myself, as to some hallowed spot. Since then, that sanctuary has been open to you only, and you can testify whether you have found it worthy of you; you know whether, since you have occupied its throne and altar, I have ever failed, one single day or minute, to prostrate myself on my knees before you in adoration, or have ever turned my gaze or my soul away from you. This proves, my beloved, that my former backsliding was only superficial, not inherently vicious; that my wound was accidental, not a loathsome, devouring canker; that I love you now, and am thereby made whole.

JULIETTE.

Tuesday, 10.45 a.m., May 2nd, 1837.

I am following up my letter immediately with another, because I am alone, and the moment is propitious for me to open my heart to you from the very bottom. Racket and pleasure are a hindrance to meditation, and at this moment I am rapt in contemplation of you and your beloved image. I see you as you are, that is to say, a God-made man to redeem and rescue me from the infamous life to which I had so long been enslaved. What Christ did for the world you have done for me: like Him, you saved my soul at the expense of your repose and life. May you be as blessed for this generous action as you are adored by me for it. I should have loved you, devil or angel, bad or good, selfish or devoted, cruel or generous—I must have loved you, for at the mere sight of you my whole being cries out: *I love you!* Would that I might proclaim it on my knees, with hands clasped and heart on lips: *I love you! I love you!* The talk we had last night kept me from sleeping, but I do not complain; there are moments when sleep is a misfortune. I needed to rehearse one by one all your words, to collect carefully those which must remain for ever enshrined in my bosom as treasures of consolation and love; the less generous ones you uttered, I have consumed in the flame of my soul; nothing remains of them but ashes, dead as the ashes of my past.

Do not turn away in disgust from the scratches I have sustained in falling from my pedestal, as you might from hideous and incurable wounds. I repeat again, my beloved, because it is the truth: misfortune there has been in my life, but neither debauchery nor moral turpitude. Henceforth there can be nothing but a sacred, pure love for you. I am worthy of pardon and affection. Love me; I crave it of you.

JULIETTE.

Thursday, 11.15 a.m., May 11th, 1837.

Good morning, my dear little man; I have bad weather to announce: rain, snow, hail, wind, and, in addition, an abominable cold in my head which does not help to resign me to a day already filled with clouds. I love you—do you know that? and I admire you for your beautiful soul. It is splendid of you, my great Toto, to have raised your voice so powerfully in defence of the poor, dead King.[66] You alone had the right, for you only are above suspicion; you only are influential enough to compel the impious, pitiless world to listen to your indulgent and religious voice. If it were possible for me to love you more, I should do so for this; but from the first day I saw you I have given my whole heart and thoughts and soul unreservedly into your keeping.

How I love you, my adored Victor, how I love you! In that short and much-misused word is contained all my soul, all the bloom of a devotion that has opened out under the sun of your gaze. Good-bye, my own.

JULIETTE.

Friday, 8.30 p.m., June 2nd, 1837.

MY LITTLE MAN,

You must make up your mind to take my love or leave it. Compare my life with yours, and see whether I do not deserve that you should pity and love me with all your might. I am all alone, I have neither family nor fame, nor the thousand and one distractions that surround you. As I say, I am alone, always alone; it even seems probable that I shall not see you to-night, while you will be spending your evening in feasting, talking, and visiting your uncle, whom may the devil fly away with. Everybody can get you except me; the exception is flattering and well chosen. I am so unhappy that I am going to bed and shall probably cry my eyes out—I am more inclined for that than for laughing. If you succeed in cheering me up to-night, I shall know you for a great man, and a still greater sorcerer; but you will not attempt it. I may be as sad and miserable as I like, and I am certain you will never interfere.

Good-night, Toto; I am going to bed. Good-night, be happy and gay and content; your poor Juju will be unhappy enough for both. I love you, Toto.

JULIETTE.

Wednesday, 1.30 p.m., June 10th.

I love you before all things, and after all things. I love you, love you, love you! I have just written to Mother Pierceau that I shall send Suzanne to her to-morrow. I forgot to ask you exactly how much money you brought me yesterday, and also for cash, for yesterday's expenses. I will do so to-night. I try hard to keep my accounts accurately, yet I am always in a muddle at the end of the month, and always either above or below what I ought to have. I do my best, but nothing seems to bring my sums out right.

I think there is going to be a big storm. The sky is lowering like yesterday, and the weather still more oppressive. Try not to get wet, and come and fetch your umbrella before it begins to pour.

What a delightful afternoon we spent yesterday! I wish we could have it over again, even if we had to be soaked to the skin. I shall never forget the Bassin du Titan.[67] The pretty turtledove that came to slake its thirst in it seemed to recognise us, and wait for its drink, until you scattered drops of poetry into the mossy, flowery grooves, surrounding its edges.

Heavens! what precious pearls you squandered yesterday in that magnificent garden, at the feet of those peerless goddesses, which seem to come to life when your glance rests upon them—what flowers upon those lawns, peopled with joyous children! How all those gods and goddesses, heroes, kings, queens, women, nymphs, and children, must have quarrelled over the treasure you lavished upon them! I was sorry to go away. I should have liked to go back in the moonlight and gather up all those jewels upon which you set so little store. Oh, I must return there very soon, and we will at the same time revisit our Metz, where we have enjoyed so much bliss. That journey will bring us happiness, and I long to make it. I love you, my great Toto. Forgive this scribble; it looks absurd now, and indeed it must needs be so, for I was inebriated with love when I wrote it. My thoughts stagger and fall upon the paper, because they have drunk too deeply of my soul, and know not where they are.

JULIETTE.

Thursday, 3.45 p.m., July 27th, 1837.

I must contribute my scribble in acknowledgment for the delightful lines you have just written in my little book.[68] My voice will sound like the cackle of a hen after the song of a nightingale; but that is the law of nature, so I do not see why I should be silent, because I have heard you. It was rash of you, my dear little man, to put down the date you suppose was that of my birth; but, as I am too honest to contradict you, I accept it and affirm that, since those days when you were a little boy studying *Quintus Curtius*, you have developed, and far outstripped all those you revered and admired when you were an urchin of seven—while I have remained the poor, uncultured girl you know. It is pretty certain that education could have added but little to my barren nature; the weeds of the sea-shore do not gain much from cultivation. On that point, thank Heaven, I have nothing to complain of. No one worried much about me until you appeared upon the scene; but you came, my great and sublime poet, and you did not disdain to cull the little scentless flower prinking itself at your feet, to attract the sunshine of your glance. I bless you for your goodness. I know that a father and mother look down upon you from the realms above, and love you for the happiness you have given to the poor little daughter they left solitary on earth. I weep as I write, for it is the first time I have really looked into my innocent past, and my loving heart. I bless you, my generous man, on earth, as you will be blest in heaven. May all those dear to you participate in this benediction, and in the joys and riches of this world and the next!

JULIETTE.

Thursday, 9 a.m., September 21st, 1837.

GOOD MORNING, MY BELOVED.

The anniversary of our return to Paris has been sadder still than the day itself, since you have not been with me at all, either last night or this morning. I am upset in consequence. I have not yet taken off my nightcap. I am cross. Shall you be at Auteuil all day? What a disappointment for poor Juju, not to speak of Claire, who has to take her chance of my temper when I am cross, and that idiot Madame Guérard, who has put me to the expense of a stamp merely to say that she thinks she is getting fat, and that she wishes you good morning. How thrilling!

I love you, dearest Toto; I love you too much, for I am miserable when you are away. I wish I could care comfortably, like you, for instance, who feel neither better nor worse, whether I am near or far. You are always the same; love never makes you miss the point of a joke, or a hearty laugh, nor fail to notice a grey cloud, the Great Bear, a frog, a sunset, the earth, water, gale, or zephyr. You see everything, enjoy everything, without a thought for poor old Juju, who is being bored to desperation in her solitary corner. Which of us two is the best lover, eh? Answer that it is I, Juju, and you will be speaking the truth. Yes, I love you. Try not to stay away from me all day. Love me for being sad in your absence.

JULIETTE.

Saturday, 6.30 p.m., September 23rd, 1837.

You are making yourself more and more of a rarity, my beautiful star, so that I become chilled, and gloomy as an antique, moss-grown statue, abandoned in the wilds of some deserted garden. I am not angry with you, but I do wish you were less busy and more lover-like. You have quickly resumed your fine Paris appearance, my beloved little man, whilst I still cling to my travelling disguise. You ought surely to have waited for me to take the initiative, if only for the sake of manners. Whom are you so anxious to please, my bright boy? Who is the favoured one you aspire to put in my place? In any case, I warn you that I shall not be sly like Granier,[69] but that I shall fall upon your respective carcases with frank blows of a cudgel, mind that! Now you may go in search of your charmer, if you are prepared to see your bones ground to powder for my use.

If you come early this evening I shall be so happy, so cheery, so content and good, that you will never wish to leave me again; but, if you delay, I shall be exactly the reverse, and you will have to coax and love me with all your might to comfort me.

You are letting your letter-box get over-full again. Toto, Toto, I shall make a bonfire of its contents if you do not come quick and secure them. Mind what you are about!

JULIETTE.

Wednesday, 12.45 p.m., November 22nd, 1837.

I really believe you do it on purpose; but you may be certain that I shall pay you back in the same kind: indifference for indifference; *donnant donnant* is my motto.

Now let us talk of other things. What do you think of the taking of Constantine? I cannot believe the present Ministry will survive long as at present constituted; Thiers and Barot may be called upon at any moment to form a new cabinet. What is your opinion? The commercial crisis is still making itself felt in the markets; oils of every description have gone down; for instance, rape oil which was at 47 is now only at 45. A recovery is looked for next year, but I have my doubts about it, haven't you?[70]

. . . .

Do you not agree with me that all this points to a revolution in the near future, which will entail sinister results for Wailly's Government? For my part, I view with consternation the removal of the Carlists from St. Jean Pied de Port to Paimbœuf, after a sojourn at St. Ménéhould. I am already sick of the recital of the horrors which disturb the digestion and the tranquillity of the citizens, of whom you are the chief ornament. Pray accept the expression of my distinguished consideration.

JULIETTE.

December 5th, 5 p.m., 1837.

How kind you are, my Toto, to have come and relieved the suspense I was in as to what had happened in Court.[71] Heavens, how well you spoke! I was so moved and so convinced while I listened, that I forgot even to admire you, yet I have never known you finer or more eloquent. Why must the case be adjourned for a week? Is it to allow time for intrigues against the incorruptible consciences of my lords the judges? I should have given worlds for the verdict to have been delivered to-day; first because it would relieve you of an anxiety as annoying as it is fatiguing, secondly because I myself crave repose, and since this devil of a lawsuit has come on the scene I cannot sleep at night, and lastly because I shall then see you oftener, or at least so I hope.

While I was waiting for you just now I copied a few passages from the letters of Mdlle. de Lespinasse about the C. D.[72] and the S.[73] of her period. Her opinions then, fit our own times absolutely: the same absurdities, the same platitudes, and the same petty triumphs! It would be pitiable were it not so grotesque. Nothing seems to have altered in the last sixty years; there are the identical *bourgeois* in the identical Rue Saint Denis, the same men and women of the world—nothing is missing. They have not grown old, they are still in good health. Stupidity and bad taste are the best agents for the maintenance of society in all its pristine foolishness. Here am I drivelling on just as if I knew what I was talking about. It would be a nice set-out if I attempted to write! I might just as well present myself as a candidate for the Senate. Please forgive me. Your lawsuit is the cause of my chatter, but I will not transgress again. I love you far too much to go out of my way to make a fool of myself.

JULIETTE.

Receipts for the Month of December 1837

Dec.		Frs.	Sous.	Liards.
Cash in hand		4	0	3

1. Money earned by my Toto	51	4	0
4. Cash from my darling	5	10	0
6. Money earned by my dear one	44	0	0
9. Cash from my Toto's purse	10	0	0
12. " " " " " "	5	0	0
13. " " " " " "	7	0	0
14. Money earned by my darling	45	0	0
17. Cash from my adored one	10	2	0
18. " " " " " "	4	2	0
19. Money earned by my beloved	60	0	0
22. Cash from my Toto	2	0	0
24. " " " " "	10	0	0
26. " " " " "	3	0	0
28. Money earned by my Toto	102	12	0
30. Money earned by my darling	100	9	0
Plus the money for the earring and ring	2	0	0
Total	466	19	3

Expenditure for the Month of December 1837

	Frs.	Sous.	Liards.
Food and wine	99	2	3
Coal	1	1	0
Lighting	21	6	0
Household expenses and postage	16	0	0
Baths, illness	8	1	0½
General expenditure	29	8	0
Incidental expenses and pocket-money	5	8	0½
Dress	41	5	0

Incidental expenses and pocket-money	5	8	0½
Dress	41	5	0
Washing	16	5	0
Debts and pawnbroker	151	6	0½
Wages	20	13	0
To the Lanvins	4	2	0½
Total	413	19	5
Cash in hand	53	0	0
	466	19	5[74]

To Toto: 9 luncheons.

Dinners to 10 persons.

In all, about 19.

Sunday, 1.45 p.m., January 21st, 1838.

Good-morning, my dear one, good-morning, my big Toto. How did you manage to fit into your bed? You must have curled yourself up into five or six hundred curves. One grows at such a pace in the space of an evening like last night[75] that you must have become gigantic by this morning, though you were already greater than any one else in the world. I have grown, too, for my love equals your beauty, equals the praises and admiration lavished upon you; so, unless one is prepared to state, against all logic, that the container is smaller than the contents, I must have grown and even surpassed you—without vanity. Love exalts as much as glory does, and I love you more than you are great. Yes my Toto, yes my dear Victor, I dare affirm it because it is true. I love you more than you are great.

How did you spend the night, adored one? I hope you did not work, tired out as you were, and in that horrible little icehouse. I cannot think of that room without shivering from head to foot. I shall be very glad when I hear that it is closed and warmed. Unfortunately that does not promise to be soon, and meanwhile you suffer and freeze, and I torment myself about you.

I adore you, my beloved Toto. I would die for you if you would promise always to think lovingly of me; even without that condition I adore you, my Victor.

JULIETTE.

Must it always be my lot to wait, dearly beloved? I thought I had given proofs sufficient of courage and resignation all this time, to have earned my reward now. Of course I know you must have had the whole of Paris in your house to-day, but if you cared for me as I do for you, you would leave all Paris, and the world itself, for me. What good is the back door, if not to enable you to evade importunate people, and fly to the poor love who awaits you with so much longing and affection? Why carry *four keys* in your pocket, like the gaoler in a comic opera, if you do not make use of them on the proper occasion? I am very sad, my Toto. I do not think you care for me any more. You are as splendidly kind and generous as ever, but you are no longer the ardent lover of old days. It is quite true although you will not admit it out of compassion for me. I am very unhappy. Some day I shall do something desperate to rid you of me, for I cannot bear to realise the coldness of your heart, and at the same time to accept your generous self-sacrifice.

You know I have always told you that I will accept nothing from you if you do not love me! I love you so much that if I could inspire you with my feelings, there would be nothing left for me to desire in this world.

JULIETTE.

Monday, Noon, February 12th, 1838.

Good-morning, my dear little man. How are you this morning? I am very well, but I should be still better if I had seen you and breakfasted with you.... I am arranging to go to *Hernani* to-night. I hope there will be no hitch, and that the promise of the bills will at last be fulfilled. I am longing for the moment. It is such ages since I have seen my *Hernani*, and it is such a beautiful creation! I wish it were already night, and I were in my little box, with dear little Toto sitting at the back, where I might reward him with eyes and lips for every beautiful line. You are not jealous? Yes, I want you to be jealous! I want you to be jealous, even of yourself, or else I shall not believe that you love me.

Good-morning, Toto. All this nonsense simply means that I dote on you and think you beautiful and great and adorable. You did not come last night—probably because there was to be a rehearsal this morning. Try and behave properly at it, for I have Argus eyes and shall come down upon you myself, like a thunderbolt, in the midst of your antics. Meanwhile, take care of yourself; do not get cold feet or a headache like mine; it would be a great nuisance.

Dear soul, if you had the least regard for your health, you would have your flannel underclothing made at once. I assure you you would find it very comfortable. I am sorry now that I let you take the stuff away, for if I had it still, I should force you to do all this. It is not that I want to worry you, my adored one, for I know how many other important things you have to think of, but this is one of the most pressing; that is why I should like it done. I love you, my Toto, with all my strength, and more yet. I press my lips in spirit upon your eyes and hair.

JULIETTE.

Wednesday, 12.15 p.m., March 7th, 1838.

Good-morning, my dear little beloved. How are your eyes, my Toto? It torments me to know that you are suffering so much, for however brave and uncomplaining you may be, I can see quite well that you are in pain.

If you knew how I love you, my dear one, you would understand my trouble and grief when you suffer. I suppose you are going to the rehearsal this morning. I wish the first performance[76] was to be this evening, for I am trembling already. Generally, I only begin to shiver on the day itself, but this time my terrors have set in twenty-four hours in advance. I hope my fears will have been vain, like so often before, and that your beautiful poetry will prove all-conquering as ever. To-morrow my soul will animate the spectators. I shall inspire enthusiasm in the discriminating, and strangle, by sheer force of love, the hatred and envy of the scum who would dare criticise your magnificent *Marion*, for whom I have so special a partiality.

AUTOGRAPH AND DRAWING BY JULIETTE DROUET.

I express myself awkwardly, but I feel all this acutely.

JULIETTE.

Wednesday, 7.30 p.m., March 7th, 1838.

MY DARLING,

I see you very seldom, but it is not your fault, I know. I look constantly into my heart, whence you are never absent, and there I see you growing daily nobler, greater, and dearer. So to-morrow is *the great day!* Ardently as I have desired its advent, I now dread it more than I can say. However, up till now I have always been very frightened, and nothing has happened, so I hope it may be the same this time. Besides, how could the disapproval of a few miserable wretches and idiots affect the magnificent verses of *Marion?* It will only prompt the sincere and intelligent portion of the audience to do you instant and brilliant justice. I am no longer afraid. I am as brave and strong as love itself. Put me where you like—I do not care—all places are equally good to applaud from, just as all moments are suitable for adoring you. Good-bye, my love.

JULIETTE.

Thursday, 12.45 p.m., March 8th, 1838.

Good-morning, blessed one. I am quite upset. If your success to-night is in proportion to my fright, you will have the most magnificent triumph of your life. I hardly know what I am doing; I am shaking like a leaf, I cannot grasp my pen. I must try to pull myself together for this evening. It is absurd of me to be such a little craven; besides, what harm can a *cabal* do you? None! It can only enhance your greatness, if such a thing be possible; so, I am ashamed of my cowardice. I am horribly stupid to dread a thing which certainly will not happen, and if it did, would not injure you. Now that is enough! I will not fear again, and I will admire and applaud my *Marion* in the very face of the cabal. I will give them a hot time to-night! Bravo! bravo!! bravo!!! I feel as if I were there already, and the happiest of women.

My little darling man, are you not soon coming to me? I do so long for you. I feel as if you had been very cold to me lately. In the old days, a first performance did not prevent your coming to make love to me. Heavens, what torture it is to have to doubt you at a moment when I am so desperately in need of you! I love you!

JULIETTE.

Friday, 1.45 p.m., March 9th, 1838.

You are adorable, my great Victor. I wish I could express myself as earnestly as I feel, but that is impossible; I am tongue-tied. So the great performance is over! What a fool I was to be frightened, and how rightly I placed my confidence in that great noodle the public, which is so slow and so hard to work up, but when once started, boils over so satisfactorily. What a magnificent success, and how thoroughly justified! What a beautiful piece, what lovely verses! and the fascinating poet! Everything was understood, applauded, admired. It was delightful. My soul was raised heavenward with the Play. Dear God, how magnificent it was!!!!!!!!!!! I must be there again to-morrow, and every night. Surely I have the right!

I love you, my Toto, I adore you with all the strength of my soul. I wish I could go out—it is such a fine day. I kiss your beloved hands.

JULIETTE.

Sunday, 12.15 a.m., March 11th, 1838.

Good-morning, my beloved one, good-morning, handsomest and greatest of men. I cannot speak as well as some of the people who pay you such beautiful and sincere homage, but I feel from the bottom of my soul that I admire and love you more than any one in the world. All the same, I am sad and discouraged. I can see that you place no reliance on my intelligence, that my last years are flying by without earning what they easily might: a position, and a provision for the future. I am not angry with you. It is not your fault if you are prejudiced against me to the point of allowing me, without regret, to waste the last few years of my youth. Possibly my desire to create for myself an independent position, and to remain ever at your side, has given birth to the delusion that I possess a great talent which only requires scope. However that may be, I am in despair, and I love you more than ever. You are good to look at, my adored one, you are great in intellect, my Victor, and yet I dare proffer my devotion, for it is as genuine as your beauty and as deep as your genius. I adore you.

JULIETTE.

Tuesday, 11.30 a.m., April 10th, 1838.

Good-morning, my soul, my joy, my life. How are your adored eyes, my Toto? I cannot refrain from asking, because it interests me to hear, more than anything in the world. I am always thinking about them. I long for the 15th of this month, for then I shall have the right to insist upon your resting, and I shall certainly exercise it. My dear love, what joy it will be for me to feel your dear head leaning against mine, to kiss your beautiful eyes, and to make certain that you do not work. The weather is lovely this morning. It carries my thoughts back to our dear little annual trip, when we were so happy and so cosy together. We are not to have that felicity this year, and really I do not know how I shall endure it when the time comes at which we used to start. It will be very hard and difficult, and I doubt whether my courage and reason will suffice to enable me to bear the greatest sacrifice I have ever made in my life. My dear one, it will be sad indeed; I wonder whether I shall be equal to it.

I love you, adore you, admire you, and again I love and adore you.

JULIETTE.

Tuesday, 7.45 p.m., April 10th, 1838.

My love, I am writing to you with joy and worship in my heart. You were so kind and tender and fascinating to me to-day that I seemed to feel again the savour and rapture of the days of old. My Toto, my adored one, fancy if your love were to flower again like some brilliant, sweet-scented spring blossom! With what ecstasy and reverence I would preserve it fresh and rosy in my breast. Poor beloved, your work has done to our idyll what the winter does to the trees and flowers—the sap has retired deep into the bottom of your heart, and often I have feared it was quite dead; but now I see it was not: it was only lulled to sleep and I shall possess my Toto once more, beautiful, blooming, and perfumed as in those glorious days of our first love.

I who am not a sensitive plant of the sun like you, have yet come better through the trial, and if I bear no blossom, I have at least the advantage of preserving my leaves ever green and alive; that is to say, I have never ceased to love and adore you. Indeed that is true, my own, I love you as much as the first day.

JULIETTE.

Sunday, 11 a.m., April 22nd, 1838.

You see, darling, by the dimensions of my paper, that I am preparing to go and applaud my *Marion* this evening. I will not reproach you for not having come this morning. In fact, in future I shall not allude to it again, for nothing is more unsuitable or ridiculous than the solicitations of a woman who vainly appeals for the favours of her lover. Therefore, beloved, as I am to live with you as a sister with a brother, you will approve of my refraining from reminding you in any way of the time when we were husband and wife.

It is still very cold, my maid says; although the sun is shining in at my windows, it has left its warmth in the sky. It resembles the fine phrases of a suitor who no longer loves; his words may be the same, his expressions as tender, his language as impassioned, but love is lacking and those words which scintillate as the sun upon my windows, fail to warm the heart of the poor woman who had dreamt of love eternal.

You will probably see Granier this morning.[77] I hope so, so that you may not be worried any more about that business. I also hope Jourdain will come to-morrow about the chimney. It is unbearable that one should have to wait upon the whim of a workman for a job which might be finished in a few minutes, and that would please you so much. I have read with pleasure the verses that came to you in the newspaper from Guadaloupe; they show that you are admired over there as much as here, and that you have fewer enemies abroad than at the Académie Française. I am furious with that little imp called Thiers, who although he is not a quarter of a man as far as size goes, yet permits himself to cherish the rancour of a giant. Miserable little wretch! If only I were not a woman, I might castigate you as you deserve!

And you, my Toto, so great and so wonderful, I adore you!

JULIETTE.

Thursday, 10.15 a.m., August 2nd, 1838.

Good-morning, my little beloved. Do you still need a secretary? I am quite ready. Come; it is so delightful to dip my pen into your glorious poetry, and watch the shining and coruscating of those precious gems which take the shape of your thoughts. Dédé could not be more delighted and dazzled than I am, if she were given the diamonds and jewels of the crown of England to play with for an hour. Oh, if I could only have spent the night with my Cæsar and his noble companions, I would have followed him without fatigue wherever he wanted to go, even as far as.... But you would not allow it, you jealous boy; you feared comparison, and you were perfectly right, for I like well-dressed men. Good-morning, my Toto. My left eye is very bad; it is swollen and painful. If this continues I shall no longer be in the position of regretting that I cannot lend you my eyes in exchange for your own. I love you, I adore you. Do not be too long before coming to me.

I am longing for you with all my might.

JULIETTE.

Wednesday, 9.45 p.m., August 15th, 1838.

My dear little man, I love you. You are the treasure of my heart. I wish we were already in our carriage galloping, galloping far, and farther still, so that it might take us ever so long to get back.

Since you have hinted at the possibility of my playing in your beautiful piece,[78] I am like a somnambulist who has been made to drink too much champagne. I see everything magnified: I see glory, happiness, love, adoration, in gigantic and impossible dimensions—impossible, because I feel you can never love me as I love you, and that my talent, however considerable, can never reach to the level of your sublime poetry. I do not say this from modesty, but because I do not think there exists in this world man or woman capable of interpreting the parts as you conceived them in your master mind.

I love you, my Toto, I adore you, my little man, you are my sun and my life, my love and my soul.

All that, and more.

JULIETTE.

Monday, 8 p.m., September.

Are you proposing to cut out all the dandies and bloods of the capital? My congratulations to you. I was only waiting for some such sign to give myself up to an orgy of wild and eccentric toilette. Heaven only knows the extravagances I mean to commit in the way of shoes, silk stockings, gowns, hats, light gloves, and bows for my hair! You will, I suppose, retaliate with an assortment of skin-tight trousers, strings of orders, and more or less absurd hair arrangements. Delightful indeed! There only remains for one of us to live at the Barrière de l'Étoile and the other at the Barrière du Trône, to dazzle the dwellers of the town and suburbs, as well as strangers from abroad. Capital!!!

My sore throat has come on again and you are not here to cure it. If you think this pleasant you are quite wrong, and if I followed my own bent I should deprive you of your functions as doctor-in-chief of the great Juju. I am determined to forgive you only if you come to supper with me presently. Seriously, I cannot understand why you keep away, seeing that your Play is in rehearsal, that this is our holiday time, and that I adore you. I am almost tempted to be a little jealous, only unfortunately, when I mean to be only slightly jealous, I become very seriously so; therefore I try as much as possible to spare myself that discomfort. You would be sweet and kind, my Toto, if you would come and eat my frugal dinner with me to-night and … I am going to concentrate my thoughts upon you, so as to magnetise you and bring you back in the shortest possible time to your faithful old Juju who loves and adores you. My first proceeding is to kiss your eyes, your mouth, and your dear little feet.

JULIETTE.

My beloved little man, you are so good and sweet when you see me that it is a pity you should see me so seldom, and that you should forget me as soon as your back is turned. To punish you, I am not going to write you two letters to-day; partly in consideration for your dear little eyes, and partly because it would be unfair to reward indifference and coldness in the same degree as affection and assiduity. Pray do not take the above expression, "dear little eyes," in an ironical sense—I mean it on the contrary as an endearing diminutive; your "dear little eyes" signify to me my adored, beautiful eyes, the mirrors of my soul, the stars of my heaven, everything that is most beautiful and fascinating, gentlest, noblest, and highest.

I love you, my Toto. I kiss your ripe red lips, your dazzling teeth, your little hands, and your twinkling feet. I am writing only your little daily bulletin, because your eyes are bad, and you have no time to waste; neither do I wish to tire or bore you, but only to make you love me a little bit.

JULIETTE.

Thursday, 8.30 p.m., November 22nd, 1838.

My little treasure of a man, you were sweet to select my hovel for a resting-place from which to write your laudatory remarks upon Mlle. Atala Beauchêne,[79] commonly called Beaudouin. It gave me a chance to admire your charming profile and kiss your beautiful shining locks. I thank you for that happiness, and I consent to your inditing daily effusions concerning that lady, if only you do so in my room and under my eyes.

As you promised to come back presently, the chances are that you will not return. I have half a mind to undress, light my fire, and set to work to bruise poppy-heads; for my provision is almost at an end, and later on I may be busy at the theatre, if Joly[80] persists in his crazy idea of giving us a whole week's rehearsals of a piece which is only to be played four months hence. It is an inducement to use the time at my disposal now, to prepare your little daily remedy.

I love you, Victor, I love you, my darling Toto.

JULIETTE.

Monday, 6 p.m., April 15th, 1839.

Why is it, my little beloved, that you always seem so jealous? You take the bloom off all those scraps of happiness your dear presence would otherwise give me, for nothing chills one's embraces so much as the vexed, uneasy mien you usually wear. It would not even be so bad if you did not accuse *me* of that same constrained, annoyed look; but the more suspicious you are, the more you think it is I who am cross, although this is simply the effect of the glasses through which your jealousy views me. Never mind, I love you and forgive you, and if only you will come and take me out a little this evening and show me part of *Lucrèce* I shall be happy and content. What a beautiful day! I would have given days and even months for the chance of strolling by your side wherever your rêverie led you. Alas, it is I who am sad, and with excellent reason! As for you, you old lunatic, what have you to complain of? You are adored, and you are free to accept and make use of that sentiment as much and as often as you desire; perhaps that is why you desire it so seldom.... But let us talk of other things. Please love me a little, while I give you my whole soul.

JULIETTE.

Sunday, 6.30 p.m., October 27th, 1839.

Here I am at my scribbling again, my Toto. It is a sad pleasure, if any, after the two months of love and intimacy which have just elapsed. Here I sit again with my ink and paper, my faults of spelling, my stupidity and my love. When we were travelling I did not need all this paraphernalia to be happy. It was enough for me to worship you, and God knows whether I did that! Here I do not love you less—on the contrary—but I live far from you, I long for you, I worry about you, I am unhappy—that is all. Still, I am not ungrateful or forgetful; I fully appreciate that you have just given me nearly two months of bliss. I still feel upon my lips the touch of your kisses, and upon my hand the pressure of yours. But the felicity I have experienced only throws into greater relief the void your absence leaves in my life. When you are no longer by my side, I cease to exist, to think, to hope. I desire you and I suffer. Therefore I dread as much as death itself the return to that hideous Paris, where there is naught for lovers who love as we love— neither sunshine, nor that confidence which is the sunshine of love— nothing but rain, suspicion, jealousy, the three blackest, saddest, iciest of the scourges which can afflict body and heart. Oh, I am wretched, my Toto, in proportion to my love; it is true, my adored one, and it will ever be thus, when you are not with me.

JULIETTE.

Friday, 10 a.m., November 1st, 1839.

Good-morning, my dear little beloved, my darling little man. You told me so definitely yesterday that my handwriting was hideous, and my scrawl nothing but a horrible maze in which you lose both patience and love, that I hardly dare write to you to-day, and it would take very little to make me cease our correspondence altogether. We must have an explanation on this subject, for it is cruel of you to force me to make myself ridiculous night and morning, simply because I love you and am the saddest and loneliest of women. If my love must be drowned in my ignorance and stupidity, at least do not force me to make the plunge myself. There was a time when you would not have noticed the ugliness of my writing; you would only have read my meaning and been happy and grateful. Now you laugh, which is shabby and wicked of you. This seems to be the fate of all the Quasimodo of this world, moral and physical; they are jeered at: form is everything, spirit nothing. Even if I could constrain my crabbed scrawl to say, "My soul is beautiful," you would not be any the less amused. Therefore, my dear little man, pending the moment when I can join in the laugh against myself, I think it would be as well to suspend these daily lucubrations. Besides, the moment has come when I must turn all my time and energies towards making my position secure. Nothing in this world can turn me from my purpose, for it is to me a question of life and death, and Heaven knows that in all these seven years I have never failed to tell you so whenever there has been an opportunity. I count upon you to help me, my beloved. I am asking you for more than life—for the moral consummation of our marriage of love. Let me go with you wherever my happiness is threatened, let me be the wife of your mind and heart, if I cannot be yours in law. If I express myself badly, do not scoff, but understand that I have a right to put into words what you yourself have felt, and that I insist upon defending my own against all those women who get at you under pretext of serving you. I will have my turn, for I love you and am jealous.

J.

Friday, 6.30 p.m., November 1st, 1839.

You are good, my adored one, and I am a wretch; but I love you while you only permit yourself to be loved; that is what makes you so tranquil and me so bitter. My heart is weighed down by jealousy this evening and nothing less than your adored presence will suffice to calm me, for I carry hell and all the furies within my soul. I wish I could be sewn to the lining of your coat to-night, for I feel I am about to encounter some great danger that I can only defeat by not leaving your side. If my fears are well-grounded, I shall probably fail in averting the doom that threatens me, for you will not be able to stay with me all the evening. The compliments and flattery you will receive will take you from me. I cannot deny that I am unhappy and jealous, and would much rather be with you at Fontainebleau, at the Hôtel de France, than in Box C. of the Théâtre Français, even when *Marion de Lorme* is being played. Kiss me, my little man; you are very sweet in your new greatcoat, but you had not told me you had been to your tailor. I shall keep up with you by sending for my dressmaker. I do not mean to surrender to you the palm for smartness and dandyism. Ha! who is caught? Toto! Toto!

Résilieux is beaming, Claire is happy, Suzanne is an idiot; such is the condition of the household. I am all three at the same time, plus the adoration I profess energetically for your imperial and sacred person. Kiss me and be careful of yourself this evening.

JULIETTE.

Monday, 12 noon, November 4th, 1839.

Good-morning, treasure. It is twelve by my clock, which is several hours fast, but I have been up some little time. I have dressed my child, and she is now practising on the piano. I spent the night thinking over what you said, my adored one. One luminous phrase especially stands out and scorches my soul. Perhaps you only said it idly as one of the compliments one is constrained to make to the woman who loves one? I know not, but I do know, that I have taken the assurance you gave me that you have never really loved any woman but me, as a sacred thing, unalterably true. I adore you and had never felt even the semblance of love until I met you. I love and adore you, and shall love and adore you for ever, for love is the essence of my body, my heart, my life, and my soul. Believe this, my treasure, for it is God's own truth. Your dread of seeing me re-enter theatrical life will quickly be dissipated by the probity and steadiness of my conduct. I hope, and am certain of this. You have nothing to fear from me wherever I may be. I adore you, I venerate you. If I could do as you wish and renounce the theatre, that is to say my sole chance of securing my future, I would do so without hesitation and without your having to urge it, simply to please you. But, my beloved, I feel that it were easier to relinquish life itself than the hope of paying my creditors and making myself independent by earning my own living. If I were to make this sacrifice I am sure my despair would bring about some irreparable catastrophe that would weigh upon you all your days.

My adored one, do not try to turn me from the only thing that can bring me peace and make me believe in your love. Help me and do not forsake me unless I give you just cause to do so. Spend your whole life in loving me, in exchange for my unswerving loyalty and adoration.

Kiss me, my little man.

I love you.

JULIETTE.

Friday, 4.45 p.m., November 15th, 1839.

I wrote the date and hour on this half-sheet of paper, thinking it was blank. I explain this, in order that your suspicious mind may not again draw a flood of insulting deductions from a thing that has happened so simply and naturally. You upset me just now when you said good-bye, because you said cruel things. It was a bad moment to choose. Your manner to me is enough to discourage an angel, and I have begun to ask myself whether it is possible to love a woman one does not esteem. If you esteemed me you would not for ever suspect my words, my silence, my actions, my conduct; if you loved me you would know how to appreciate my honesty and fidelity, whereas even in the tenderest moments of our most intimate communion, you never fail to say something cruel and disheartening. I often say one might almost imagine you were under a promise to someone to tire out my love by inflicting pain upon me on every occasion; but I hope you will never succeed in doing this.

I suffer, I despair at heart, but I love you so far, and I hope for both our sakes that I always shall. I cling to my love even more than to your esteem, for the latter is a poor blind thing that cannot distinguish night from day, candle-light from sunshine, or an honest woman from a harlot.

THE BRIDGE OF MARNE. Drawing by Victor Hugo (Victor Hugo Museum).

My love is more clear-sighted. It was attracted at once by your physical and spiritual perfection, and has never confused you with any other of the human species. I love you, Toto. Torment me, drive me to desperation if you will, but you shall never succeed in diminishing my affection. My head aches, little man, and the thoughts that fill it at this moment are not calculated to cure its pain. I press my hand upon my brow to crush thought, and I open my heart to all that is good and tender in my love for you. Good-bye, Toto. I adore you. Good-bye. We were very happy this morning; let us try to be so again very soon.

In the meantime I adore you.

JULIETTE.

Wednesday, 8.45, November 20th, 1839.

I am in despair. I wish I were dead and everything at an end! The more precautions I take, the more I purge my life, the less happiness I achieve. It is as if I were accursed, and I often feel a wild desire to behave as if I were, and crush my love underfoot. I am so unhappy that I lose all courage and hope for the future. You were very good to me when you were going away, but that does not prove that when you come back presently you may not be the most offensive and unjust of men. I sacrifice to you one by one all my actions, even the most insignificant; I am careful inwardly and outwardly to cause you no sort of offence, and yet I am unsuccessful! My struggles only fatigue and dishearten me. On the eve of taking the great step which would bind us to each other even closer than we already are, would it not be better for us to break off our relations, and put a stop to the whole thing instead? I can understand now the generosity of Didier, who elects to die upon the scaffold forgiving Marion with his last breath, rather than live persecuting and torturing her with the recollection of her past, and with suspicions a thousand times more painful than death and oblivion. Ah, yes, I can understand a Didier like that.... I suffer! Ah, God, people who do not love are very fortunate! I love you, and I know that failing some violent remedy I shall continue to suffer and care for you. I admit that all these things I write are absurd, and that it would be wiser to throw this letter into the fire, and keep to myself the thousand and one follies inspired by my despair.

JULIETTE.

Monday, 5.30 p.m., December 16th, 1839.

You did well, my adored one, to come back after the painful incident we had just gone through. If you had not, I should have been wretched all the evening. Thank you, my beloved Toto, thank you, my love. You looked very preoccupied, my treasure, when you came up the first time. I gathered that Guirault's letter had something to do with this, and that you were meditating your answer. Beyond that, I did not take much notice, for I was too furious with you to be able to think of anything.

If you knew how much I love you, and how faithful I am to you, my adored one, you would be less suspicious. Suspicion is an insult that makes me frantic, because, it proves to me that you do not believe in either my honesty or my love. Jealousy is another thing: one can be jealous of a face or of a person, because however sure one may be of one's own superiority, one may still fear that some beast or monster may be preferred to oneself;

but jealousy, I repeat, is different from everlasting suspicion of one's actions and even of one's negative conduct and inaction. Finally, I differentiate between jealousy and suspicion; I feel there is a great gulf between my jealousy and yours, and yet I love you more than you love me—you cannot gainsay that—if you admit it, I will pardon all your misdeeds and adore you and kiss your dear little feet. *Hurrah! I am to have my wardrobe! Hurrah!*

You will not be an Academician, but you will always be my dear little lover.

JULIETTE.

Thursday, 5 p.m., January 16th, 1840.

I love you, my Toto, and am sad at seeing you so seldom. But I know how much you have to do, my little man, so am not angry with you—still that does not prevent me from being horribly sad.

Money melts in my pocket. I was reading yesterday a description of Monsieur de Sévigné, the son, which applies wonderfully to me. "He had no hobbies, did not entertain, gave no presents, wore plain attire, gambled not at all, had only one servant and not a single horse on which to ride out with the King or the Dauphin; yet his hand was like a crucible wherein gold is melted." I am rather like that. I do not give many presents, I wear the same dress for a year at a time, I only do expensive cooking when you are coming to dine with me, I have only one servant, and yet money disappears in my establishment like snow under the rays of the sun. With me, it is not my hand that is the crucible, but my past life, which is like an abyss that all the money in the world would find it difficult to fill. That is why I am sad. Love me, my Toto, and above all do not kill yourself with working for everybody as you do without respite. I can sell something I do not want, whereas your health and repose are indispensable to my welfare and tranquillity. Remember that, my dear one, and do not be over scrupulous at the expense of the real consideration which makes my happiness. When shall I see you again, treasure?

JULIETTE.

Sunday, 1.15 p.m., March 22nd, 1840.

Good-morning, my beloved Toto. I read the manuscript of "Didine" over again last night, and I shed all the tears I had restrained in your presence. I am more convinced than ever that you committed an act of unfaithfulness against our love when you composed those lines. I do not see how you can hope to persuade me to the contrary, or wonder that I am wounded to the quick by such a mental and spiritual lapse. Jealousy is not excited only by infidelities of the senses, but primarily by such an infidelity as that which you have committed in writing these verses and concentrating your gaze and your thoughts upon that young girl, while my whole heart and soul were raised in prayer for you in that church at Strasbourg. I will never go back there, either to the church or to the town. There is an end of that. Would to God we had never gone there at all! I should have preserved one illusion more, and suffered one sorrow less. Well, well, it is not your fault. You wished to carry away the memory of that woman, as you could not possess her person, and you have written some very beautiful lines which prove, in the same degree as my pain, what a profound and striking impression she produced upon you. I hope you may never experience a jealousy so well-justified as mine about any woman you may love in the future; for myself I desire a speedy recovery from the most miserable infatuation in all this world.

JULIETTE.

Monday, 6.45 p.m., June 1st, 1840.

I am writing to you in the company of Résilieux, my love, but that does not restore to me the gaiety I have lost since this morning. That woman and her persistence annoy me more than I can say. When I think of the close confinement in which I live and realise the depth and devotion of the love I bear you, I am indignant to the bottom of my heart that a wretched woman of the street should dare to cast the eye of envy upon a passion which constitutes the religion and adoration of my whole life. If I listened to my own inclination, I should make a terrible example of the hussy and her low caprice, and no other would venture an attempt to capture your affections for many a long day. I am wretched since this morning. I think myself plain, old, stupid, badly dressed—and all because I tremble for the safety of my love, because I am afraid for my poor little slice of happiness. Alas! alas! my Toto, I care too much for you; it is crazy of me. I did so hope that when your family was settled in the country, you would sometimes come and take me out with you—but, on the contrary, in a whole month I have only been out once with you; for I do not count those two evenings at the theatre, when I drove there and back in a carriage. It would be a cruel jest if you considered those as going out with you. I am not well. I have rushes of blood to the head and heart, but you do not care. I shall not do my monthly accounts to-night; my head aches too badly. Perhaps I may try to-morrow. The laundress has been here and I have paid her; I shall probably get the grocer's bill to-morrow, but I shall certainly not pay it unless you have plundered some passer-by to-night. Meanwhile, I love you, my Toto. Dinner has just been announced; I shall not be as happy as yesterday, for you are not dining with me; but perhaps as

I am alone I shall be able to ruminate over my good fortune, for I was hardly able to realise it at all yesterday with all those females about.

JULIETTE.

January 7th, 9.30 a.m., 1841.

Good-morning, my darling Toto, to whom I dare not yet give his prospective title, for I am very doubtful of the integrity of old Dupaty. I hope you will not keep me waiting too long for the result of the rabid voting of the opposing parties.[81] The contest becomes more and more curious and interesting. I wish it were already four o'clock.

The weather is not very propitious for that moribund scoundrel. It would be difficult to let him down through the window, and still more so to transport him to the place where we do not wish him to be. If the computation is correct, the mortal illness of the old wretch should give you the place by a majority of one vote at the first scrutiny; but what about a black-ball? Perhaps this time it will come from the ignoble creature who walks under the filthy, greasy, hideous hat of that beast Dupaty. I wish we were already at this afternoon, that I might know what the foul old man has dared to do. Until then I shall look at my clock many and many a time. Try, my love, to come at once and tell me the result whatever it may be. I shall at least have the pleasure of seeing you, which will add to the joy of your nomination or console you for your defeat.

By the way, you were so shabby last night that one might suppose you were preparing to contest the palm of bad dressing with that old pickpocket Dupaty. I shall forgive you your untidiness if you are successful. I love you.

JULIETTE.

Thursday, 6 p.m., January 7th, 1841.

I am enchanted for everybody's sake, my dear Academician, that at last you are elected. There you are at last, thanks to the seventeen votes of your friends, and in spite of your fifteen adversaries. You are an Academician. Hurrah!

I wish I could have witnessed with my own eyes the grimaces of all those contemptible old things, and heard the profession of faith of that horrible Dupaty; you ought to indemnify me by showing me your own beautiful countenance for a little more than a paltry five minutes as you did just now. I love you, Toto, as much as the first day and more than ever. But, alas, I dare not believe the same of you, for I do not see much proof of it, as my maid would say. The fact is that whether as an Academician, or a candidate, or nothing at all, I hardly see you more than an hour a day. This is neither novel nor consoling; it becomes more and more sad and painful. Think of that, my love, and come very soon after you have read my letter.

I love you.

JULIETTE.

Sunday, 10.45 a.m., April 11th, 1841.

Good morning, my beloved Toto, my adored little man. How are you, my darling? I am afraid you may have tired yourself last night reading your splendid speech to me. Poor beloved, it would be a calamity that my pleasure should cost you so dear; it would be unjust and cruel. I hope it is not so, my adored one, and that you have not been punished for your kindness.

What a magnificent address! and how stupid it is of me only to appreciate it inwardly, and to be incapable of expressing my feelings better than by inarticulate grunts. It is not my fault, yet since I have learned to love you I have not been able to resign myself to my limitations. Every time the opportunity presents itself to admire you I am furious with myself and should like to slap and kick myself—though my poor body would have no time to recover between the assaults, for every single thing you say and do is as admirable and striking as your written works. So I should be kept busy. Fortunately you do not object to my want of intellect; you realise the quality and proportions of my love. All my intelligence and being have turned to spirit, to idolise you. I may be only a goose outwardly, but inwardly I am sublime with devotion. Which is best? I cannot tell, it is for you to decide. Meanwhile I am the most fortunate of women to have heard the beginning of your beautiful speech, and I love you with all my strength.

JULIETTE.

Thursday, 4.30 a.m., June 3rd, 1841.

Good morning, my adored little man, my beloved *Monsieur l'Académicien*! How are you, my Toto? I am very much afraid you will be horribly tired before this afternoon, poor treasure![82] I think you should have had the speech printed a day earlier, and have kept this night free for resting.

I really do not know how you will manage to deliver your address after these several days of grinding fatigue, and a night spent in correcting the proofs at the printing-works. Nobody but you can accomplish these feats of endurance. Still, my beloved, it is time you changed a mode of living which must kill you in the long run. I hope you are going to spend the remaining few hours in your bed.

I already feel as agitated as if I were going to make the speech myself. I shall be in a desperate state of mind until you have finished and Salvandy begins to speak. I shall have this fearful lump on my chest until then.

Whatever happens I adore you.

JULIETTE.

June 3rd, 5.30 p.m., 1841.

Where shall I begin, my love? At your divine feet or your celestial brow? What shall I express first? My admiration? Or the adoration that overflows my heart like your sublime genius surpasses the mediocre creatures who listened to you without understanding, and gazed at you without falling upon their knees! Ah, let me mingle those two sentiments that dazzle my brain and burn up my heart. I love you! I admire you! I adore you! You are truly splendid, noble, and sublime, my poet, my beloved, light of my eyes, flame of my heart, life of my life! Poor adored beloved; when I saw you enter, so pale and shaken, I felt myself swooning, and but for the support of Madame Démousseaux and Madame Pierceau, I should have fallen to the floor. Happily nobody noticed my emotion, and when I came to myself and saw your sweet smile answering mine and encouraging me, I felt as if I were awaking from a long, painful dream, though only a second of time had elapsed.

Thank you, my adored one, for sparing a thought to the poor woman who loves you, at that solemn moment—I should have said, that supreme moment, if the assemblage had not consisted for the greater part of tiresome blockheads and vile scoundrels.

Thank you, my good angel, my sublime Victor, my illustrious *child*. I saw all your dear little family;[83] lovely Didine, charming Charlot, and dear little Toto who looked pale and delicate. I kissed them all in spirit as I did their divine father.

I love you.

JULIETTE.

Thursday, 2.30 p.m., July 8th, 1841.

While you are lording it at the Académie[84] I am weeping and suffering at home. You might have spared me this pain by inviting me to attend the sitting, or else staying away yourself. I must warn you, my Toto, that this sort of sacrifice and torment is unendurable, and if it happens again I do not know what I may do rather than resign myself to it.

We are not living in the East, and you have not *bought* me, thank Heaven! I am free to cast off the yoke of proceedings which are neither just, nor kind, nor affectionate. I swear by all I hold most sacred in this world, namely my love, that I will not submit a third time to be thus flouted. If you knew how furious and miserable I am feeling at this moment of writing, you would not venture to inflict a third trial of the kind upon me. In any case pray keep my letter as a *definite announcement* of what I am capable of doing if you are so cruel as to persist in your present line of conduct. Meanwhile I am doing my best to avoid taking any definitely fatal step, but I warn you that I cannot much longer remain mistress of myself.

JULIETTE.

1 a.m.

Hell in my heart at noon, Paradise at midnight, my Toto. I love you and have full confidence in you.

Friday, 7.45 p.m., November 19th, 1841.

I HAVE IT! HURRAH!! Fancy, it has been here all the morning, yet nothing warned me! My heart did not beat faster than usual, the earth did not tremble, the skies did not fall, in fact everything remained in its humdrum, normal condition, as if nothing unusual had happened—and it was here all the time! I possessed it in my room, under my eyes! Verily it can hardly be credited, and if anybody but myself said so I should not believe it. But what you must believe, my love, for indeed it is true, is that I love you and that you are the kindest, most charming, best, handsomest, most generous, most noble, and most adored of men. That is what you have got to believe, because it is God's own truth. The cabinet is fascinating, but what is still nicer is the way you gave it to me. "The manner of the gift is better than the gift itself," was once said by some one whose name I have forgotten. When you are the donor, the proverb is still more applicable. If you had all the treasures of the universe to bestow, you would do it with a grace that would enhance the value of the gift a thousandfold. As for me I am mad with delight, for I believe you love me. I may tell you now that last night I cried helplessly at the thought of how much younger and handsomer you are than I. I anticipated the moment when you will no longer be able to love me, and my heart contracted so that I should have suffocated without the relief of tears. I feel I shall certainly die the day you cease to care for me, and I know that no other woman can ever worship you as I do. But I trust that day will never dawn, will it, my angel? There are no wrinkles in the heart, and you will see my face only in the reflection of your attachment, eh, Victor, my beloved? The while I wept and mourned, you were thinking of me, my poor sweet, and bringing me the cabinet. We were both performing an act of love, mine gloomy, yours, charming and considerate like everything you do. I hope your present will bring us both happiness, and that you will adore me as long as I shall admire my dear little cabinet—that is, for ever.

I HAVE IT! WHAT HAPPINESS! I should like to put it in the middle of the room on a golden table, or in my bed, or carry it in my arms, on my heart, anywhere in fact where it could be seen and touched. Meanwhile I will give it a good cleaning to-morrow. It is rather too late to-night. I must do some copying, and dine, and send you back the scribble you entrusted to me yesterday, so I will put off till to-morrow—principally because I shall have a better light then. I will clean it in bed, drawer by drawer. It will be a delightful occupation.

I love you, I love you, Toto, I kiss you and adore you, Toto.

JULIETTE.

Wednesday evening, 6.30, February 9th, 1842.

Do you really want me to write Toto, even when my heart is breaking, and my soul brimful of discouragement? I obey, but if you would only listen to me, you would allow me to discontinue these daily scrawls, which have never served any purpose but that of betraying the measure of my stupidity and making you tire of a love become absurd by dint of reiteration. I feel you only insist out of kindness, but it seems futile to continue this childish babble, which deceives neither you nor me, and gives me no indication of what is passing in your mind. It would be better, my beloved, to inure me gradually to a catastrophe which may be nearer than I guess, than to make efforts to leave me an illusion which neither of us really shares nowadays. A sad ending to all our past happiness! God grant it may not be altogether buried. This does not prevent me from doing you full justice, my friend. You are kind with a kindness full of pity and divine indulgence, but you no longer cherish for me the love of a man for a woman. Do not pretend otherwise, for you cannot delude me. I bear you no grudge my Victor, neither should you bear me any, for it is no more your fault than mine, that you do not love me while I still love you—not our fault, but God's, Who distributes unequally the amount of love we may each expend during our lives. Happy he or she to whom the smaller sum is apportioned—so much the worse for him or her whose heart is inexhaustible. Now, my beloved Toto, I will torment you no longer. I will even try to make myself agreeable, though, alas, what woman can be agreeable when she is no longer loved! But I shall do my best, and that, coupled with your natural generosity, may still retard for a few days the greatest misfortune of my life. Fear nothing from me, my Victor. You have to-day received the last expression of my choler. One may strike, and even kill, while one feels oneself beloved, but one must spare the man who no longer cherishes one.

You see, my Victor, that you have nothing to be afraid of, but I beseech you to let me off these daily scribbles about things that have neither point nor reason.

I demand this of your goodness.

JULIETTE.

Thursday, 2.30 p.m., February 10th, 1842.

My beloved, my adored Victor, thank you! You remove hell from my heart, and replace it with paradise. Thank you! My life, my spirit, my soul, bless and adore you. What a letter, my God! I wanted to read it kneeling; happy tears poured down my cheeks. You love me, my dear one! It must be true, for you declare it in the loveliest, sweetest language of the whole world. You love me although I am ill-tempered, violent, stupid; you love me my good angel, because you know that your love is the breath of life to me, and that without it I could no longer exist. I also love you, but only God and myself know how deeply. Yesterday when you left me, I was on my knees praying and kissing with tears the footsteps I could hear fading away in the street. I could have flung myself out of the window and died at your feet. My despair, then, was as poignant as the bliss I felt just now when I read your adored letter. My Victor, my love, my life, my joy, I love you more than ever! I implore your forgiveness, I throw myself at your feet and embrace them. Thank you, my treasure. You must be very happy, for you have done a lovely thing in writing me the most charming, the kindest, the most wonderful and most adorable letter that ever issued from your heart.

JULIETTE.

Thursday, 9.30, April 30th, 1842.

Good morning, my adored Toto. How did the little invalid sleep last night? As for you, I do not even ask, my poor dear, for I know you spend all your nights working. I love you, my poor angel. I do not know what else to say, because that is the only thought in my heart and soul; to love you always and for ever. Here comes the bright sunshine that is going to cure our poor little man at once.[85] I have not seen a finer spring since the one we spent strolling about the heights of Montmartre together. I cannot think of it without tears of regret for the days that are gone, and of gratitude to Providence for those few moments of most perfect felicity. I would give half my life to have it again, my beloved Toto; and it depends only upon you—if you wished it, we could easily recover the happiness of those days. Why do you no longer desire it? I know you have to work, but so you did then—*Claude Gueux, Philosophie Mêlée, Les Voix Intérieures, Les Chants du Crépuscule, Angélo, Les Rayons et Les Ombres* and *Ruy Blas*, are there to prove it. In those days you loved me better than you do at present. Alas, I love you more than ever, or rather, as much as the first day!—that is, with all my soul.

JULIETTE.

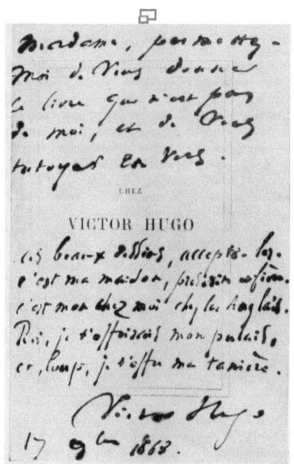

A DEDICATION BY VICTOR HUGO TO JULIETTE DROUET.
The original belongs to M. Louis Barthou.

Saturday, 6.30 p.m., August 20th, 1842.

I am a strange creature—at least you think so, do you not, beloved? But what you take for eccentricity, caprice, bad-temper, is really love, but an unhappy love, mistrustful and anxious. Everything is to me a subject of dread almost amounting to despair. Thus this visit to the Duchesse d'Orléans, whither I quite admit you were kind enough to take me, was simply a torment on account of the hour and the circumstances: I, badly dressed, barely clean, and that woman under the prestige of a great sorrow[86] which, next to physical beauty, is the surest way to your heart. I frankly confess that however gallant my love may be, and whatever reliance I may place upon your loyalty, I am not easy when I have to fight and struggle without weapons. This result of a *surprise* and a hurried rush through Paris in a cab may seem excessive to you, and verging on hysteria; but the fact is, my adored one, that my love, so long repressed, is verily degenerating into a disease, almost into frenzy. Everything hurts me. I am afraid of everything. I am a poor thing needing much compassion for loving you so. If these incoherent expressions do not force upon you the realisation of the depth of my devotion, it must be that you no longer care for me, or indeed have never done so; but if on the contrary you do understand, you will pity and pardon me, and love me all the better, and I am the happiest of women.

JULIETTE.

February 14th, 11.15 a.m., 1843.

Good morning beloved Toto, good morning adored one. I love you. When I heard you describing last night the impression produced upon you by the rehearsal of *Lucrèce* and more especially by the singing of the guests, I seemed to feel it all myself. The fact that my love has not grown a day older, that my admiration is still on the increase, that I think you as handsome and as young as ever, makes it easier for me to go back to the feelings of those days. Looking into my heart, I seem to feel that all this adulation and joy and feast of glory and love began yesterday. Alas, those ten years have left traces only upon my poor countenance, and have been as harsh to it as they have been indulgent to your charming features.

I express this somewhat crudely, as I always manage to do, but it is not my fault, my love, nor any one else's. I love you. Therein consist my intelligence, my wit, my superiority; beyond that I am as stupid as any other animal.

You must be very busy to-day with the two rehearsals,[87] and the Maxime[88] worry which falls upon your devoted head, not to speak of the *great business*! I dare not expect you to-night till very late. Well, my dearly beloved, I know you do not belong to me, so I will resign myself as cheerfully as may be, and put a good face upon your absence. Try to think of me, my dear little man; that is all I venture to ask at this moment. As for me, there is no more merit in thinking of you and loving you than in breathing.

I love you, Toto, as much as life.

JULIETTE.

Where are you? What are you about, my adored one?[89] In what condition is your family? What state are you in yourself? what will happen to us all in our despair, if God be not merciful to us! Since you left me I can think only of your arrival at home. I imagine the scene: the despairing sobs of your children, the expression of your own frightful grief, so long and sternly repressed. All those tears and sufferings fall back upon my heart and rend it. I cannot bear more. My poor head is on fire and my hands burn like live coals. I want to pray and cannot; all my faculties, all my being, turn to you. I would give my life to spare you a single pang. I would have sacrificed myself in this world, and the next to save your adored child. My God, what will become of me if you stay away much longer, when I have refrained with such difficulty from sending to get news of you? I have begged Madame Lanvin to come to me this afternoon and bring her husband, so that if, as I fear, I have not seen you before then, he can go and ask for news of you under the name of Monsieur St. Hilaire. My heart aches, my poor treasure, when I think of all you are enduring. I feel I cannot much longer bear not seeing you. I shall commit some act of folly if you do not come to my assistance. I exhausted my strength and courage on that awful journey, and during last night and to-day. I have none left now to endure your absence. I picture to myself your wife ill, and you also; in fact, I am like a mad thing in the extremity of my anxiety and grief. I am trying to occupy myself mechanically, in order to bring nearer the moment when I shall see you, but my efforts only make every minute of waiting seem like a century, and all the fears my heart anticipates, become frightful realities against which I cannot struggle. My adored Victor, whatever be your despair, mine is greater still; for I feel it through my love, which makes it a hundred times worse and multiplies it beyond all human calculation. Never has man been so idolised by woman as you are by me, and the poor angel we mourn knows it and sees it now, as God knows and sees it, and she will forgive, as He does, I am certain. I think of her, poor beloved, as an angel of heaven. To her I shall direct my prayers, that she may give you the strength and courage you need. To her also I shall address myself in the hour of death, that the good God may take me with all of you into His Paradise.

My adored Victor, it is more than five o'clock, and you have not yet come. What shall I do! What can I think, or rather what am I to fear? We are in a terrible cycle of misfortune, and God only knows when it will end. My Victor, before giving way to despair, think of mine, remember that I love you more than life.

JULIETTE.

Sunday, 5.45 p.m., October 8th, 1843.

I have been working all the morning my beloved, or rather scribbling on paper—only to please you, for I doubt whether my labour will be of any use to you; still, I am trying hard, and if I cannot do *better*, I am doing *my* best. I cannot do more. I am trying more especially to forget no detail, which makes me occasionally note down trivialities, little futile, insignificant things. My search among our memories is like the botanising of a child who is as apt to collect couch grass as the more useful and rarer plants. However, I am doing my best, and better still, I am obeying you. Would you believe that, although I have been writing the whole day, I have not yet reached *Auch*.[90] My mind and pen rather resemble the fantastic equipage we drove thither, but there is less risk in the present venture. The worst that can happen is that we should tumble promiscuously into a muck heap of absurdities and nonsense which leave no bruises, whereas we risked our necks several times in the course of the thirty-three miles between Tarbes and Auch.

I should love to see you, my Toto. The day, though filled with joyous recollections of our journey, has seemed long and sad to me. Nothing can take the place of one of your embraces. The remembrance of the greatest happiness cannot weigh against one glance from you. I realise it more to-day than ever before; therefore, do try and come, my beloved Toto. It will give me courage and patience to get through the evening. I love you too much, you see, but I cannot help it; it is no fault of mine.

JULIETTE.

Sunday, 7.15 p.m., November, 1843.

I think of you my beloved, I desire you, I love you. Ah yes, I love you my adored Toto, you may be sure of it, for it is God's truth. My little Claire and I talk of you and nothing but you. We love you and bless you. The poor little child will not be with me much longer, and I can already see her poor little face wrinkling up with sorrow; but I try to be cheerful and to remind her of the fortnight's holiday which will soon come. We love the pictures of your dear little Toto, and his pretty home. We gaze at them with eagerness and affection, we are all eyes and heart. At this moment Claire is reading Ulric's poems,[91] while I am writing to my beloved Toto with a heart full of gratitude and devotion. May the happiness you bestow upon me, be yours also, my love! May a just pride sustain you, for you have saved two souls, the mother's and the daughter's! I feel ineffable things I dare not express, for fear of vulgarising them by the mere fact of putting them into words. Do not delay long ere you come, my darling Toto. If you knew the joy and radiance you diffuse in this house, you would indeed hasten your steps. Alas, I am foolish, for have you not children of your own whom you must also make glad! I am envious of them, but not cruel enough to deprive them of their bliss—only I beg of them to hurry with their enjoyment, so that my turn may come.

Did you give Dédé the sachet? Did Toto take back his quince jelly? Meanwhile, I am giving Suzanne a whole evening to herself, and making my little rogue read *Le Musée des Familles*. I should love to give you a good kiss, but I know you will not come for it. You have not the sense to do so.

JULIETTE.

Monday, 11.15 a.m., July 22nd, 1844.

Good morning my beloved, my sweet, my darling little Toto. How are you? Are you less sad and painfully pre-occupied than yesterday, my adored one? Alas, it is unlikely ... your grief and sorrow are not of those that time can soften. You have the painful faculty of feeling things far more acutely than do other men. Genius does not only pertain to the brain, it belongs above all to the heart. My poor dear one, I love you; I suffer when you suffer; be merciful to us both, I implore you.

My little Claire went away this morning. She was more resigned than usual, for she has a holiday of three days in prospect, beginning next Saturday. The poor little thing is very devoted to us; her sole happiness is to be with us. She complains of not seeing you often enough, and I back her up in that. You must try to give us at least one evening out of the three she will spend at home. Verily I am not very cheerful company for the poor child when I am alone with her. I am so absorbed in my love that sometimes I do not speak to her twice in the day, however much I try to bring myself to do so.

I have copied Méry's verses, because I do not wish to deprive Mademoiselle Dédé of his autograph. I can understand her setting store by it, poor darling, so I shall make a point of returning it to her. Only (and it is you I am addressing now) you must give me just as many as you give her. You must not lose your good habits, my darling, for I am sure it would bring us bad luck. Therefore you must bring me all your letters as you used to do. I promise to divide them conscientiously with dear little Dédé, and you know quite well that I am a woman of my word. I adore you.

JULIETTE.

Thursday, 4.45 p.m., October 20th, 1844.

I have sent to Barbedienne, my adored one, but Suzanne has not yet returned. I am writing to you meanwhile to make the time hang less heavy. I hope to goodness I may be able to procure that lovely medal![92] Since I have glimpsed the chance of possessing it, I feel my disappointment would be greater than I could bear, if I failed to get it. Good God, how slowly that girl walks! Fancy having to trust to legs like those on such an occasion! I could have gone there and back ten times, since she went. May the devil fly away with her, or rather, precipitate her right into the middle of my room with his cloven foot, providing only that she brings the longed-for medal!

JULIETTE DROUET IN 1846.
Bust by Victor Vilain (Victor Hugo Museum).

Here she is! Ah! Victor, do not be angry! Victor, I am at your feet—Victor, I will be reasonable for the whole of the rest of my life if only you will let me add 15 fr. to the sum you promised me. Oh, Victor, I have not time to wait for your answer and yet I fear to annoy you. Ah, no, you are too kind to be angry with your poor Juju who loves you with such absolute admiring, devoted love! You will look at her with your gentle, ineffable smile, and say I was right—surely, yes, you will. Three cheers for Toto! Juju is a clever woman ... at heart. Yes, it is quite true and I am the happiest of women.

JULIETTE.

Tuesday, 9.30 a.m., September, 1845.

I have just been gardening, beloved. I am soaked with dew and all muddy, but I have spent three hours thinking of you without any bitterness. My eyes were as moist as my flowers, but I was not weeping. While I busied myself with the garden, I reviewed in thought the lovely flowers of my past happiness. I saw them again fresh and blooming as the first day, and I felt close to you, separated only by a breath. As long as the illusion lasted I was almost happy. I should have liked to pluck my soul and send it to you as a nosegay. Perhaps what I am saying is silly, yet it is the sort of nonsense that can only issue direct from the tenderest, most passionate heart that ever lived. For nearly thirteen years past, I have never once written to you without feeling my hand tremble and my eyes fill. When I speak of you, no matter to whom, my heart swells as if it would burst through my lips. When I am dead, I am certain that the imprint of my love will be found on my heart. It is impossible to worship as I do without leaving some visible trace behind when life is over.

My beloved Victor, let your thoughts dwell with me, so that my days may seem shorter and less dreary; and do try to surprise me by coming to-night. Oh, how happy I shall be if you do that!

Meanwhile, I love you more than I can say.

JULIETTE.

Saturday, 8 a.m., September 27th, 1845.

Good morning my beloved, my soul, my life, my adored Victor. How are you? I hope yesterday did not tire you too much. I forgot until you reminded me that you have been forbidden to walk much, but I do trust it did you no harm; did it, Victor darling? As for me I felt no fatigue, I seemed to have wings. I should have liked to place my feet on all the paths we traversed together eleven years ago, to kiss the very stones of the roads and the leaves on the trees, and to pick all the flowers in the woods, so keenly did I fancy they were the very same that watched us pass together all those years ago. I gazed at you my adored Victor, and in my eyes you were as young and handsome, nay handsomer even, than eleven years ago. I looked into my heart and found it full of the same ecstasy and adoration that animated it the first day I loved you. Nothing was changed in us or about us. The same ardent, devoted, sad and sweet affection in our hearts, the same autumn sun and sky above our heads, the same picture in the same frame; nothing had changed in eleven years. I would have given a decade of my life to stand alone for ten minutes in that house that has sheltered our memories for so long. I should like to have carried away ashes from the fireplace, dust from the floors. I should have liked to pray and weep, where once I prayed and wept, to have died of love on the spot where once I accepted your soul in a kiss. I had to exercise superhuman self-control not to perpetrate some act of folly in the presence of that girl who showed us so indifferently over a house I could have purchased at the price of half the rest of my life. Fortunately, thanks to her profound ignorance of our identity, she noticed nothing, and we were each able to bring away a tiny relic of our former happiness. Mine must be buried with me when I die.

Beloved, did you work late last night? It was very imprudent of you if you did, after the fatigue you underwent during the day. To-day, you must be very careful and not walk much. I shall be extremely stern with you. My antiquarian propensities shall not make me forget, like yesterday, that you are still convalescent and must hardly walk at all. And you will obey me, because little Totos must always obey little Jujus, as you know.

Kiss me, my adored Victor, and may God bless you for all the happiness you give me.

JULIETTE.

Saturday, 9 p.m., May 2nd, 1846.

I cannot nerve myself to the realisation that I shall not see you this evening my sweet adored beloved; yet it is all too true. This is the first time in fourteen years that I have not slept in a room belonging to you.[93] Consequently I am feeling quite forlorn. Everything conspires to harrow me. Just now when I left you I longed for death, and the tears I drove from my eyes trickled inwardly to my sad heart. If this anxiety about my child, and the separation from you, are to last long, I do not think I shall have strength to endure them. I am vexed and disgusted at the tone of those about me. I am ashamed and indignant at my inability to remove myself from it, however I may try; then when I remember you, so generous, so loyal, so noble, so kind and indulgent, my bitterness evaporates and nothing remains in my heart but admiration, gratitude, and love for your divine and fascinating self.

When I got back, I found my child in a raging fever. I gave her fresh compresses, and now she is sleeping. God grant she may do so all night, and that the change of ideas and surroundings and air may have a good effect upon her health. I shall in that case have less cause to grudge the sacrifices I am voluntarily making to that end. Meanwhile, I am a prey to fearful anxiety, and am suffering the uttermost from the absence of what I love best in this world, above life, above duty, above everything. Good-night, beloved. Think of me. Sleep well, and love me.

JULIETTE.

Tuesday, 3.45 p.m., 1846.

I love you, my Victor. Between every letter of those five sweet words there lurk depths of maternal anguish and sorrow. Gloomy reflections mingle with my tenderest thoughts. My life at this moment is divided between my poor little daughter whom I already mourn in anticipation, (for I feel that these few days of illness are but snatched from Eternity), and my adoration for you, from which no preoccupation, even of the most terrible and sinister character, can long distract me. On the contrary, my love is all the greater for the trials and sufferings God sends me. I love you selflessly, as if I myself were already over the border. My heart is racked, yet I adore you.

Claire's condition is the same as yesterday; only the weakness, which, but for the doctor's plain warning I might have attributed to the heat, has increased. The night was not very bad; the poor little thing suffers hardly at all. She seems to have no firmer hold on life than life has upon her. Apathy and profound indifference characterise her illness. Only her father has the power to rouse her for the few moments he is with her. He came this morning and happened to meet the doctor,[94] who, it appears, is not quite so despondent as Monsieur Triger;[95] but what does that prove?

I have not been able to get her up at all to-day. She lay in bed in a state of profuse and constant perspiration. The various tonics she takes fail to produce any effect whatever. The exhaustion increases hour by hour, which means that death is coming nearer. I pray, but I obtain neither solace nor confidence. The good God disdains my prayers and rejects them, I know—yet I love and admire Him in His beneficent, lofty, noble, generous and beautiful works.

I love Him as His saints and angels in Heaven love Him. What more can I do to find favour in His eyes? He deprived me of my mother at my birth; now He is about to snatch my child from me. Is that His justice? I do not want to blaspheme, but I am very miserable, and if I do not see you, if you cannot come to-day, I do not know what will become of me. Despair fills my soul, but I love you. God may crush my heart if He so wills, but the last breath from it shall be a cry of love for you, my sublime beloved.

April 29th, 9 a.m., 1847.

Good morning, my adored Victor. My thoughts and soul and heart go out to you in this greeting. I hope I shall see you before you go to the rehearsal, for if I do not, I shall have to wait till this evening, which would increase my depression. From now until the anniversary of the terrible day on which I lost my poor child, every hour and minute is punctuated by the recollection of the sufferings of that poor little thing, and of the anguish I went through. They are painful memories, impossible to exclude from my thoughts. Last night while I lay sleepless I seemed to hear her, and in my dreams I saw her again as she looked at the close of her illness. I am worn out this morning. All the pangs and fatigues of the last moments of her life weigh down my heart and limbs. It may be that I shall find comfort in prayer, and I shall pray better by her side, buoyed up by the hope that she will hear me and obtain for me resignation enough to bear her absence without murmur or bitterness. It was you who gave me the courage to live. All that a heart can gain from consolation, I found in your love; but there is a grief surpassing all others and beyond human aid, for which only God can provide, and to Him I must address myself to-day.

JULIETTE.

Thursday, 8 a.m., May 6th, 1847.

Good morning, my all, my greatly loved Toto. How are you this morning? Did you gather in a good harvest of glances, smiles and flattery yesterday from the women you met? Were you the cause of many incipient passions, or were you yourself ensnared by those females, like any beardless student or bald-headed peer of the realm? Tell me, how are you after your evening at Court? For my part, I have a very sore throat and am feeling fearfully cross. I have a longing to scratch which I should love to vent upon the face of some woman or even upon yours—or better still, upon both. I am sick of playing the gentle, sheep-like woman. I intend to become as fierce as a hyena, and to make your life and everything depending upon it a burthen to you. I mean to make a terrible example of you, so that people shall say as you pass by, that it is a woman who has been outraged, but a Juju who has avenged herself! Meanwhile, to begin with, I am going to wrest from you somehow, two silk dresses, a lovely hat, two pairs of smart shoes; and if you do not confess your crime, I will punish you to the tune of torrents of tea-gowns, pocket-handkerchiefs, and silk stockings. I am capable of anything if you drive me too far.

JULIETTE.

Tuesday, 12.45 p.m., June 6th, 1848.

The more I think of all that is going on in Paris at this moment, my beloved, the less do I desire the success of your election.[96] We must let this frenzy of the populace which knows not what it wants and is in no condition to distinguish the true from the false, or evil from good, exhaust itself first. When it is worn out with turning in its own vicious circle of disorder, violence, and misery, it will come to heel and humbly crave the assistance of incorruptible, strong, sane politicians, among whom you are the most incorruptible, the strongest, and the sanest. I say this in the simplicity of my heart, without any pretension to be other than a mere woman who loves you above all things, and trembles lest you should enter upon some undertaking that might jeopardise your life without saving your country. Therefore I pray that this candidature, to which you have been driven in self-sacrifice and generosity, may not succeed. If I am unpatriotic, I accept the blame, but I do think that in this instance my feeling is in accord with the best interests of France. It would not be the first time that the heart has proved cleverer than the brain. It has happened too often in my case for me to marvel. Pending our next meeting, I kiss you from my soul, I adore you with all my strength.

JULIETTE.

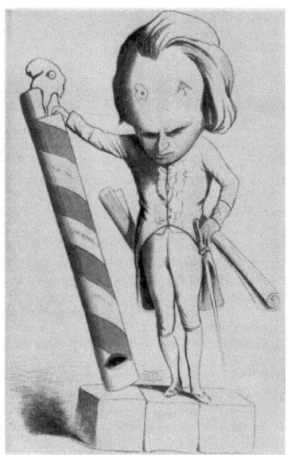

VICTOR HUGO, RÉPUBLICAIN.
Political caricature, 1848.

Monday, 9 a.m., July 9th, 1849.

I am hurrying, my love, for I wish to be at the door of the Assemblée at noon precisely, in order to secure a good place.[97] I wish the great moment had arrived, for I am already feeling stage-fright, and it will go on increasing until I see you descend from the tribune. I thought this morning that I could not experience any other sensation than happiness at seeing you, but now I begin to understand what fear is. Yet when I say fear, I am hardly correct; for I mean something more indefinite, which is rather the suspense before a great joy, than the stupid emotion of cowardice or funk. In any case, I am very agitated; I wander aimlessly about the house, and feel as if the longed-for moment would never arrive. My blessed love, my great Victor, my sublime beloved, I kiss in spirit your noble forehead with its generous thoughts, your beautiful eyes so gentle and powerful, your fascinating mouth, which has the happiness of speaking all your divine thoughts. I prostrate myself before the most beautiful and most sublime thing in the whole world, namely, your dear little person and your profound genius.

I do not ask you to think of me before your speech, adored one, but afterwards I entreat you to spare me one glance to complete my happiness.

JULIETTE.

Wednesday, 12.30, February 6th, 1850.

Think of me, my adored one, and do not permit yourself to be ensnared by the mercenary blandishments of that woman.[98] I am in the throes of a jealousy so terrible, that the hardest heart would be moved to pity, and the most intrepid would fear me; for I am suffering, and I am capable of anything to avenge a despicable treachery. Alas, my poor adored one, this is not what I should like to say, or what I ought to say. I realise that threats are powerless to hold you. I believe if the statistics of infidelity could be drawn up like those of crime, it would be shown that the severe penalties of the code of love are more apt to drive lovers into breaches of its laws than to bind them together. I am sure of it, and I wish I could convert my natural ferocity into bland indifference, in order to remove from you the stimulant of a forbidden Rachel; but it is no good—I shall never manage it. Therefore, I implore you for the sake of your personal safety and mine, to be honourable and prudent in your dramatic relations with that dangerous and perfidious Jewess. Try not to prolong your literary and theatrical consultation beyond the strictly necessary limits, and to come and fetch me before three o'clock.

I should be so grateful to you, my adored little man, for you would thus abridge the moments of my torment. Meanwhile I am very unhappy and anxious and worried. I try to hearten myself up by remembering the last promises you made me. When do you intend to keep them, I wonder? God knows!

JULIETTE.

Saturday, 8 a.m., April 6th, 1850.

Good morning, my adored one, my sublime beloved. How are you? Did you have a better night, or did fatigue and excitement prevent you from sleeping? When I think of the admirable speech, so religious in character, so noble, self-abnegating, and conciliating, that you delivered yesterday[99] at the risk of your health, and then reflect upon the senseless uproar, and idiotic and violent interruptions it provoked, I feel only hatred, contempt, and disgust, for political life. It is revolting that a man like you should be the butt of the irresponsibility of all the parties. It is hateful, abominable, infamous, that scoundrels without talent, wit, or feeling should dare argue with you and should be accorded an attentive hearing where you only meet with insults. Really, my treasure, the more I see of political life, the more I regret the time when you were simply the *poet* Victor Hugo, my sublime love, my radiant lover. I revere your courage and devotion, but I am hurt in my tenderest feelings when I see you delivered over to the beasts of an arena a thousand times less discriminating than that of ancient Rome. Therefore, my beloved Victor, I have conceived a loathing, not only for your antagonists, but also for the form of government which imposes this Sisyphus life upon you. If I had the power to change it, I can assure you I should not hesitate, even if I had to deprive you for ever of your rights of citizenship. Unfortunately, I can do nothing beyond cordially detesting those who obstruct your work. I pity you, bless you, admire you, and love you with all my soul.

JULIETTE.

Saturday, 3 p.m., June 29th, 1850.

I have just watched you go with inexpressible sadness, my sweet and beautiful beloved. With you have departed the sunshine, the flowers, the pleasant thoughts, the hopes that link past happiness with future bliss. Nought remains to me but my love, a poor hermit whose regrets have been her sole bedfellows this long time. When you turned the corner of the street, something luminous, soft, and sweet, seemed to die within me. From that moment I have been as depressed and desolate as if a great misfortune had befallen me. Alas, it is in fact the misfortune that weighs down my whole life, namely, your absence. Since politics have monopolised your time, happiness has eluded my grasp. Will it ever return? I doubt it, hence my despair. I am greatly to be commiserated, my beloved, in that I have constituted your eyes my illumination, your smile my joy, your words my bliss, your love my life—so that when you are away, all these are simultaneously snatched from me. I am not certain of seeing you to-night, still less to-morrow. What is to become of me? What am I to do with this poor body bereft of its soul when you are not by? Tell me if you can. Explain if you dare. Meanwhile, I adore you.

JULIETTE.

Monday, 10 p.m., July 7th, 1851.

What I had foreseen has happened, my beloved, even sooner and more painfully than I had feared. Does this fresh crisis foreshadow my speedy recovery? I dare not hope it, for I feel that my disease is incurable. I tell you so in the frankness of my despair. I neither can nor will deceive you, beloved, and my anxiety, far from diminishing, augments with every minute. I am suffering the torment of the most humiliating and poignant jealousy. I know that for seven years you have *adored* a woman you think beautiful, witty and accomplished.[100] I know that but for her sudden treachery,[101] she would still be your preferred mistress. I know that you introduced her into your family-circle, that she is of your world, that you can meet her at any moment, that you promised her you would continue your intimacy with her, at all events outwardly. All this I know—yet you expect me to feel my own position secure! Surely I should need to be idiotic or insane to do that. Alas, I happen to be instead a very clear-sighted, miserable woman.

Midnight.

Beloved, thanks to you and thanks to your tender perseverance and inexhaustible kindness, I am once more, and this time for ever I hope, the sensible, sanguine, happy Juju of the good old days. But if I am to be quite as I was then, you must suffer no longer, my little man—you must be as strong as three Turks, and love me as much as a hundred Swiss-guards. On those conditions I shall be happy! happy!! happy!!!, but pending that great day, try to sleep soundly to-night, not to be unwell to-morrow, and to forgive me for loving you too much.

JULIETTE.

Saturday, 8 p.m., July 26th, 1851.

I trust you, my beloved, and believe everything you say. I yield my soul to the hopes of happiness you have held out to me. My heart is full of love and security. I love you, I am happy, I am at peace, I forget all I have suffered. I remember only the tender, loyal, encouraging words you uttered just now. Felicity has succeeded despair—I quit hell and enter Paradise. I love you and you love me, nothing can be sad any more. You will see how I shall resume my interest in life, how I shall smile, how happy I shall be, and what confidence I shall have in you. I do not know whether we shall be able to carry out all the adorable plans you sketched just now, but I experienced great happiness in anticipation while I watched you making them, and knew myself so closely associated with them. I felt as if all my past sorrows were transfigured into happiness to come. I listened, and my heart was filled with joy. Thank you, my Victor, thank you, my beloved. Do not be anxious about me any more; now that you love me I shall get well. I shall be happy again, you will see. I am beginning already, so as to lose no time in rewarding you for your goodness and gentleness and patience. I am awaiting you with my sweetest smiles, my tenderest caresses.

JULIETTE.

Monday, 12.45 p.m., July 28th, 1851.

This is the hour I begin to expect you, my Victor; each second that lags past with the slowness of eternity crushes my hopes as quickly as I conceive them. What is to become of me all this wretched day if I may not see you? Oh, I thought myself stronger, braver, more resigned; but now I see I have used up all my strength in the horrible struggle I have been going through this last month. What will happen to me, shut up here, all alone with that terrible anniversary, the 28th June, 1851? How can I evade its ghastly grip, how keep myself from suicide, from the desperate hankering after death? Oh, God, how I suffer! I implore you, do not leave me alone here to-d....[102]

Midnight.

This letter, which was begun in delirium and mad jealousy has ended, thanks to you my ineffable beloved, in the happy calm of confidence and the sacred joy of love shared. May you be blest, my Victor, as much as you are respected, venerated, adored, and admired by me—then you will have nothing further to desire in this world or the next.

JULIETTE.

Saturday, 8 a.m., August 2nd, 1851.

Good morning, man that I love; good morning, with all my joy and smiles and soul and happiness and love, if you had a good night and are well. I felt sure your dear Charles' depression could not stand against an hour of your gentle and persuasive philosophy. You have the marvellous art of extracting good from evil, and consolation from despair, and there is irresistible magic in your eyes and smile; your every word is full of seduction. I, who only linger in this life in the hope of seeing you every day, should know something of that. What the joys of eternity in Paradise may be I cannot tell, but I would sacrifice them all for one minute of your true love. My Victor, my Victor, I love you. You will see how sensible I am going to be, and how I shall give way to all the exigencies of your work, and the consideration required by your position as a political personage. I am ready, my Victor; dispose of me how you will; whether happy or unhappy, I shall bless you. I trust the bad atmosphere you were compelled to breathe for several hours yesterday did not injure your throat. I am eagerly awaiting this afternoon to learn this, and to see you. Until then, I love you, I love you, I love you.

JULIETTE.

Friday morning, September 12th, 1851.

Good morning, and forgive me my poor sweet beloved, for nothing was further from my thoughts than to torment you as I involuntarily did yesterday. My foolishness does not include malice, and I respect you even in my most violent bouts of despair. Besides, you had just been telling me something that ought to increase my clinging to life, namely, my responsibility for your tranquillity, your fortune, your genius and existence. Without accepting in its entirety this exaggerated view of my own importance in the grave situation you find yourself in, my persecuted love, I have grasped that I should be unworthy of the position, were I to allow my troubles to weigh in the balance, against your safety. Therefore, my Victor, you have nothing to fear from me, so long as my poor brain retains a glimmer of reason, and my wretched heart a scrap of confidence in your loyalty.

I spent part of the night reading over your old letters, especially those of *May 1844*,[103] and I shed more tears over your desecrated tenderness and sullied affection, than you can have squandered kisses upon that woman, during the seven years of your treachery to me. If life could escape through the eyes, my sufferings would long ere this be terminated; but like sorrow, the soul is not so quickly exhausted, though God only knows where it finds sustenance. As for me, my adored one, I love you without being able either to live or to be healed. I am ashamed of my incurability, and I gratefully compassionate the superhuman efforts you make to restore me to courage.

JULIETTE.

Thursday, 10.45 p.m., October 23rd, 1851.

You know my dear little man, that I need no encouragement to give way to epistolary intemperance. When time permits, I am always ready to fling myself unrestrainedly into a sea of lucubrations without sense or end. But this time I have more than a mere pretext for giving rein to my harmless mania; I have two days full of the most radiant joy and happiness that could befall a woman who lives only by and for her love. Whole volumes would not suffice to enumerate and describe them, and even your sublime genius would not be too great to express the splendid poetry of them. I felt as if a little winged soul sprang from each one of our embraces and flew heavenward with cries of jubilation and joy. Your love penetrated my soul and warmed it, as the rays of the sun pierce through the fogs and melancholy of autumn, and reach the earth to console it and lay the blessed seed of hope within her womb. I rejoiced in the bliss, watered by tears, that precedes and follows love and sunshine, in that season of life and nature. Though my heart is bestrewn with the dead leaves of past illusions, I feel new sap rising within it, which awaits only your vivifying breath to bring forth the flowers and fruits of love.

My adored Victor, my soul overflows with the accumulated joys of those two days of life by your side under the eye of God. I relieve myself as best I can by pouring out the surplus of my enchantment upon this paper. Sleep well, my adored one, I love you and bless you.

JULIETTE.

Thursday, 8 a.m., November 6th, 1851.

Good morning, my sweetheart, my adored one. I wish my kisses had wings, that you might find them on your pillow at your awakening. If you only knew how much I love you, you would understand that for me there is life, heart, and soul, only in you, by you, and for you. Yesterday when I passed your old house in the Place Royale, all the memories of our love and happiness awoke again within me. I stood awhile before it, caressing its threshold with my eyes, fingering the knocker, pushing the door ajar to peer in, as I should look at the inside of a reliquary, or touch some sacred object. Then I went into the garden to gaze up at the windows whence you sometimes looked down upon me. I wandered all about the district in the same sweet, sad tremor I experience when I read over your old love-letters. I traced our past happiness upon every stone of the pavement, at every street-corner, on the shop-signs—everywhere I found memories of our kisses among those surroundings where I enjoyed happiness for so long, where you loved me and I adored you—where, eight years ago, I would gladly have lain me down to die if God had left me the choice.

JULIETTE.

BRUSSELS,
Wednesday, 1 p.m., December 17th, 1851.

Beloved one, I wish the first sheet of paper I use, the first word I write, in this hospitable country, to be a message of love from me to you. It is surely the least I can do, since my every thought, my life and heart and soul, pass through you before reaching the common objects of this world and returning to me. Is it indeed possible that you are safe, my poor treasure, and that I have nothing further to fear for your life or liberty? Is it true that you love me, and that you deign to rely upon me in the difficult passages of life? Is it conceivable that I am henceforth happy and blest among women, and that I have the right to raise my head and bask openly in the sunlight of love and self-sacrifice! Ah, God, I thank Thee for all the gifts and joys and blessings Thou dost bestow upon me to-day, in the revered and adored person of my sublime beloved! All my efforts shall be directed towards deserving them more and more. All my gratitude is for Thee, my God!

JULIETTE.

BRUSSELS,
Wednesday, 3.30 p.m., December 17th, 1851.

Do not worry about me, my beloved, for I never love you better or more tranquilly than when I know you are attending to your family duties and busying yourself with securing the peace and comfort of your wife and children. Pray devote yourself entirely to the service of your noble wife for the time of her sojourn here. Do not deny her any of the little pleasures that may divert her mind from the heavy trials she has just undergone. Let my resignation and courage, my consideration and devotion, help to smooth the rough places of life for her as long as she remains with you. Give her all the consolation and joy in your power. Lavish upon her the respect and affection she deserves, and do not fear ever to wear out my patience and trust in you.

I see you coming my adored one. Bless you.

JULIETTE.

BRUSSELS,
Monday, 3.30 p.m., January 19th, 1852.

I had set myself a task, beloved, before writing to you, in order to earn that sweet reward. I have just completed it, and without further delay I proceed with my insignificant vapourings, in the intervals of copying two most interesting stories. I am not writing for your benefit, but for the pleasure it gives me to babble a few tender words to you in default of the kisses and caresses I cannot give you at this distance.

My Victor, as you do not wish me to be sad, and hate to feel that I am unhappy, and dread the sight of my pain, you must adopt the habit of telling me everything frankly and under all circumstances. Your deceptions, however trivial and kindly meant, hurt me far more than the harshest of truths (if you were capable of harshness towards any creature). I declare this without bitterness and in the form of an appeal, my beloved. Do not hide anything from me. Try to manage that your answers to the admiring letters certain women address to you, should be written at my house rather than elsewhere. Do not delay telling me things until I have guessed them for myself, or circumstances have betrayed them. No hints can be unimportant where jealousy is concerned, and there is no happiness without complete confidence. Therefore, my beloved, I implore you with all the urgency my soul is capable of, to tell me everything—even the ownership of those *opera glasses*, and about the *Hügelmann* notes, of which I have several here, forwarded from Belle-Île, and certain names and addresses; and about those actresses you protect with so much solicitude, and the machinations of the bluestockings who apply to you for mysterious nocturnal interviews, under pretext of enlisting your pity or your literary sympathy—about Mdlle. Constance, too, in spite of her significant name and reassuring age. I want to know everything—I must know everything, if you are really concerned for my peace of mind, and health, and happiness. Then I shall become calm, patient, happy; my pulse will beat evenly, I shall grow fat and smiling. Does not all that make it worth while for you to be frank, loyal, and ever faithful towards me?

JULIETTE.

BRUSSELS,
Monday, 1 p.m., March 22nd, 1852.

You may give me something to copy for you now if you like. I have nearly finished that foolish scrawl, so if you want to utilise my time, you can send me anything you like. I am quite at your disposal. Meanwhile, I am mending your underlinen and my own, and watching the clouds sail above my narrow horizon. I envy them without having the courage to follow their example and allow myself to be driven by chance winds or caprice. I am too lazy, bodily and mentally, to move. I recline in my chimney corner, cosily humped up, and my soul lies torpid within me. I am not exactly unhappy, neither am I sad in the true meaning of the word—but I am uneasy and depressed. I feel a threatening influence in the atmosphere about me. What it is, I cannot precisely say, but I am under some evil thrall. I am sure there is a mystery between us that you are trying to conceal, and that fate will force me to discover sooner or later. Perhaps it would be safer not to try to hide things from me—it would certainly be more loyal and generous; but as neither prayers nor tears can induce you to give me your full confidence, I will await my fate with resignation. After all, as long as you arrange your life to suit your own feelings and tastes, I have no right to complain. I have never meant to force myself upon you in any case; therefore, my Victor, whatever happens, you may be sure I shall place no obstacle in the way of your happiness and glory. I love you with all the pride of my inferiority.

JULIETTE.

BRUSSELS,
Sunday morning, July 18th, 1852.

Good-morning, my Victor. I will do exactly as you like. So long as my love is not called into question, what does it matter how, and when, my body changes its *habitat* and moves from Brussels to Jersey? Therefore, my

Victor, I make no objection to starting at the same time as you. Between the pain of a twenty-four hours' separation, and the mortification of travelling with you as a total stranger, my poor heart would find it hard to choose. It is quite natural that I should sacrifice myself to appearances, and respect the presence of your sons by this painful incognito, but it seems cruelly unjust and ironical that it should be required of my devotion and fidelity and love, when it was never thought of in the case of that other woman, whose sole virtue consisted in possessing none. For her, the family doors were always open, the deference and courteous protection of your sons exacted; your wife extended to her the cloak of her consideration, and accepted her as a friend, a sister, and more. For her, indulgence, sympathy, affection—for me, the rigorous application of all the penalties contained in the code of prejudice, hypocrisy, and immorality. Honours for the shameless vices of the society lady—only indignities for the poor creature who sins through honest devotion and love. It is quite simple. Society must be considered. I will leave for Jersey when and how you will.

I am quite ready to copy for Charles. I fear he may find my bad writing more tiresome than useful, but I shall do my best, and I will get some better pens. He had better send me the manuscript as soon as possible. From now till then I am, my Victor, at your absolute disposal.

JULIETTE.

JERSEY,
Thursday, 9 a.m., December 2nd, 1852.

Good morning, my divine, adored love. When one considers what the infamous trap laid for you on December 2nd has inspired you to write, one is tempted to give thanks to Providence. It almost seems as if that dastardly crime had been committed for the aggrandisement of your renown, and the better instruction of the nations. I do not think any scoundrel will ever be found bold enough to repeat the offence, after reading your fulminating poems. Just a year ago, on this day and at this hour, I learnt the news of the *Coup d'état* through poor Dillon. Knowing how closely it concerned me, the worthy creature rushed to my house from the Faubourg St. Germain to warn me, and place her services at my disposal, which meant at yours, for she is a brave, noble woman. From that moment until the day I received your dear letter from Brussels announcing your safety, I lived in a state of nightmare. I only woke again to life and happiness when I found myself in your arms on the morning of December 14th in the Customs shed at Brussels. Since then, my beloved Victor, my sublime Victor, I have never let a day pass without thanking God for rescuing you so miraculously, nor have I ceased for one minute to admire and adore you.

JULIETTE.

DRAWING BY VICTOR HUGO, SIGNED "TOTO."
Unpublished, belonging to the Author.

THE FLOWER AND THE BUTTERFLY.
Drawing by Victor Hugo for Juliette (Victor Hugo Museum).

Good morning, my life, my soul, my joy, my happiness.

Dear adored one, from yesterday until the 14th of this month, there is not a moment that does not recall to me the dangers you were exposed to a year ago,[104] and the terrors and inexpressible anguish I endured all through those awful ten days. A year ago, at this very hour of the morning, you stood in the Faubourg St. Antoine, alone, holding and challenging a frantic mob lost to all sense of reason and restraint. I can see you now, my poor beloved, calling upon the soldiers to remember their duty and their honour, threatening the generals, withering them with your contempt. You were terrible and sublime. You might have been the Genius of France witnessing in an agony of bitter despair, the accomplishment of the most cowardly and despicable of crimes. It is an absolute miracle that you escaped alive from that spot which echoed with the solitary force of your heroic fury. When I think of it I still feel terrified and dazzled.

JULIETTE.

Good morning, my poor flayed, mutilated darling. How I pitied you yesterday during the long-drawn-out massacre of your masterpiece,[105] which however, like an Immortal, emerged from the ordeal finer and in better fettle than ever. As for me, my treasure, I could only admire and envy your heroic impassivity in the face of that frightful profanation. I could hardly sit still, so vexed and irritated did I feel at the audacity of those wretched strolling mountebanks. Yet Heaven knows how hard they must have worked to be even as ridiculous as they were. One cannot be really angry with them, but it is impossible to recall them individually without laughing till the tears run down one's cheeks. That is what I have been doing ever since I came out of that horrible little theatre, for I did not sleep very much. My thoughts were busy with you, my adored one; I was seeing you again in imagination, handsome, young, triumphant, as you were at the original performance of your *Angélo.* I felt all the tenderness and adoration of those old days surging up again in my heart.

JULIETTE.

Good morning, my too-dearly loved little man. I am cleverer than you, for I do not need lenses, paper, chemicals, and sunshine, to reproduce you in every form within my heart. Love is a splendid stereoscope; it throws all the photographs and daguerreotypes in the world, into the shade. It can even, if the need exist, convert black jealousy into white confidence, and force into relief the smallest modicum of happiness, the slightest mark of love. That being so, I hardly know why I desire so ardently to multiply your dear little pictures around me, unless it is that I wish to compare them with those of my inner shrine. Whatever be the reason, I do implore you, my dear little man, to give me one as soon as possible; it will be such a pleasure to me. Meanwhile my poor persecuted hero, I cannot tell what trials the future may have in store for you, but as long as a breath of life remains within me, I mean to expend it in defending, guarding, and serving you. My faith in the power of my love amounts to superstition; I feel that so long as I care for you, nothing irretrievably bad can happen to you. This is neither pride nor fatuousness on my part; it is a sort of intuition that comes to me, I think, from Heaven above.

JULIETTE.

JERSEY,
9 p.m., Thursday, January 6th, 1853.

If the soul could take visible shape, you would perceive mine at this moment, my sweet adored one, bending over you and smiling. If kisses had wings, you would feel them swooping about your dear little person in clouds, like joyous birds upon a beautiful flowering bush. Unfortunately, my soul and kisses have to pass and repass before you invisible, and perhaps even unsuspected by you. But that does not deter me, and I am drawn irresistibly to you by the need of living in your atmosphere. My thoughts sit boldly at your side wherever you are. However my chastened personality may bend under the contempt and disdain of the world, my love rears itself proudly in the consciousness of its superiority. While you leave my body standing outside, it enters hardily with you and leaves you not. This may not be very tactful of me, but it is the mark of an ardent and loyal heart. And after all we are living "on an Island." I can see you, making eyes at your neighbour on the left, and signalling to the one opposite. I want you to be mine absolutely, body and soul, and I do not mean to share one little bit of you with anybody. You must make up your mind to that, and content yourself with enjoying the cosmopolitan cookery of that Hungarian Lucullus.[106] I will allow you to gorge like four Englishmen and drink like one Pole, but I shall not take my eyes off you and shall watch your every movement. I think you laugh a great deal for a grave man with a handsome mouth, and your hands are enough to bring a blush of envy to the paws of all those exiled females! They suffer by comparison—so much the better! Hold your tongue, drink, turn your head my way at once, and keep it there.

JERSEY,
Tuesday, 12.30 p.m., February 1st, 1853.

I really mean what I said just now, my dear little boy. Instead of posing interminably in front of the daguerreotype,[107] you could quite well have taken me for a walk if you had wanted to. Anyhow, pretexts for keeping away from me will never fail you, and the fine weather will now add many to those already on your list. Therefore I ask you in all good faith, what use am I to you in this island, apart from my functions of copyist? I do not wish to reopen this eternal discussion in which you never tell me the truth, yet I shall never cease to protest against a state of things so foreign to true love, and so little conducive to my happiness. And now, my dear little man, you may amuse yourself, and make daguerreotypes, and enjoy the glorious sunshine in your own way. I, for my part, shall make use of solitude, desertion, and shadow, to bring to a head an attack of depression which will easily develop into a great big sorrow. I shall study how to make the most of it. Meanwhile I smile prettily at you, after the fashion of a stage dancer executing the final pirouette which has exhausted her strength and left her breathless. Brrrr.... Long live Toto! Long live worries and all their kith and kin! Long live love!

JULIETTE.

JERSEY,
Thursday, 9 p.m., April 28th, 1853.

I come to you, my beloved, as you are unable to return to me this evening. I come to tell you I love you without regret for the past or fear for the future. I come to you with a smile on my lips and a blessing in my bosom, with my hand upon my mutilated heart and my eyes full of pardon, with my purity restored and my soul redeemed by twenty years of fidelity and love, with my delusions swept away and my faith shining. I come to you without rancour, sustained by divine hope. I come with the maternal devotion and the passionate tenderness of a lover, with a mind instinct with reverence and admiration, a resignation and piety like to those of God's martyrs, and I constitute you the supreme arbiter of my fate. Do with me what you will in this life, so long as you take me with you in the next. I sacrifice my feelings to the virtue of your wife and the innocence of your daughter, as a homage and a safeguard, and I reserve my prayers and tears for poor fallen women like myself. Lastly, my adored one, I give you my share of Paradise in exchange for your chances of hell, considering myself fortunate to have purchased your eternal bliss with my eternal love.

JULIETTE.

Whatever you may say, my sweet one, to retard the gradual cessation of my daily yarns, you cannot stay the progress of the natural law, even when assisted by my passive submission to your will. Why continue this custom of writing to you twice a day, when the pretext for doing so has faded from our joint lives? If I were a woman of parts, I could substitute imagination and shrewd observation for love-making; but as these are entirely lacking in me, I have nothing to record in those bulletins where kisses and caresses once occupied the chief place. Now, when I have said good morning and alluded to the state of the weather, I have nothing more to say, because I am stupid. Your influence alone can extract what is in my heart. For this reason, my dear one, these scribbles became blank and aimless, from the moment the happiness that once dictated them began to die away and degenerate into a friendship despoiled of all pleasure and voluptuousness. I do not reproach you, my adored one, any more than I reproach myself for not being still the woman you loved beyond everything—still it might be better to discontinue this daily record of the change, and to give up the piteous babblings which no longer have even the excuse of wit.

JULIETTE.

How one's brain scintillates from living for ever within four walls! What sparkling and varied incidents one experiences in this existence of a squirrel in a cage! For my part I am so inspired by it that I hardly know where to commence. Let us, therefore, proceed in due sequence; my cat, which has been slumbering for the last two hours on its right ear, has just turned over on to its left.

Père Nicotte, abandoning the ploughshare, announces for Thursday, September 29th, the sale by auction of three fat hogs, a sow with her eight sucking pigs, three yearling bulls, another rising two, and other items too numerous and too peculiar to enumerate.

Births: August 5th. Blanche Laura, daughter of Mr. Harper Richard Hugo.

The annual dinner of the Society will take place on the above-mentioned day. Those intending to be present, and those proposing to furnish fruit for the same, are urgently requested to send in their names on or before the preceding Saturday.

What more do you want? Eleven pigs, not including the sow, three yearling bulls, not including the one rising two, a daughter of your own, and permission to invite yourself to a dinner of the Society, and even to furnish the fruit for it. If all this does not attract you and stir the very marrow of your bones, and tempt your appetite, you must be dead to the promptings of sensibility, paternity, and sensuality. In that case, go to bed and to sleep, and leave me to myself—the more so, as I do not happen to possess an accommodating table,[108] to furnish me with ready-made apparitions. Remember, I have to be my own Dante, Æsop, and Shakspere, whereas you catch the dead fish that the spirits of the other world attach to your lines—a proceeding practised in the Mediterranean long before those tittle-tattling tables were thought of. Pray accept my most tender sentiments.

JULIETTE.

JERSEY,
Sunday, 10 a.m., January 1st, 1854.

I love you so much, my darling, that I cannot find anything else to say to you. My poor spirit is ready to give way under the weight of too much love, like a bough bending under an abnormal show of fruit; but my heart has strength enough to bear without flinching the infinite tenderness, admiration, and adoration I feel for you.

What a letter, my adored one! I read it with my heart in my eyes. It seemed to penetrate word by word like sun-rays into the very marrow of my bones. My Victor, your hopes are mine, your will, mine, your faith, mine; I am what you deserve that I should be; I live only for you and in you. To love you, serve you, reverence you, adore you, are my only aspirations in this world. Where you are, I shall be; where you struggle, I shall watch; when you suffer I shall pray, when you are threatened I will defend you, save you, or die. I tell you all this pell-mell and anyhow, my adored Victor, for it is impossible for me to discipline my thoughts when they fly in your direction—they are less amenable to common sense than to my heart and soul, which are in ecstasy since this morning. I know not what trials may still be in store for you, my sublime, persecuted love, but I can answer for my own courage and devotion to you. Like you I associate our two angels with all my prayers and hopes and joys and love. I constitute them your guardian angels and to them I confide your life, that is, mine, your heart, that is, my happiness. I send you enough kisses to make a connecting-rod from my mouth to yours.

JULIETTE.

GUERNSEY,
Monday, 7.30 p.m., July 21st, 1856.

It shall not be said that your adored name ever appeared before me in its dazzling nimbus without being saluted by my heart with a triple salvo of love, oh, my dearly beloved, and without the outpouring of all the perfume of my soul at your divine feet. Although I am very tired, almost ill, I cannot let this day pass without giving you my tenderest, sweetest, most love-laden greetings. Others may bring you flowers and pay you handsome compliments, but I offer you twenty-three years of tried fidelity free of human stain. It is all I have to bestow—it may be insignificant, but it is my all. Such a thing cannot be bought; it is accounted among the treasures of God. In His keeping you will find it, when the gifts of Heaven shall replace those of Earth. Meanwhile, to show you that I still belong to this sphere, I send you my beautiful violet robe brocaded with gold; but I specially stipulate that it should form part of the decoration of your own room, rather than that you should hang it in the gallery. Still, if you prefer to use it elsewhere I leave you free to do as you like, for your pleasure is my sole desire. You must not imagine that my generosity is entirely disinterested, because that would be a great mistake. I am sure you would not wish to remain in my debt, and that you will therefore give me a little drawing for your birthday. This is my request—now bring me your cheeks that I may kiss them without stint, and do be discreet to-night with the women who will come to offer you birthday greetings! Keep your heart entire and intact for me.

JULIETTE.

GUERNSEY,
Friday, 1.45 p.m., December 12th, 1856.

Adored one, I am sending Suzanne to get news of your dear little sick child.[109] Although night is coming on, I hope I may get a good report; this weather is enough to give an attack of nerves to anybody at all disposed that way. You saw Suzanne yourself, my darling, yet someone is knocking—fancy if it should be you! It is! What happiness!

How good, how ineffably good you are, dear kind father, to have come yourself to reassure me about the little feverish symptoms that are beginning to show themselves to-night in your little girl's condition. Let us hope they will yield to remedies this time, and that the night may prove more calm and satisfactory than the day just passed. Meanwhile thank you with all my heart, thank you with all my soul, for allowing me to share your family hopes and fears and joys and troubles. Thank you. If God hears and grants my prayers, as I trust with sacred confidence He will, your adored child will soon be restored to health and happiness.

JULIETTE.

GUERNSEY,
Monday, 7.30 p.m., April 13th, 1857.

If you say another word I shall seize them all,[110] so there! I shall certainly not place my house, my rooms, my old age, my tables, chairs, carpets, water, ink, my virtue, great and small, at your disposal, to be rewarded by seeing masterpieces pass under my very nose on their way to Teleki, Mademoiselle Alix, and other trollops of her calibre. I must have some too; castles, moonlight scenes, sunrises, and fog effects. If you are not prepared for a quarrel, you must give me at least my share. Ah, here you come! I am not sorry to see you....

JULIETTE.

JERSEY,
Saturday, 4 p.m., July 1st, 1857.

Darling beloved, I begin my letter in the hope of its being interrupted shortly, and completed this evening with a lighter heart; but I so need to love you that I must take the initiative, my adored one. I have just read the sad, tender poems you gave me to copy. I see you coming....

8.45 p.m.

I have just finished copying those adorable verses, so poignant through their very restraint,[111] and I weep for my own grief as well as yours, my poor afflicted friends. The shadow which has fallen across your lives is black night in my case, for all the radiant joys of family life were wiped out with the death of my only child. When I think of my forlorn infancy bereft of father and mother, and of what my deathbed will be, without the loving tears of a child of my own, I feel as if a curse were laid upon me for the expiation of some hideous crime. Yet, oh God, I am not ungrateful to Thee, far from it; I feel indeed with the deepest gratitude of heart and soul how good Thou art! May you be as greatly blest as you are loved by me, my Victor. You are divinely grand and sublime. I kiss your dear little feet and your angel's wings. I worship you on my knees.

JULIETTE.

JERSEY,
Tuesday, 2.30 p.m., July 2nd, 1857.

Yes, since you wish to hear it, I love you, my little man; but I could demonstrate it much more intelligently by working something for you on canvas, than by daubing this poor little sheet of paper with hieroglyphics. If perchance death should surprise us before you have destroyed these crude ebullitions of my heart, inquisitive folk will experience keen disappointment; they will find it difficult to distinguish the traces of an overmastering passion in such a petty mind as mine. I hope you will be provident enough and generous enough to spare me this humiliation beyond the grave, by burning gradually all those poor letters that are so ineffective the moment they have crossed the threshold of my soul. Meanwhile I continue to obey you with entire submission, and my love for you is greater than your genius—that is to say, I love you, love you, love you, without being able to find anything to compare with the magnitude of my infatuation.

JULIETTE.

GUERNSEY,
Saturday, 8 p.m., December 19th, 1857.

Although unwell and fatigued, my beloved Victor, I cannot leave this little home where we have loved each other, without penning a grateful farewell for all the felicity it has sheltered during the year I have lived in it. I trust I may be as happy in my beautiful new house as I have been here in my hovel. The sadness I feel to-day is nearer akin to nerves than to real sorrow. Please forgive it, my adored Victor, if you have misunderstood and thought for a single instant that you were to blame for it. Far from reproaching you for the difficulties of my situation, I admire your ineffable kindness and bless you from the bottom of my heart for all the trouble you are taking to house me handsomely. It was difficult, but of what are you not capable when you set your mind to a thing? I think without affecting the false modesty of a collector, that you have succeeded, and I thank you with all the strength of my loving soul, which asks no better than to be happy in the new paradise you have just prepared for me.

JULIETTE.

GUERNSEY,
Friday, 11 a.m., July 16th, 1858.

My beloved, my beloved, my beloved, what sin have we committed that God should strike us so cruelly in your health and my love! Unless it be a crime to love you too much, I do not feel guilty of aught. What shall I do, my God, what will become of me! Victor ill and away from me! I dread lest, as I write, you should almost hear my sobs and guess at my despair, from these reckless words.

I had anticipated this trouble and thought myself able to face it. I know it is imperatively necessary that you should remain at home, yet my whole being rebels at this separation as at a cruel injustice, and the greatest misfortune of my life. Why, why, why am I like this, oh, my God? Yet I possess courage, Thou knowest! Thou knowest also that I desire his speedy recovery and love him with a devoted, illimitable love. My adored Victor!

Why then, is the reason of this gloomy and profound despair which robs me of strength and reason? Oh, God, dost Thou hate me? Have my offences been graver than those of other women like me, that Thou shouldst chastise me so mercilessly! Oh, I suffer, Victor, I love you, I am wretched!

JULIETTE.

GUERNSEY,
Saturday, Noon, July 24th, 1858.

Another short spell of courage and patience, my poor gentle martyr, and your deliverance will be complete. The doctor has just assured me so. I shall soon be able to rejoice at your convalescence without the poignant dread of a frightful disaster mingling itself with my joy. In the delirious delight this good news gave me, I kissed the doctor's kindly hands, which have become sacred to me since they have ministered to you. The poor man was surprised and moved by my emotion, and looked quite embarrassed—almost shy of my gratitude—but I was proud of it. Why should not a woman kiss the hands that have saved the life of the man she adores, when so many men kiss the idle fingers of the women who betray them.

Rosalie arrived a few minutes after the doctor, to fetch your egg, and found me weeping and smiling. I explained the reason to her. The girl has surprised me in tears so often that I fear she will take me for a cry-baby by temperament, though God knows, I do not lay claim to hyper-sensitiveness. But how could I have remained calm during your long, painful illness. For, my beloved, one can afford to admit now, that you have been in grave danger the last twelve days. Happily all is over, you are saved and I thank God on my knees and adore you.

JULIETTE.

GUERNSEY,
Wednesday morning, August 4th, 1858.

At last, at last, at last, beloved, I have reached the blessed moment when I shall see you again! I am so happy that words and breath fail me. Oh, my adored one, how have I managed to live so far away and separated from you for so long! Three weeks ago I should have thought such a sacrifice beyond my strength, yet to-day I am almost afraid I am seeing you too soon; for my solicitude takes fright at the idea of any imprudence that might augment or prolong the sufferings you have only just overcome. The worthy doctor assures me there is no risk for you in the short walk from your house to mine, but I have been so wretched during your illness, and I love you so much, that my heart knows not to whom to hearken. My beloved, my joy, my life, my happiness, be prudent! I adore you, I await you, my love.

JULIETTE.

GUERNSEY,
Monday, 8 a.m., June 13th, 1859.

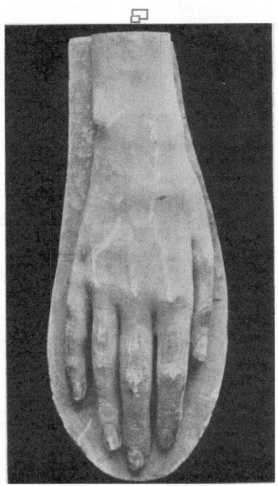

JULIETTE DROUET'S HAND.

Good morning, my adored one. I say it with all the tenderness which had to be disguised owing to the presence of your kind and charming son, during the lovely fortnight we have spent at Sark. Everything there was a feast for mind and heart. One thing only was lacking for my complete happiness; freedom to love you aloud and in all frankness. Now there need be no obstacle to the passionate expansion of my soul, but it is in the silence and solitude of my house, without the joys, smiles, sparkling wit, and poetical atmosphere you and your son spread before my dazzled eyes, during the splendid fortnight I spent with you both; so true is it that one cannot have everything at the same time here below, and that perfect happiness is attained only in Heaven. But while our two souls are travelling thither, the one assisting the other, I am grateful to God for the radiant fortnight He has just given me. I thank Him with a full heart, and beseech Him to repay you and your dear Charles with as many fruitful and glorious years as you have given me days of happiness in the tender intimacy of Sark. As usual, my words are inadequate to express my feelings, but you will understand, my beloved, and restore the balance between the two.

I hope you spent a good night, my sweet love. I am waiting for you to give you as many kisses as you are able to carry. Until then I adore you with all my soul.

Tuesday, June 14th.

May God preserve you from all evil, my beloved, and permit my love and blessing to constitute the whole happiness of your life.

JULIETTE.

GUERNSEY,
Thursday, 4.30 p.m., February 16th, 1860.

You sat at this very spot just now, my sweet love, writing in my little red book, (record of our love), the very things my own heart feels and would have dictated to you, could it have spoken aloud—so certain is it that my life belongs absolutely to you, and that my thoughts take birth from your glances. Like you, I have faith in our radiant future in the life beyond; like you, I pray to die as near you as possible, cradled in your arms, whenever it please Heaven. If I hearkened only to the voice of my selfishness, I should plead that it might be now, but I am too conscious of the sublime mission you are called upon to accomplish towards humanity in this world, to dare put up such an impious petition. I will wait bravely, patiently, reverently, in prayer and adoration, until it please God to call us unto Himself.

Thursday evening, 7.30.

I resume my scribble where I left it when you came back this afternoon, my darling beloved—not to add anything of value, but to continue for my own pleasure the sweet dialogue between my heart and my love. I thank you for our dear twenty-seventh anniversary, which you made memorable by words so luminous and a tenderness so penetrating and sacred. I thank you for myself, whose pride and joy and veneration you are; I thank you on behalf of my nephew and his family, for the immense honour you have conferred upon them by writing to their son. Lastly, my beloved, I kiss your feet, your hands, your lips, your eyes, your brow, and I only cease through fear of wearying you by this over-flow of caresses.

I love you.

JULIETTE.

MONT ST. JEAN,
Monday, 8 p.m., June 17th, 1861.

Dearly beloved. Whilst you are expanding among the tender delights of family life, I am invoking all my physical and moral strength to prevent myself giving way under the sadness of your absence. As long as my eyes could distinguish the omnibus, that is to say, as far as the *Betterave Renaissante,* I watched your progress along the Gronendael road. Beyond that point, I was forced to relinquish the sweet illusion that I could still see the dear little black speck on the horizon, and to acknowledge that nothing lay before me but the endless void of your twenty-four hours' absence. So, as I did not know what to do with myself or how to kill time, I walked by a fairly easy field-path as far as the church at Waterloo, and came back by way of the village, without however visiting the church, notwithstanding the pressing invitation of an old woman who called me her dear friend. I got back to the hotel at six o'clock precisely, and spent the half hour before dinner freshening myself up by washing from head to foot; then I put on a dressing-gown and went down to our little dining-room, where I ate without hunger and drank without thirst, so dismal and forlorn am I when you are no longer present. I must have been pretty fully convinced of the impossibility of accompanying you to Brussels without exposing your movements to undesirable criticism, to accept the sad alternative of remaining here alone. But that certainty is no comfort whatever, and I am just as miserable as if it had been in my power to make the expedition with you. Certainly, human respect is a horrid beast, more malevolent and worrying than even midges and their poisonous sting, and all the ammonia in the world is powerless against it.

I am well fitted to make the comparison seeing that my arm is already healed, while my heart suffers more and more. Dear adored one, do try, on your part, to spend profitably this interval which is costing me so dear. Be happy; I love you, bless you, and adore you.

JULIETTE.

GUERNSEY,
Tuesday, 8 a.m., February 17th, 1863.

Good morning, my beloved. In full daylight and glorious sunshine, in love and happiness, good morning. Again I greet you, like that first day thirty years ago, when my eyes followed you along the Boulevard after you left me. My soul winged flights of kisses to you when you looked round for one more glance at my window before turning into the Rue du Temple. That picture remains for ever graven upon my mind; I can assert with truth that everything remains the same in my heart as the night I first became yours. These thirty years of love have passed like one day of uninterrupted adoration, and I feel now younger, more virile, and more capable of loving you, than ever before—heart, body, soul, all are yours, and live only by you and through you. I smile upon you, bless you, adore you.

JULIETTE.

GUERNSEY,
Sunday, 10.30 a.m., April 26th, 1863.

Good morning, unutterably dear one. May all the blessings of heaven and earth rest upon you and those you love. I slept very well and hope you did the same. My headache has gone and I feel as sturdy as an oak-tree. I do not in the least desire a great house whence I shall not be able to see you in the mornings, and I should much prefer to keep my own little perch upon which my heart poises so happily while I watch you moving about your home. Having made my protest, beloved, you shall dictate to me the letter I must write to notify the landlord that he need not move out to-morrow. We can settle when you come, what time I must be ready, so as not to lose one second of our little walk up the hill. I am so happy at the thought of remaining near you, that I feel as if I had already substituted youthful wings for my old legs. Even my garden is gay, and cries out to me by the mouths of its lovely flowers: *don't go away*! Health is where happiness is, and happiness means loving each other, side by side, eyes upon eyes, soul with soul. Therefore, I shall stay here. That is quite settled.

GUERNSEY,
Friday, 7.30 a.m., October 30th, 1863.

Good morning, good morning, and again, good morning, my dear, wide-awake person. You must be very well to-day, judging by the energy with which you are shaking your rugs to the four winds. I hope that signifies a good night, good health, lively love, and all the rest of it. As for myself, I slept little, but soundly. I got up before gun-fire this morning, and had already finished my dressing when I saw you on your balcony. What a privation it will be for me, my adored man, when I can no longer watch you in the mornings, moving about your house. I do not feel as if I should ever get accustomed to it, and I think of it with apprehension, for there is a proverb that says, "Out of sight, out of mind." If you gave up loving me, or worse, loved me less, what should I make of life in that great empty drawing-room?

At this moment, I am trying to numb these reflections by the contemplation of the marvels you are creating in that future house of mine; but at the bottom of my heart, I know I shall always mourn this poor little lodging, where my eyes could watch over you, caress you, guard you, preserve you, and adore you. The more I think of it, the more oppressed I feel, and the more I blame myself for having exchanged the happiness of every moment, for a comfort I shall hardly have leisure to appreciate, and for health which did not require amelioration. My poor beloved, forgive these regrets which are only dictated by love, and this anxiety which also means love. Try not to let the separation of our houses entail that of our hearts; try to love me as heartily there as here, and do not let yourself be enticed away from me by anybody. On those conditions I promise to live happily in the splendid rooms you have prepared for me.

J.

GUERNSEY,
Wednesday, 1.30 p.m., June 15th, 1864.

Dearly beloved, I cannot forsake this little home where we have loved each other for eight years, without imprinting a kiss of gratitude upon its threshold. I have just gazed my supreme farewell at your beautiful house, which has so long been to me the polar star of my heart's wanderings. Alas, I am lengthening out the moments as much as possible; I cannot bring myself to leave this dear little house, which I had made the shrine of my cult for you. I should like to carry away the walls against which you have leaned, the floors you have trodden, and even the dust your feet have spurned. I fear lest my sadness be observed by those who cannot understand it, and the efforts I make to seem unconcerned increase the constriction of my heart, and drench my eyes with tears. Oh, my adored beloved, how you will have to love me and give me all the time at your disposal, to console me for the immense grief I am experiencing to-day in quitting your neighbourhood, that is to say, in losing sight of it! How you will have to double and treble and quadruple your love, to replace the dear memories I leave behind me! May God protect me and may the dear souls of our angels follow us to the new home, and bless us till our last hour!

I adore you.

J.

GUERNSEY,
Thursday, 5.30 a.m., June 16th, 1864.

Where are you, my beloved? My eyes seek you vainly, you are no longer there to smile upon me; it is all over—I shall never again see the little roost whence you used to blow kisses and wave your hand so tenderly. I am alone now in my fine house, alone for ever; for there is no further chance in this life of having you near me. I shall never again live in your immediate intimacy, as I have done for the past eight years.

Loyally as you may endeavour to bridge over the distance between our abodes by coming to me oftener in the day-time, the separation of our two existences must ever endure. I know it by the blank depression I am feeling this morning. I would give a hundred thousand houses and palaces, and the universe itself, for that little slice of horizon where my heart projected itself night and day. I am ashamed of having been so mean-spirited as to barter my daily happiness against a chimerical amelioration of health. I am punished for my transgression, my dearest. I carry death in my heart. Forgive me! I would gladly smile at you, but at this moment I feel incapable of doing so. Forgive me for loving you too much. I hope you had a good night. I hope you gazed upon my dark, empty house and gave it one sigh of regret. I hope you love me and are conscious of my absence. May God preserve you from all evil, dearly beloved, and may your love remain whole and intact in severance as in propinquity. I bless you, and adore you. A kiss to all our dear memories.

J.

GUERNSEY,
Sunday, 8.30 a.m., June 11th, 1865.

It would take very little to make me stay in bed till noon. I am ashamed of myself and well punished, for I have not seen you this morning, and have not yet heard whether you had a good or a bad night. I hope you were clever enough to sleep uninterruptedly from the moment you laid your head on the pillow, till that of your uprising. I shall be very glad if I have guessed right. Meanwhile, my sweet treasure, I send you a smile and a blessing. I am listening at this moment to the joyous cheeping of my tiny chicks over a saucer of milk that has just been put before them. I am also watching two white butterflies darting after each other among my roses, like twin souls in Eden. The flowers are blooming, love-making is going on all around, and my heart is overflowing with tenderness and adoration for you. The further I progress in life, the more I love you; you are the beginning and end of my being. I hope everything of you, and my soul trusts you, all in all. You are my radiant and divine beloved.

J.

Sunday, 7.30 a.m., December 2nd, 1866.

Good-morning, my adored one, bless you. I can afford to smile on this date, abhorred of all worthy folk: December 2nd.—because it is, for me alone, a joyful anniversary. If my gratitude is an offence towards humanity, I humbly ask pardon of God and man. I am tormented at the thought that you may have slept badly. If I could be reassured on that point, I should be quite happy this morning. Unfortunately, I can only find out much later when you come here to bathe your dear eyes. The mention of your eyes reminds me of your poor wife's sight. Surely, if the doctors were not certain of curing her, they would not keep her so long in Paris, away from all her belongings, in winter weather? My desire for her complete recovery of a sense of which she has made such noble use in her beautiful book *Victor Hugo, raconté*, makes me look upon her delay in returning, as a happy presage of future recovery. I ask it of Heaven, with love.

J.

GUERNSEY,

Wednesday, 8 a.m., January 1st, 1868.

I thank you, dearest, for letting me have a share in your prayers, when you plead to God not to separate us in life or in death. It is what I pray all day long; it is the aspiration of my heart and the faith of my soul. I am not a devout woman, my sublime beloved, I am only the woman who loves and admires and reverences you. To live near you is paradise; to die with you is the consecration of our love for all eternity. I want to live and die with you. I, like you, crave it of God. May He grant our joint prayers!

I feel as you do, my beloved, that those two dear souls hover above us and watch over us and bless us. I associate them with all my thoughts and sorrows and joys, and I place my prayers under their protection, that they may convey them direct to the foot of the Great White Throne. I bless them as they bless me, with all that is loftiest and holiest and most sacred in my soul. I am stopping at almost every line of this letter to read your adorable one over again, although I already know it by heart. I kiss it, talk to it, listen to it, and then begin all over again. I love you.

J.

GUERNSEY,

Thursday, 7 a.m., May 7th, 1868.

Dearly beloved, I am rather less worried since I have seen you and exchanged a kiss with you; yet I know you slept badly. I can feel that you are ailing and sad. I pray God to give you happiness again as soon as possible, in the form of a second little Georges all smiling and beautiful; meanwhile, I beg Him to let my love be the balm that will heal your wounds, until the day of resurrection of the sweet child for whom you weep.[112]

I hope He will hear and grant my petitions on your behalf, and that you will be restored to some degree of calmness and consolation. When you write to your two dear sons, Charles and Victor, do not forget, I beg, to thank them from me for the little portrait. Tell them I love them and mingle my tears with theirs.

I adore you, my great one, my venerated one, my sublime mourner.

J.

BRUSSELS,
Sunday, 7.30 a.m., August 2nd, 1868.

Again I have slept better than ever, beloved. I trust it has been the same with you. I was very proud and pleased at my walk with you and your family last night, but I felt somewhat shy and ill at ease. Please permit me to decline any further invitations of the kind. Should the occasion arise again, which is improbable, I think good taste and discretion demand that I should hold myself aloof from your family affections, and only associate myself with them at a distance, or in my own home. As this feeling, or scruple, whichever you may like to call it, could not be expressed in the presence of your dear children yesterday, I consented to go with you, while intending to call your attention privately to the embarrassment such an incident would cause me, if it should happen again. I think you will probably agree with me, and approve of my sacrificing my pleasure to your tender family intercourse.

J.

BRUSSELS,
Wednesday, 8.30 a.m., August 26th, 1868.

My poor beloved, I pray God to spare you and your dear children the misfortune which threatens you at this moment in the loss of your angelic and adorable wife. I hope, I hope, I hope. I pray, I love you, I summon all our dear angels above to her assistance and yours. I pray God to make two equal shares of the days remaining to me, and add one to the life of your saintly and noble wife. My beloved, my heart is wrung, I suffer all you suffer twice over, through my love for you. I do not know what to do. I long to go to you, I should love to take my share of the nursing of your poor invalid, but human respect holds me back, and my heart is heavier than ever. Suzanne has only just come from your house, and I already want to send her back again, in the hope that she may bring me less disquieting news than that which I have just received. Oh, God have mercy upon us and change our anguish into joy!

BRUSSELS,
Thursday, August 27th, 1868.

My beloved, in the presence of that soul which now sees into my own,[113] I renew the sacred vow I made the first time I gave myself to you; to love you in this world and in the next, so long as my soul shall exist, in the certainty of being sanctioned and blessed in my devotion by the great heart and noble mind which has just preceded us, alas, into eternity.

BRUSSELS,
Friday, 8 a.m., August 28th, 1868.

I placed your sleep last night under the protection of your dear one, my beloved, and implored her to remove from your dreams all painful memories of the sad day just past. I hope she heard me and that you slept well. Henceforth, it is to this gentle and glorious witness of your life in this world, now your radiant protectress in Heaven, that I will appeal for the peace and happiness you require, to finish the great humanitarian task to which you have pledged yourself. May God bless her and you, as I bless her and you.

The more I think over to-night's mournful journey, the more convinced I feel that I ought not to take part in it. The pious homage of my heart to that great and generous woman must not be exposed to a wrong interpretation by indifferent or ill-natured critics. We must make this last sacrifice to human malignity, in order to have the right to love each other openly afterwards; do you not agree, my beloved? Afterwards, may nothing ever come between us here below, nor above—such is my ardent desire!

J.

BRUSSELS,
Friday, 5.30 p.m., August 28th.

My heart and thoughts are with you and your beloved dead. I am sad and heart-broken, not for the angelic and sublime woman who now shines out in the world of spirits while we here below regret her, but for you, my poor sad man, to whom she was a holy and meek companion; for your dear children whose joy and pride she was; for myself, to whom she was ever a discreet and considerate protectress.

My heart is torn by your grief, my poor afflicted ones; my eyes rain all the tears you are shedding. Dear treasure, I beg your wife to obtain for you the courage you need. May her memory remain with you, sweet and gentle and benign as was her exquisite person in life. I entrust you to her as I confide myself to you, and I bless you both.

J.

GUERNSEY,
Tuesday, 2 p.m., February 1st, 1870.

Since I have seen you, my great beloved, I am feeling much better. Your smile has completed my cure. It may be an illusion of my eyes and heart, but at this moment I seem to feel the breath of spring. Perhaps it proceeds from the nearness of the anniversary of the first performance of *Lucrèce Borgia*, which is to be acclaimed and applauded by an enthusiastic public to-morrow night, just as it was thirty-seven long years ago. Bonaparte may do his best to-morrow against this magnificent play, he will get no good out of his police-engineered cabal. I think he will hardly dare risk such an infamous attempt, but I wish it was already Saturday, that we might be quite easy. Meanwhile, I love you after the fashion of Princesse Négroni.

JULIETTE.

GUERNSEY,
Monday, 8.30 a.m., February 14th, 1870.

Good morning, my dearest. Did you sleep better last night, my great, little man? Were you warmer? How are you this morning? It is indeed tedious to have to wait until this afternoon to hear all this. I am trying to moderate my impatience by doing things for you. I have already selected your two eggs, put fresh water into your finger-bowl, and a snow-white napkin on your plate. Suzanne is making your coffee, which perfumes the whole house, while I trace these gouty old "pattes-de-mouche," which are to lay all the tender nonsense of my heart at your feet. I am beginning early, as you see, to be certain that they arrive in time. The thaw has begun. I was quite hot in the night, though I must admit I had taken measures to that end; so I slept excellently, as you can judge by the state of my spirits. But what I really want you to take note of is, that I adore you.

J.

GUERNSEY,
Saturday, 7.45 a.m., May 21st, 1870.

My heart, my eyes, my soul, are bewildered, my beloved, so overwhelmed are they with tenderness, admiration, and happiness! What an adorable letter, and what a marvellous surprise! How good you are to me! How generous and charming! Words fail me, and the best I can say is: I love you! I love you! I threw my arms around old Mariette's neck, and almost embraced Marquand himself in the delirium of my delight. What a splendid frame for that lovely little mirror! It contains everything: flowers, birds, a shelf, little Georges' sweet face above, and your beautiful verses for wings. How can I thank you adequately, or describe my gratitude? Fortunate am I to have eternity before me in which to bless you. I kissed my dear little letter before everybody, but I would not read it until just now when I was able to bolt my door. I always read you thus, my adored one. My soul demands privacy for the better understanding of your sublime words, and I never finish the reading of them without feeling transported with love and almost prepared for the next world. I love you!!

Mariette told me you had spent a very good night. Is it really true? I slept capitally, too, and am feeling more than well. I have been looking about for a place for my new treasure, but have not yet decided on one. I shall leave it to you to choose its proper place in my museum of *souvenirs*. Meanwhile, I have covered it away from the dust and put it in the shady drawing-room. As soon as I have read your adorable little letter again, I shall go back and have another look at it.

J.

VICTOR HUGO, BY RODIN.

GUERNSEY,
Friday, 5 a.m., August 18th, 1870.

At all hazards I must send you my morning greeting, though I trust you are sleeping too soundly to hear it. You have slept so little and so badly for many nights, that it would be only fair that this night should be long and good. As for me, I hardly slept at all, but I do not mind and am hardly surprised, as it is a habit of mine. But the thing I feel I cannot become inured to, is the apprehension of the perils you are about to encounter on your journey to Paris, ranging from the loss of your wealth to the death of your love for me—either would finish me. I think with terror of the tortures of all kinds I shall undergo there; my courage fails me and craves mercy in anticipation. I have fought all night against the wicked temptation to desert my post in a cowardly manner before even meeting the enemy— not an enemy that can be fought with fire and blood, but one that stabs you smiling. But I have not even the courage of cowardice; I am ready to suffer a thousand deaths if only I can preserve you from a single danger. You must live at any cost, that you may be enabled to complete your glorious task, and be happy, no matter how or with whom. My duty is to devote myself to that end, whatever betide. If I go under in the execution of it, so much the worse for me, or possibly, so much the better. To serve you and love you is my mission in this world—the rest does not concern me.

J.

Thursday morning, July 20th, 1871.

This is your patron-saint's day, my great beloved. Others will congratulate you with flowers and music and expressions of admiring gratitude and emotion, but nobody will love you more than I do, or bless and adore you as you deserve to be loved, blessed and adored!

I hope this anniversary may be the beginning of a new year less sinister and sad than the last, and that your dear grandchildren will give you as much joy and happiness as you have had sadness and misfortune in the past. I say this hastily, as best I can, with emotion in my old heart and thrills of joy in my soul. As I sit scribbling, I hear your voice calling me and I rush towards you just as in the early days of our love.

I kiss your hair, your eyes, your lips, your hands, your feet. I adore you.

JULIETTE.

PARIS,
Thursday, 10.15, January 18th, 1872.

Good morning, my great and venerated one. I kiss one by one the wounds of your heart, praying God to heal those that ache worst. I beg Him to give me strength to help you carry your heavy cross to the end. I ask Him, above all, to give me that which, alas, is lacking in my nature, namely, that infinite gentleness without which the most perfect devotion is unavailing. Since the day before yesterday, my poor, sublime martyr, my heart has been wrung by the new blow that has fallen upon you,[114] and I weep helplessly, without power to check my tears. God Who gave you genius makes you pay heavy toll for that favour, by overwhelming your life with the pangs of sorrow. My beloved, I beg you to tell me how I may serve you. I will do anything you desire. I will use my whole heart and strength in your service.

I love you.

J.

This is your birthday, beloved—the anniversary of anniversaries, acclaimed in Heaven by the great men of genius who preceded you upon earth, and blessed by me ever since the day I first gave myself to you. We used to celebrate it with all the sweetest instruments of love; kisses, words of endearment, letters, all were pressed into service to make this date, February 26th, a perfume, an ecstasy, a ray of sunshine. To-day these winged caresses have flown to other realms, but there remains to us the solemn devotion that better becomes the sacred marriage of two souls for all eternity. In the name of that devotion I send you my tenderest greetings and beg you to let me know how you spent the night. I hope your little breach of regulations yesterday did not prevent you from sleeping. As for me, I slept little, but I am quite well this morning, thanks to the influence of this radiant date. I ask little Georges and little Jeanne to kiss you for me as many times as you have lived minutes in this world. My dearly beloved, I bless you.

J.

This is a day of sunshine: God, in His Heaven above, and little Jeanne under my roof. I hardly know—or rather, perhaps I do know which is the brighter of the two, but I am not going to tell you, for fear of making you too proud. What a beautiful day, and what an adorable little girl! But what a pity we cannot all enjoy these spring-time delights together, walking and driving, in town and country-meadows. I am really afraid the good God will weary of us and pronounce the fatal dictum: "IT IS TOO LATE" when at last we make up our minds to take our share of life, sunshine, and happiness. The terrible part is that whether innocent or guilty we shall all suffer alike for *your* transgression, for divine justice is very like that of man. As for me, I enter my protest from my little retreat, but it serves no purpose except that of an idle pastime; it does not even keep me from adoring you.

J.

My beloved, I do not desire to turn your successes into a scourge for your back, but I cannot help feeling that my old-fashioned devotion cuts a sorry figure amongst the overdressed *cocottes* who assail you incessantly with their blandishments and invitations. This fantastic chase has gone on for a long time without extorting from you any sign of weariness or satiety. As for me, I long only for repose—if not in this life (which seems difficult in my case to obtain), then in the immobility of death, which cannot long be delayed at the pace I am going. I ask your permission to begin preparing for it by giving up my daily letters. That will be something gained; the rest will come gradually, little by little, till one fine day we shall find ourselves quite naturally on the platform of indifference, or of reason, as you will prefer to call it. From to-day on, therefore, I place the key of my heart on your doorstep, and will wander away alone in the direction of God.

J.

Dear adored one. All your desires in life, as well as mine, are granted to-day if your dear Victor has spent a good night, as I hope. I am anxiously waiting for Mariette's return to know how the dear invalid is....

My poor beloved, I am in despair—I have just seen Mariette, who tells me that your poor son is in high fever at this moment.[115] I do not know how to tell you; I do not think I shall have the strength to do so. Dr. Sée has been sent for and Mariette has just gone back to hear what he thinks of this relapse. Oh, Heaven have mercy on us! I hardly dare breathe or even weep, so greatly do I dread betraying to you the misfortune which threatens you, my beloved. How can I ward off the fate that is hanging over you? What can I say or do? My brain reels! Ought I to tell you everything— would it be wrong to conceal from you the imminent sorrow that is going to wring your heart once more? I know not, but I lack the courage either to speak or to be silent; I am in despair, yet I dare not make moan. I suffer, I adore you. Pity me, as I pity you. Let us love each other under this cruel trial, as we should if Heaven were opening its gates to us.

J.

Go, dearest, try to find in a solitary walk, which may prove fruitful to the world, some solace for the painful agitation of your heart. My thoughts follow you lovingly and bless every one of your steps. Do not worry about me in the new arrangements of your life. Whatever you settle shall be accepted by me. For forty-one years I have followed that programme, and I will do so now, more than ever. Provided you love me as I love you, I desire nothing more from God or you. The advice I give you, apart from my own personal concerns, is always practical and in your own interest and that of your dear grandchildren. I should feel I had failed in my duty if I kept the least of my ideas from you, whether good or bad, insignificant or stupid. I love you and adore you, body, heart and soul.

J.

PARIS,
Tuesday, 12.30 p.m., February 17th, 1874.

Dear one, there is rather more bustle about us than usual on this our sweet and sacred anniversary. We have the little excitement of your two adorable grandchildren, which we had not expected, but which is all the more delightful for that. The perfection of happiness would have been to take them ourselves to that famous circus which little Georges already knows, and little Jeanne dreams of; but the bad weather and the remains of my influenza counsel a pusillanimous prudence. It is not without regret, beloved, that I impose this sacrifice of one of our most precious joys upon you, but I feel I cannot do otherwise to-day. As for the dear little things, their pleasure will, fortunately, not be marred in any way. So long as they can revel in the antics of Mr. and Mrs. Punch and their august family, they will not mind whom they go with. That being the case, Mariette is a sufficient escort to the promised land of Auriol and Punch.

As for ourselves, dearest, I trust that our two souls, communing together, will not miss those fascinating little witnesses of our love over much.

J.

PARIS,
Wednesday, 7 p.m., March 11th, 1874.

He whose heart is younger than his years suffers all the sorrows of his age. This aphorism contains in a few words the secret of the turmoil I involuntarily bring into your life, while I myself suffer like a soul in damnation. Still, I must not allow this ridiculous folly to be an annoyance to you; I must and will get the better of it, and leave you your liberty, every liberty, especially that of being happy whenever and however you like. Otherwise, my poor beloved, you will very shortly come to hate the sight of me. I know it, and it terrifies me in anticipation. So I am determined to crush my heart at all costs, that I may restore peace and happiness to yours.

J.

PARIS,
Saturday, 1.45 p.m., April 4th, 1874.

I thank you dear one, for having been loyal enough to tell me this morning that you had written another poem to Madame M. I thank you also for having offered to read it to me, and not to send it to her till afterwards. I accepted this respite in the first instance, but I realised later that *what is delayed is not lost*, and that I should gain nothing by struggling against being bracketed with this *statue inhabited by a star*, and that I was simply putting myself in the absurd position of the ostrich that tries to avert danger by hiding his head in the sand. Therefore beloved, I beg you to act quite freely, and to send the verses dedicated to your beautiful muse whenever you like. Once the poetry has been written, it is quite natural that you should intoxicate each other without consideration for me. Besides, in my opinion, infidelity does not consist in action only; I consider it already accomplished by the sole fact of desire. That being settled, my dear friend, I beg you to behave exactly as you like, and as if I were no longer in the way. I shall then have leisure to rest from the fatigues of life before taking my departure for eternity. Try and be happy if you can.

J.

JULIETTE DROUET ABOUT 1877.

Permit me, my great beloved, to offer you my three-score years and ten, freshly completed this morning. Give the poor old things a friendly reception, for they are as blazing with love for you now, as if they had only been born yesterday. I commission little Jeanne to give you seventy million kisses for me to-day, not one less, but a few more if she likes. I hope little Georges' nose has not bled since yesterday, and that he slept well like the rest of you. I slept like a top, and am splendid this morning. I feel a degree of youthfulness that must proceed from the seventy springs I have absorbed so freely. The sky itself contributes its birthday greeting by pouring its measure of sunshine upon us. Therefore, long live love, for us in the first place, (for a little selfishness will not harm happiness,) and in the second, long live love for all whom we love. May you be blest, my beloved, in all those you care for. I adore you.

J. PARIS,
Thursday, 10.45 p.m., May 7th, 1874.

Dear, dear one, the separation I dreaded as a veritable calamity is now an accomplished fact. God grant it may not be the beginning of the end of my happiness. My heart is full of sad presentiment. The distance that separates us is like a broken bridge between our hearts, over which neither joy nor hope may pass henceforth. I cherish no illusion; from this evening forward, all intimacy between us is over, and my sweet horizon of love is for ever clouded. I try to give myself courage by reflecting that the happiness I lose is gained by you in the affection of your two dear grandchildren. I tell myself that this compensation should be sufficient for me; still I am in despair, and I can hardly help shedding floods of tears, as if some irreparable misfortune had befallen me when you walked away just now. I accustomed myself far too speedily to a happiness that was only lent to me for a little while. But however short-lived it proved, I bless you, and pray God to turn my regrets and sorrow into a future of joy and kisses and ecstasy for you and your two little angels.

J. PARIS,
9.30 a.m., Sunday, June 21st, 1874.

I had hoped that nothing would happen to disturb the sanctity of this sad anniversary,[116] and had counted on the assistance of the angels of death to defend me from the aggressions of the devils of life. Alas, I was sadly at fault, for never was a more audacious or more cynical attempt made against my peace of mind. One might think that the mangled remains of my poor heart were a target for the arrows of those emissaries of vice! I declare myself vanquished without a fight, and ere my reason finally succumbs, I mean to place my bruised heart in shelter, far from the flattering intrigues of which you are the fortunate hero.

3 p.m.

You wish me not to be anxious, not to relinquish a tussle in which I am unarmed? It is more generous than wise on your part, for what happened to-day, happened yesterday, and will again to-morrow, and I have no strength left, either physical or moral. This martyrdom of Sisyphus, who daily raises his love heavenward only to see it fall back with all its weight upon his heart, inspires me with horror, and I prefer death a thousand times over, to such torture. Have mercy upon me! Let me go! It shall be wherever you will. Do not run the risk for yourself and me of my committing some frightful act of folly. I ask you this in the name of your daughter and mine—in the name of little Georges and your dear little Jeanne. Give me a chance to recover from these reiterated attacks. I assure you it is the only remedy possible, or capable of effecting my cure. You will hardly notice my absence; the children of your blood, and those of your genius, and the rest, will easily fill the void of my absence, and meanwhile I shall regain calmness. I shall become resigned and perhaps be cured, and in any case it will be a respite for you as well as for me. I assure you my treasure, that it will be a good thing for you. I beg you to let me try it. The abuse of love, like the abuse of health, brings suffering and death in its train. The soul may have a plethora, as well as the body. Mine suffocates under its own weight. Let me try to lighten it in solitude and the contemplation of our past happiness. I beg and implore it of you—I ask it in the name of those you mourn and love.

J. Paris,
Monday, 6 p.m., February 16th, 1875.

My dearest, your letter burns and dazzles me, and I feel humbled by it, because physically I know myself to be so far beneath your ideal; but morally, when I look inward and see my soul as your love has transformed it, I am arrogant enough to think myself above it, and to have no fear of the moment when I may reveal to you its resplendent purity in the eyes of God. Pending this, sublime and divine treasure of mine, you must shut your eyes to the sad reality of my old, sickly body, and await with patience the rejuvenation promised in Heaven. I pray God to allow me to live as long as you, because I do not know how I could exist a single minute without you, even in Paradise with our holy angels. I hope He will grant my ardent prayer, and that we shall die and rise again together on the same day and at the same hour. To ensure this, I must put my health on a level with yours, which will be difficult, for I am very feeble. I try to, every day, without much success so far, but I am counting on the spring to give me a push up the hill, so that I may continue to pace the road at your side. This evening, if nobody comes, and if Madame Charles leaves us early, I shall beg you to let me do *Le Passus* with you. I should like to celebrate the day by something brave and wholesome. I hope I shall manage it. I love you, bless you, and adore you.

J. Guernsey,
Tuesday, 7.45 a.m., April 21st, 1875.

Good morning my great, good, ineffable, adorable beloved. I pray Heaven to bless you in Heaven as I bless you here below. I hope you slept as well as I did, that you bear me no grudge for the irritability born of excessive fatigue, and that you do not love me less on account of it. My confidence in your inexhaustible indulgence lends me courage to proceed with the sad business that brought me here.[117] The thought that we shall never return to these houses of ours, where we loved and suffered and were happy together, makes my heart as heavy as if we were already attending our funerals. This fresh break between the sweet past of our love and the short future that remains to us in this life, makes the present very painful. But I am not unthankful for the compensations that await us in Paris in the society of your dear grandchildren—far from it! I shall smile upon them and bless them with my last breath, as the tangible angels of your happiness and mine. I am doing my best to be ready to start on Tuesday morning. I regret not being able to carry away every relic of our love, from the soil of the garden, to the air you breathe. By the way I have a petition to make to you, but am ready to submit to a refusal if you do not approve of granting it. I want you to allow me to give Louis the two splendid drawings of St. Paul and the Cock, which are really mine to dispose of, since you gave them to me long ago. Some mementoes are more prized by an heir than mere money, and I should like to leave these from you to my kind and worthy nephew, if you consent. Meanwhile, as I said before, I will bow to a refusal, even if you give me no reason, for I adore you.

J. PARIS,
Tuesday, 7.45 a.m., October 5th, 1875.

Good news from your dear little travellers. The top of the morning to you, and long live love! The telegram, which came after I was in bed, that is to say after eleven o'clock, is dated from Genoa, and says they arrive the day after to-morrow at Madame Ménard's, and will write at once from there. Meanwhile they send you thousands of kisses, of which I make bold to reserve a share, before being quite certain that I am meant to do so. This long delayed arrival in France heralds their speedy return home, which is not at all displeasing to me—*on the contrary!* My gaze, night and morning, at their dear little portraits in no degree replaces their kisses, their sweet faces, and the joyous little shrieks one hears all day long. At last we are touching the end of our long abstinence and shall soon be able to devour them whole. Meanwhile I continue to feed upon your heart, to whet my appetite.

J. PARIS,
Sunday, 5 p.m., November 21st, 1875.

Dear beloved, your promise to take me every day to Versailles, if you are obliged to return to the Assemblée, fills my heart with such joy that I have been humming all the merry songs I used to sing. It is long since I have done such a thing. What would it be if some lucky event sent us all back to Guernsey, never to leave it again ... or at least, not for a very long time! What enchantment, what a starlit dream, if God were to give us that bliss a second time! I think I should promptly return to the age I was when I received your first kiss. Fortunately for France, God will not grant this selfish wish, but He will forgive me for entertaining it I hope, for I cannot help loving you beyond everything in this world, and it does not hinder me from being satisfied with whatever happiness He is pleased to vouchsafe, so long as you are content, and love only me, who adore you.

J. PARIS,
Tuesday, 8 a.m., April 25th, 1876.

My treasure, I pray God not to separate us in this life or the next. That is why I am anxious to be with you in the crowd that will rush to see and hear you at the cemetery to-day.[118] I know by experience that your enthusiasm borders on imprudence, so I want to press my body to yours as closely as our souls are riveted, so that whatever befalls you on this sad occasion, may include me. As the love animating our hearts is identical, it is only fair that our fate should be the same. I wish this evening were safely over, that I might be satisfied that everything has gone off well; for I am afraid if poor Louis Blanc attends the mournful ceremony in his present state of ill-health and weakness, he may not be able to get through it. I shall not be easy until we are at home again. Meanwhile I pray Heaven and our angels above to watch over you and preserve you from all danger. I bless, love, and adore you, for all eternity.

J. PARIS,
Wednesday, 7.30 a.m., April 26th, 1876.

I thank you with sacred emotion, my dear one, for your inclusion of me in the sublime and magnificent exordium you pronounced yesterday on the noble wife of Louis Blanc. I accept it without false modesty, because I feel I deserve it, and I am proud and grateful for this ante-apotheosis you made of me, a living woman, standing at the open grave of the devoted deceased. I am sure her spirit will not have grudged it, and that she blesses you from above, as I do from below, joining her prayers to mine, that God may grant all grace and divine consolation to those we love. I have already re-read your splendid oration many times to-day, and although I know it by heart, each repetition discloses some fresh beauty in it. My one cry is: I love you! I love you!! I love you!!! All my heart and soul are contained in those words: I love you.

J. Monday, 10 a.m., November 11th, 1878.

No, my beloved, you have no right to endanger your precious health and risk your glorious life for nothing. "Art for art's sake" is not permissible in your case, and we shall oppose it strenuously, even at the risk of curtailing your liberty. I am sorry, but there it is—you must make up your mind to it. There are plenty of useless men in this world who may waste their lives as they like, but you must guard and preserve yours for as long as it pleases God to grant it to you for the honour and happiness of humanity. So, my dear little man, I implore you not to repeat yesterday's imprudence, or any other, for all our sakes, including your adorable grandchildren's and mine whose health and life and soul you are. When I see you so careless of yourself I cannot help feeling you no longer love me, and that my continued presence is so wearisome to you that you want to be rid of it at any price. Then I am seized with a desperate longing to deliver you of me for ever, rather than be the involuntary accomplice of your repeated suicidal acts, which have been ineffectual so far, not through your fault, but because God intends you to go on living, for His greater glory and your own. May His will be done. Amen.

J.

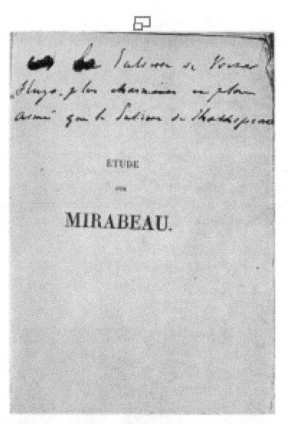

THE DEATHBED OF VICTOR HUGO.
Victor Hugo Museum.

A DEDICATION BY VICTOR HUGO TO JULIETTE DROUET.
The writing reads thus: "A la Juliette de Victor Hugo, plus charmante et plus aimée que la Juliette de Shakespeare."
The original belongs to M. Louis Barthou.

VILLEQUIER,
Friday and Saturday mornings, September 12th and 13th, 1879.

A double letter, my beloved; to-day's and yesterday's, which, for want of paper, pens and ink, I was not able to send you at the proper time, in spite of the inexhaustible fount of my love. This morning being better provided, I can let myself go in the happiness of being with you in the house of your respected friends,[119] enjoying their tender and devoted hospitality. I am proud and yet shy of sharing it with you; proud, because I think myself worthy, shy because I do not know how to thank them or to prove my gratitude. Fortunately the honour and pleasure of your presence is reward enough for those you esteem, and from whom you accept this filial friendship, admiration, and devotion. I express myself badly, but you are accustomed to grasp my meaning, in spite of the lapses of my pen; so I never worry about the confusion of my scribbles, and I end them imperturbably, as I begin them, by the sacred words: I love you. I did not venture to ask your permission yesterday to accompany you on your pious pilgrimage,[120] but I add the prayers I addressed to God and your dear dead, to the sacrifice I was forced to make to appearances. If you allow me, I shall go before we leave Villequier, and kneel beside those venerated tombs, to offer under the open sky my profound respect and eternal benediction. I shall only do it if you consent, for I should not like to offend against good taste by the outward manifestation of the sentiment I cherish in my heart for your dear dead relations. I know you slept well—thanks evidently to the calm and happy life your friends provide for you in their circle, for which I thank and bless them from the bottom of my heart. I do not know whether the weather will be favourable to-day for the excursion we planned; it is foggy so far, but whatever be the state of the barometer, I am disposed to be quite happy if you are, and to adore you without conditions of any kind. By the way, how are you going to evade the attentions of the mayor and corporation of Le Hâvre without hurting the feelings of the poor workmen who implore you to go amongst them while you are in their neighbourhood? It is not an easy problem to solve. Luckily nothing is a difficulty to you—nor to me either when there is any question of loving you with all my might from one end of life to the other!

J. PARIS,
Monday, 7 a.m., May 30th, 1880.

How beautiful, how grand, how divine!!! I have just finished that glorious reading, and am electrified by the elixir of your ardent poetry; my fainting soul clings to your mighty wings, to arrest its fall from the starry heights in which you plane, to the profound abyss of my ignorance. I was afraid I might disturb your sleep by the rustling of the leaves as I cut and devoured them greedily, never noticing that night was turning into day. Finally, fearing to be caught by you, I dragged myself unwillingly to bed at three o'clock, and have now already been up an hour, in triumphant health, rejuvenated by the virility of the thoughts your inexhaustible genius pours forth without intermission before a dazzled and grateful humanity. My hand shakes from my inward tremor, and it is with difficulty that I finish this poor little cry of admiration. Even my voice, if I tried to speak at this moment, could hardly stammer out my adoration. I am in the throes of a kind of delirium which would be painful, were it not as exquisite as the divine love which overflows from my heart.

Beloved, Heaven decrees that in the absence of your dear departed souls, your sweet angels here below should be restored to you to-day. Let us bless Him with all reverence, and be solemnly happy with the memory of those who once made our felicity, and the kisses of your adorable grand-children, who constitute your present and future content. What joy it is to see them once more, lovelier than ever if possible, and in still better health. All night I listened to every sound, that I might be the first to welcome them on the threshold. I succeeded, and was repaid by their hugs. The sun shot forth its brightest beams in their honour. As for you, divine grandpapa, I trust your horrid cold will yield to the tender caresses that await you, and that we shall have you with us in our enjoyment. The least we can hope for is an indulgence in unlimited caresses, after these three months of separation. I make a start by flinging myself into your arms.

J. PARIS,
Tuesday, 9 a.m., December 14th, 1881.

I come to fetch my heart where I left it, that is to say in yours. I return it to you, praying you not to bruise it over much by unjust and wounding tyrannies. My independent, proud nature has always borne them ill, and is now in revolt. I beg you beloved, not to constitute yourself the critic of my little personal needs. Whatever I may ask, I assure you I shall never exceed the bounds of necessity, and never will I take unfair advantage of your trust and generosity. The position you have given me in your household precludes me from placing myself at a disadvantage in the eyes of your guests by an appearance not in consonance with your means. Therefore, please, dear great man, leave it to my discretion to do honour to you as well as to myself. Besides, the little time I have to spend on earth is not worth haggling about. So, my great little man, let us be good to each other for the rest of the time God grants us to live side by side, and heart to heart.

J. PARIS,
Sunday, Noon, July 10th, 1881.

My dear beloved, I must first of all confess the fault (if it be one) I committed yesterday under the influence of the universal enthusiasm occasioned by the glorious ovation offered to you, so that you may forgive it, even if you see fit to punish me. This is my crime. Whilst you, still in the full flood of your emotion, were thanking the enthusiastic crowd, the councillors of our district approached to congratulate you and at the same time to beg for money for their schools. Madame Lockroy sent them forty francs by Georges. Failing to attract your attention, though they stood behind you, intent upon presenting their money-boxes themselves, they turned to me. In my agitated surprise, I handed them the hundred-franc note I was saving up for my birthday. I gave the note in your name, at the same time reminding them they had already received five hundred from you the day before, through their mayor. He, happening to be present, confirmed my statement. This is my transgression; if you deem it deserving of severity you need not refund the money. If you take into account the delirium and excitement of the occasion you will smile and give me back my poor little mite of which I have great need. In any case you must not scold me too much, for I am very sensitive.

J.

Wednesday, 8 a.m., June 21st, 1882.

Beloved, thank you for taking me to-day to the mournful and sweet *rendez-vous* of St. Mandé. I feel as if my sorrow would be less bitter, kneeling at my child's grave than when I am at a distance ... as if my soul could get closer to that of my little beloved, through the earth of her tomb, than anywhere else. I hope you will find your dear daughter in good health, and that we shall both return from this sacred errand resigned to the will of God, though not consoled, for that is no longer possible in this world. Thank you again, my adored one, for sharing with me the sad anniversary that recalls to you the many sorrows of your own life. I am very grateful to you, and I bless you as I love you, with all the strength of my soul.

J.

Monday, January 1st, 1883.

Dear adored one, I do not know where I may be this time next year, but I am proud and happy to sign my life-certificate for 1883 with this one word: I love you.

JULIETTE.[121]

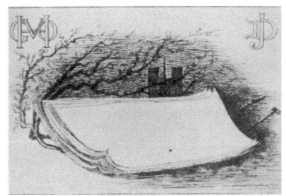

**BOOK-PLATE DESIGNED FOR JULIETTE DROUET BY
VICTOR HUGO.**
The original belongs to M. Louis Barthou.

FOOTNOTES:

[1] Her birth-certificate is drawn up in the following terms: "On April 11th, 1806, at 3 p.m. before me, Louis Pinel, mayor of Fougères and registrar of births, deaths, and marriages, Julien Gauvain, tailor, aged twenty-nine, residing at Rue de la Révolution, Fougères, presented a female child, born on the preceding day at 7 a.m., the legitimate daughter of himself and his wife Marie Caretandet; he declared his intention of bestowing upon her the names of Julienne-Joséphine. The said declaration and presentation were made in the presence of François Dorange, sheriff's officer, aged twenty-five, residing in Fougères, and François Paunier, gardener, aged sixty-eight, residing in Lécousse. This certificate was duly signed by the father and the witnesses, after the same had been read aloud to them. Signed: Julien Gauvain, François Paunier, Dorange, and Louis Pinel."

[2] She posed, not, as has been stated, and as we ourselves have erroneously printed, for statues in the towns of Lille and Strasburg, but for numerous studies of the head and the nude which Pradier afterwards made use of; thus the features of Julienne may be recognised in almost all the rough studies belonging to the first portion of Pradier's career, which are exhibited under glass in the museum at Geneva.

[3] The portrait of Victor Hugo by Devéria has often been reproduced. It is popular. Léon Noël's lithograph is less known. It is to be found either in the *Artiste* in the course of the year 1832 or in the Musée Victor Hugo. We reproduced it in the *Contemporaine* of February 25th, 1902.

[4] Victor Hugo, *Correspondance*. Letter to Sainte-Beuve, August 22nd, 1833.

[5] Victor Hugo, *Correspondance*. Letter to Sainte-Beuve, July 7th, 1831.

[6] *Lettres à la Fiancée.*

[7] Under the heading: *A Ol.* (Olympio) XII.

[8] Théophile Gautier, *Portraits contemporains.*

[9] Alphonse Karr, *Une Heure trop tard.*

[10] We heard it from Monsieur Benezit, who was often with Frédérick Lemaître about the year 1872.

[11] Théophile Gautier, *Portraits contemporains.*

[12] *Lucrèce Borgia.* First note to the original edition.

[13] She was forty-six and beginning to grow fat. According to Juliette, she told Victor Hugo that his mistress was deceitful, vain, lawless, and a flirt.

[14] V. H. Fleischmann, *Une Maîtresse de Victor Hugo,* chap. vii.

[15] Nothing remains of it now, save the name and the site. All the rest, park, garden, and dwelling, has been completely altered.

[16] In 1877 Madame Drouet, although seventy-one years old, insisted upon attending the funeral of Mlle. Louise Bertin. "I wish," she wrote to Victor Hugo, "to show in this way that I have not forgotten the marks of sympathy she gave you on my account in the early days of our love" (*Letter of April 28th, 1877*).

[17] This inn still exists, and is not changed in any way. It is exceedingly modest.

[18] It belongs now to Madame Veuve Bigot. On the left exterior wall a Versailles society has thought fit to place an inscription recording that Victor Hugo once inhabited the house. Four lines of *La Tristesse d'Olympio* follow. It would have been more correct to bracket the name of Juliette Drouet with that of the poet, for after all it was not he who lived there, but she.

[19] Here occurs the only discrepancy between *La Tristesse d'Olympio* and the letters of Juliette. Victor Hugo writes in 1837: "They have paved this rough, badly-laid road"; whereas Juliette, as early as 1835, calls it *the pavement.*

[20] *La Tristesse d'Olympio.*

[21] See also later, in the collection of letters, the one written under date of January 25th, 1844.

[22] September 27th, 1845.

[23] September 29th, 1845: "I wish I had the money to buy it all before it is desecrated." Victor Hugo understood her feeling, and a generous impulse led him to propose to buy the house. The price asked was six thousand francs. Very delicately Juliette refused. October 7th, 1845.

[24] 1834.

[25] December 15th, 1838.

[26] Théophile Gautier.

[27] In 1836 Victor Hugo was forced to take legal action against the Comédie Française. He won his case the following year.

[28] We have proofs of this in two letters from Juliette to Victor Hugo.

[29] February 1st, 1836.

[30] It will be remembered that Mlle. Maxime brought an action against the Comédie and Victor Hugo on that point, which made some considerable stir. See the articles of Monsieur Jules Claretie in *Le Journal* of February 5th, 1902.

[31] *Les Burgraves* alternated in the bill with a piece by Madame de Girardin in which Rachel played the heroine.

[32] May 30th, 1841.

[33] The removal took place in the month of February 1845. The rent and accommodation of the apartment were about the same as at No. 14. The furnishing, which Victor Hugo wished to make somewhat more luxurious, cost 2,256 francs, including the first quarter's rent.

[34] 1833.

[35] Monsieur Léon Seche, *Revue de Paris*, February 15th, 1903.

[36] Catalogue of an interesting collection of autograph letters of which the sale took place on Saturday, November 30th, 1912, page 21. Paris. Noël Charavay, 1912. In another note dated from Les Metz, Victor Hugo tells Claire "that he loves her with all his heart, and uses his best handwriting in writing to her, which is very praiseworthy in an old student like himself." And he adds, "I kiss both your little peach-cheeks." (Same, p. 22.)

[37] Autograph postscript by Victor Hugo to a letter to Juliette on May 28th, 1833, quoted above.

[38] Pradier did not fail to write a sermon on this occasion full of the unction and solecisms in which he habitually excelled.

[39] June 5th, 1841.

[40] *Les Contemplations*, Livres V., XIV., Claire P.

[41] One of the sons of the sculptor was called John.

[42] April 25th, 1845.

[43] April 27th, 1845.

[44] The thrilling episode of Victor Hugo's political adventures in 1851, by which his life was placed in jeopardy through his espousal of the cause of liberty and progress, is related by himself in *L'Histoire d'un crime*. He was forced to go into hiding in December for several days, and subsequently made his escape to Brussels in the disguise of a workman. Juliette had preceded him thither, to prepare a safe refuge for him.—*Translator's Note.*

[45] Charles Hugo, *Les Hommes de l'Exil*, p. 104.

[46] *Ibid.*

[47] May 18th, 1852.

[48] This passage constitutes the portion of the Galleries of St. Hubert situated at right angles to the two others, called respectively, Passage du Roi, and Passage de la Reine.

[49] May 24th, 1852.

[50] A packet of Victor Hugo's love-letters to Madame B. was treacherously forwarded to her by the lady in question. They extended over a period of seven years, 1844 to 1851. Victor Hugo had carried on his secret intrigue with Madame B. while he was daily visiting and corresponding with Juliette. The discovery of his duplicity almost broke her heart.—*Translator's Note.*

[51] Victor Hugo, *Correspondance*, letter to Émile Deschanel, December 11th, 1853.

[52] January 23rd, 1853.

[53] It was signed by Félix Pyat, Rougée, and Jourdain.

[54] Victor Hugo had disposed of the bulk of his furniture in June 1852, but he had stored the things he specially valued at Juliette's apartment, Cité Rodier.

[55] These remarks may be verified by the series of photographs of the poet taken by his sons during his exile and preserved in the Musée Victor Hugo. Some of the snapshots, as we should call them nowadays, are an indication of the distress of the great outlaw.

[56] *Victor Hugo Intime*, by Madame Juana Lesclide.

[57] A young girl in bad circumstances, to whom Juliette had given shelter under her own roof, and who thus requited the charity of her benefactress.—*Translator's Note.*

[58] Juliette Drouet was buried on May 12th, 1883, in the cemetery of Saint Mandé, near her daughter Claire, under a marble stone she had selected for herself in 1881. Her funeral was attended by a large body of journalists. The speech was delivered by Auguste Vacquerie. According to a letter she wrote to Victor Hugo on November 1st, 1881, she wished for an epitaph taken from one of the "sublime poems" he had addressed to her. Her desire was not gratified; the tomb does not even bear the name of our heroine.

[59] Juliette Drouet occasionally acted as the poet's secretary.

[60] This letter is not signed. The envelope is addressed: "M. Victor Hugo. A quarter to twelve, midnight. I am going to your house."

[61] Victor Hugo was then living at 6, Place Royale, in the house which is now the Musée Victor Hugo. Juliette Drouet lived not far away at 4, Rue de Paradis au Marais, which is now one of the sections of the Rue des Francs-Bourgeois.

[62] Juliette's furniture had just been seized, and her landlord was threatening to evict her.

[63] Mlle. Mars, who was rehearsing a part in *Angélo*, at the Comédie Française.

[64] There are traces of tears all over this letter.

[65] Eugène Hugo, brother of the poet, had just expired. See Number XXIX of *Voix Intérieures, à Eugène, Vicomte Hugo.*

[66] This is an allusion to the second poem in the *Voix Intérieures:* "Sunt lacrimæ...."

[67] One of the basins in the park of Versailles.

[68] Victor Hugo had given Juliette a *Quintus Curtius* in which he had formerly studied Latin. On the fly-leaf he had written a few words of dedication.

[69] A critic.

[70] Juliette Drouet here enumerates the depreciation of various stocks. The letter is of course written in a sarcastic vein induced by *pique.—Translator's Note.*

[71] This is an allusion to the lawsuit of Victor Hugo against the Comédie Française.

[72] Casimir Delavigne.

[73] Scribe.

[74] Juliette's sums were always wrong.

[75] Alluding to the revival of *Hernani* at the Comédie Française, January 20th, 1838.

[76] The revival of *Marion de Lorme* at the Comédie Française was to take place the next evening, March 8th.

[77] Granier de Cassagnac, one of the most ardent champions of Victor Hugo against the classical writers. The poet had introduced him to the *Journal des Débâts*.

[78] *Ruy Blas*. The poet had considered the propriety of casting Juliette for the part of the Queen, and had in consequence caused her to be engaged by the Théâtre de la Renaissance.

[79] The creator of the part of the Queen in *Ruy Blas*. The first performance had taken place on November 8th.

[80] Anténor Joly, Manager of the Théâtre de la Renaissance. He had intended to produce Juliette in a musical comedy.

[81] Victor Hugo had already submitted himself three times as a candidate for the Académie and was elected the fourth time, that is to say, the day Juliette wrote this letter. His chief adversary in the Académie was one of his former rivals, the Vaudevilliste, Dupaty.

[82] Victor Hugo was received into the Académie by Monsieur de Salvandy on June 3rd, 1841.

[83] The poet's children.

[84] Victor Hugo had been elected Chancellor of the Académie Française on the preceding June 24th. Charles Nodier was the President.

[85] François Victor Hugo, whose childhood was extremely delicate.

[86] This is an allusion to the recent death of the Duc d'Orléans, the friend and protector of Victor Hugo.

[87] Rehearsals of *Burgraves* at the Comédie Française.

[88] An allusion to the disagreement of the poet with Mdlle. Maxime, to whom the Comédie Française wished to allot the part of *Guachumara*, and whom he was afterwards able to replace by Mdlle. Théodorine (Mme. Melingue).

[89] This letter is written after the catastrophe at Villequier on September 4th, 1847, in which the eldest daughter and the son-in-law of the poet perished.

[90] This is an allusion to a journey Juliette and Victor Hugo had just made, the account of which had been published in *Alpes et Pyrénées*.

[91] Probably Ulrich Guttinguer.

[92] A bronze medal representing Victor Hugo, after the medallion by David d'Angers.

[93] This letter was written at Auteuil, where Juliette was living, with her dying daughter, in a house belonging to the sculptor, Pradier. Victor Hugo visited her there nearly every day.

[94] The doctor chosen by Pradier.

[95] Juliette's own doctor.

[96] Victor Hugo was then a candidate for the Assemblée Nationale.

[97] Victor Hugo was to make a speech that day on *La Misère*, vide *Actes et Paroles, Avant l'Éxil*.

[98] Mdlle. Rachel. Arsène Houssaye, who had recently been appointed Director of the Comédie Française, had just introduced Victor Hugo to the great tragedian.

[99] A speech on deportation. Vide *Actes et paroles, Avant l'Éxil*.

[100] Madame Biard.

[101] Madame Biard had sent Juliette a packet of Victor Hugo's letters to her.

[102] The word "to-day" is left unfinished in the original, thus: *aujo....*

[103] The period when Victor Hugo's intrigue with Madame Biard began.

[104] On December 2nd, 1851, Victor Hugo held a meeting of the representatives of the people, at which he drew up a proclamation addressed to the Army. On the 3rd he presided over a meeting of the Republicans in the Faubourg St. Antoine. Word was brought that the troops were marching on the Faubourg. Victor Hugo thereupon delivered an impassioned appeal to his audience, which concluded in the following terms: "On one side stand the Army, and a crime—on the other, a handful of men, and the Right! Such is the struggle. Are you prepared to carry it through?"—*Translator's note.*

[105] A troupe of actors passing through Jersey had insisted upon playing *Angélo* before the exiled poet.

[106] Teleki, one of Victor Hugo's friends in Jersey.

[107] Victor Hugo had taken up photography.

[108] An allusion to spiritualism to which Victor Hugo had just fallen a prey.

[109] Adèle Hugo, daughter of the poet.

[110] Victor Hugo's drawings. He was giving them away indiscriminately to his friends, and Juliette was jealous.

[111] Probably one of the poems commemorating the catastrophe of Villequier. They were collected and republished in *Les Contemplations*.

[112] Charles Hugo had lost his eldest son, Georges. He gave the same Christian name to the second, who, with Petite Jeanne, figures in *L'Art d'être Grand-père*.

[113] Madame Victor Hugo had just died.

[114] François Victor Hugo had just been given up by the doctors. His slow agony lasted eleven months.

[115] François Victor Hugo died in the course of the day.

[116] The anniversary of the death of Claire.

[117] The removal from *Hauteville Féerie*.

[118] Victor Hugo was to make a speech at the funeral of Madame Louis Blanc.

[119] A. Vacquerie and family.

[120] To the grave of Léopoldine.

[121] This letter is the last Juliette ever wrote.

[122] Monsieur Eugène Planès possesses the original editions of *Chants du Crépuscule, Les Voix Intérieures, Les Rayons et les Ombres,* dedicated to Juliette and annotated by herself. He has been good enough to refer to them and verify our list in so far as the three following collections are concerned. We have included in the selection only the love-poems directly inspired by Juliette. We have left out the miscellaneous pieces which were dedicated to her after they were written, sometimes at her own request.

CPSIA information can be obtained
at www.ICGtesting.com
Printed in the USA
LVHW111723011022
729743LV00007B/364